T0375559

REFLECTIONS ON SIERRA LEONE BY A FORMER SENIOR POLICE OFFICER

The History of the Waning of a Once Progressive West African Country

Ezekiel Alfred Coker, MR, JP, BEM

*Retired senior assistant commissioner of police,
Sierra Leone Police Force*

Reflections on Sierra Leone by a Former Senior Police Officer
The History of the Waning of a Once Progressive West African Country

iUniverse books may be ordered through booksellers or by contacting:

iUniverse
1663 Liberty Drive
Bloomington, IN 47403
www.iuniverse.com
1-800-Authors (1-800-288-4677)

Because of the dynamic nature of the Internet, any web addresses or links contained in this book may have changed since publication and may no longer be valid. The views expressed in this work are solely those of the author and do not necessarily reflect the views of the publisher, and the publisher hereby disclaims any responsibility for them.

Any people depicted in stock imagery provided by Thinkstock are models, and such images are being used for illustrative purposes only.
Certain stock imagery © Thinkstock.

ISBN: 978-1-4917-9102-8 (sc)
ISBN: 978-1-4917-9103-5 (e))

Library of Congress Control Number: 2016904973

Print information available on the last page.

iUniverse rev. date: 04/05/2016

Brief Particulars about Sierra Leone

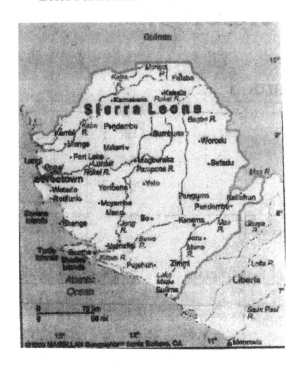

To the loving memory of my dear late maternal grandfather, Alfred Napoleon Brown, for all the sacrifices made to enhance my general welfare, particularly my education. And to the memory of Rev. Father Clarkin CSSP, former principal of St Edward's Secondary School, Freetown, Sierra Leone, for his pivotal role in advancing my secondary education.

Contents

Sierra Leone: Basic Facts

Sierra Leone is a relatively small country located on the west coast of Africa opposite the Atlantic Ocean. The area of the country is 27,699 square miles (71,740 square kilometres).

Capital: The capital, Freetown, which is also the only major port in the country, has a large natural harbour. The city's population is approximately one million.

Population: The population of Sierra Leone is about six million.

Government: The country was formerly a British colony. It was granted independence in April 1961and has a democratic system of government. It has now been a republic since 1971. The president at the time of this writing is Dr Earnest Bai Koroma.

Currency: The leone (Le)

Religion: Christian, Muslim, and traditional beliefs practiced by some.

Education: There are five colleges in the country, the oldest of which is Fourah Bay College established in 1827. FBC is also the oldest college in West Africa. The country boasts many secondary schools. CMS Grammar School, established in Freetown in 1845, is the oldest. Sierra Leone also has many primary schools.

About 60 per cent of the population is literate, to varying degrees.

Resources: The country has many natural resources, including bauxite, cacao, coffee, diamond, fish, gold, iron ore, palm kernels and rutile.

Introduction

This book is about different aspects of the history of Sierra Leone. It also incorporates some facets of my life, including my experiences in the Sierra Leone Police Force, in which it was my pleasure and privilege to serve my country.

My short memoirs are contained in part 1, "Memoirs of Borbor." Borbor is the Creole expression for a young male. When I was a young boy, my pet name was Borbor.

Sometime during the latter part of 2005, Attorney Prince Shyllon, one of my close friends, disclosed to me that he was writing a book on Sierra Leone. He said he wanted to acquire knowledge about the various activities in the country, particularly activities in Freetown prior to 1943 when he was born. He added that he was particularly interested in activities by the British during the colonial era.

A few weeks after Prince made this request, I delivered to him a few sheets, which I termed "A view of Freetown prior to 1943." Unfortunately, Prince died in January 2007 before he could get the book published.

After his death, I continued writing in my leisure time. It then occurred to me that I could not be so sharply circumscribed in what he had requested of me; therefore, I decided to write detailed particulars about all that I could remember since the early thirties onward. Consequently, the title of the previous document was transformed into "A Bygone Era in Sierra Leone." These particulars are contained in part 2.

Part 3, which is entitled "Political Upheavals in Sierra Leone", includes some of the experiences I gained regarding the political manoeuvrings and tussles in Sierra Leone during my service in the Special Branch of the Sierra Leone Police Force.

As for part 4, "The Creoles (Krios) of Sierra Leone", I realised that not too many citizens in Sierra Leone – the Creoles included – know much about the history of this ethnic group that has played a significant role in Sierra Leone's development from about the early nineteenth century to the middle of the twentieth century. I have, therefore, included herein some facts about the Creoles of Sierra Leone.

Most of the important events in Sierra Leone have not been adequately documented. I thought it desirable that I should not let some of the momentous events that have taken place in the country fade into obscurity without being placed on record for posterity. That is one of my main purposes for writing this book.

The other purpose is to compare Sierra Leone under British colonial rule and Sierra Leone when it came under the rule of Sierra Leoneans after the country had been granted independence in April 1961.

It is my sincere hope that this book will serve as enlightenment to Sierra Leoneans, especially those among the younger generation who were born after the country had gained its independence. I also hope that non-Sierra Leoneans will gain some knowledge about this small diamond-rich country on the west coast of Africa.

Finally, I wish to convey my profound thanks to one of my granddaughters, Capt. Melisa Coker, PsyD, of the US Army Medical Services Corps, for being the first to sow in me the seed that inspired me to write a book. That seed has now germinated and blossomed into *Reflections on Sierra Leone by a Former Senior Police Officer.*

PART 1

MEMOIRS OF BORBOR

chapter 1

BEGINNINGS

I was born in Freetown with the help of a traditional birth attendant locally known as "grannie". My mother, Harriett Brown, was a resident of Gloucester Village, but she had to travel to Freetown accompanied by her father and mother to give birth to me. During that time, Sierra Leone was under British colonialism. As my mother and my maternal grandparents were permanent residents of Gloucester Village, I also grew up in the village.

I was christened by Reverend E.N. Jones at the Anglican Holy Trinity Church at Kissy Road, Freetown, on 14 January 1927.

I was a parishioner at St Andrew's church at Gloucester Village and was a chorister at that church between 1938 and 1940.

MY IMMEDIATE FAMILY

My mother was an assistant dressmaker.

My maternal grandfather, Alfred Napoleon Brown, was a descendant of Liberated Africans. He was a sergeant in the Sierra Leone Police Force. He retired sometime in the early twenties, before I was born, and took residence in Gloucester, the village in which he was born and educated. I knew him as my "papa."

My maternal grandmother, Sarah Brown, was a Susu who was born in Kychom in the northern province of Sierra Leone. Later she was adopted by Creole couple in Freetown with whom she grew up before her marriage to my grandfather. She could also speak Temne, the language of another tribe in Sierra Leone. She was the only petty trader selling various consumer goods at Gloucester Village.

My mother Harriett Morpeh Brown

My father, George Ebenezer Coker, was a customs officer from the neighbouring village of Charlotte. He died in 1940 after a short illness whilst he was in his middle forties.

My education began at Gloucester kindergarten school from 1932 to 1934, after which I proceeded to the primary school at Regent Village. I started standard 1 in 1935 and stayed there through standard 6 in 1940. The teachers at both schools were all Sierra Leoneans and residents in one or other of the surrounding villages.

In 1941, my grandfather transferred me from Regent Primary School to St Edward's primary school in Freetown. After passing the Primary School Leaving Certificate in November 1941, I attended St Edward's Secondary School on Howe Street in Freetown from 1942 to 1945. Both St Edward's Secondary School and St. Edward's Primary School were in the same building. The former was on the top floor, whilst the latter was on the ground floor. The headmaster of the primary school at the time was an Irish Roman Catholic priest named Rev. Father O'Toole. The principal of the secondary school was the renowned Rev. Father Cornelius Mulchy, who was also an Irish Roman Catholic priest. Unfortunately Rev. Father Cornelius Mulchy died sometime in 1941 after a short illness. He was succeeded by Rev. Father Clarkin, who was also a Roman Catholic Irish priest.

Whilst I was at St Edward's Primary School in 1941, I was converted to Roman Catholicism.

After successfully passing the Cambridge Senior School Certificate in November 1945, I started to teach as an assistant teacher in standard 4 at St Edward's primary school from January to December 1946. In 1947, I was transferred to Cathedral Boy's Primary School, where I also taught in standard 4 from January to May 1947.

Teaching in those days was not a lucrative profession, and added to that, I was not a certified teacher. My salary was £3.10s.0d a month. Being that Sierra Leone and all the other three West African British colonies were British colonial territories, the currency that was then in circulation was the British West Africa pound sterling. The British then had a rather complex currency, which was not decimal but consisted of pound, shilling, and pence. Twelve pence equalled one shilling; twenty shillings equalled one pound. To write, say, two pounds (£), nine shillings (s), and ten pence (d), one had to write £2.9s.10d. Third-grade civil servants were earning £3.15s0d (three pounds fifteen shillings) monthly.

In 1946, the British colonial government appointed a commission of inquiry headed by a Mr Harragin, a very senior official in the British Home Civil Service, to look into the conditions of the civil service in Sierra Leone and make recommendations for improvement. Following the report of Harragin, the salaries of civil servants were raised substantially. The monthly salary of third-grade clerks was then raised to £7.0s.0d. Personnel in the other grades in the civil service also had large increases in their monthly pay. On the other hand, the salaries of teachers were not raised. At that time, I had to take care of myself, my mother, my grandmother, and my grandfather.

My appointment as a third-class customs officer on probation

As Sierra Leone was then a colonial territory of Britain, the king of Britain was the head of the government in Sierra Leone. Consequently, the department of customs was termed His Majesty's Customs. King George VI was, at that time, king of Britain.

In April 1947, I applied to the then Appointments Committee (the precursor of the Public Service Commission) for appointment in any government department as a third-grade civil servant. I was successful in the interview. Within about two weeks, I received a letter from the Appointments Committee appointing me as third-class customs officer on probation in the then HM Customs.

This photograph was taken on 7th February, 1949
at Shed 7, Old Government Wharf, Freetown, Sierra Leone.
It shows Customs Officer, Third Class, Ezekiel A. Coker (on the right)
sitting on a desk with a tally clerk of Elder Dempster Lines.
Bags of palm kernels were being shipped for export to Britain
and the Customs Officer on duty in the shed has got to tally the number of bags
palm kernels being exported for export duty purposes.
(Ezekiel Coker was then a little over 22 years of age.)

Ezekiel Coker in the uniform of a customs officer

Me in the uniform of a customs officer in 1949

I then submitted my letter of resignation from the teaching profession through the headmaster of the Cathedral Boys' Primary School.

On being employed at the HM Customs as a probationary third-class customs officer, I was at first made to work for short periods in different sections of that department, both indoor and outdoor at the old government wharf. This was intended to gain me experience of the duties in the various sections of the department.

MY TRANSFER TO THE CORRESPONDENCE BRANCH

After serving in the other sections of the HM Customs, I was transferred permanently to the correspondence branch in 1952. I was a little over twenty-five years of age. The staff at the correspondence branch worked under the direct eyes of both the comptroller and the deputy comptroller who were both British colonial civil servants. The lessons I learnt whilst I was in the correspondence branch were to provide the foundations for my future elevation in life.

One particular incident was of very great significance to me. I had only been at the branch for a few weeks in 1952 when a lesson in leadership was subtly demonstrated to me. At that time, I was not proficient in typing. The handwritten draft of a letter by the comptroller of customs to the general manager of a commercial firm was passed to me for typing, as that matter was under my schedule of work.

In those days there were no computers and printers. There were only mechanical typewriters. If a mistake was made in the spelling of a word in a typed letter, the only means of correcting the error was to scrub the misspelled word off using an eraser and retype the correct word.

That particular day, I struggled to type the letter. I had to erase and retype several words. The letter thus contained several smudges. When I passed the letter to my supervisor, he expressed doubt as to whether the typing was of a suitable standard for the comptroller's signature. Nevertheless, he passed it in to the comptroller for his signature. About half an hour later, the comptroller called both the supervisor and me into his office. He said that the letter was not typed well enough to be sent to the manager of a commercial organisation.

I made the excuse that I was not a proficient typist yet. The comptroller responded that he was not a proficient typist either, but he could have produced a better letter than the one I had typed. He advised me to make an effort to type letters more decently and concluded that he would retype the letter himself. The supervisor and I then left the comptroller's office.

After work, the comptroller spent several minutes in the office typing the letter. At about 8.30 a.m. the following morning, the comptroller called the supervisor and me into his office. He playfully asked me how I had spent the night. Then he produced the letter he had typed himself the previous afternoon and displayed it next to my own typewritten letter. He asked me which of the two letters was decent and presentable. Obviously, his own was better. There were no smudges on it. I said that his was the better of the two letters. He admonished me to try and improve the standard of my typing. I assured him that I would endeavour to do my best. Since that day, I made desperate efforts to improve the standard of my typing, and no one could find fault in my typing.

What totally impressed me was that the comptroller understood that I was not a proficient typist. But he did not castigate me. Rather, he showed that example was better than precept. That was a lesson in leadership I was able to apply years later as a supervisor and the head of a section in the police force.

My romantic involvement with Miss Edna Johnson

My younger brother had a lady acquaintance in about 1952. One day, the two of them paid me a casual visit at my residence. After a few minutes conversation, the lady said she should return to work at the female dressmaker shop where she was employed. It was my lunch break. As the dressmaker's shop was along the route from my house to the customs department, I accompanied both my brother and his lady acquaintance to the dressmaker's shop. To my surprise, among the other ladies I met at this seamstress shop (female dressmakers were called seamstress) was the light-complexioned lady who used to pass along Alcock Street several months previously but whom I had temporarily lost sight of. We all engaged in a short friendly conversation, after which I left to return to work.

The next day, I visited the seamstress shop – my main motivation being to see and converse with the fair-complexioned lady. Gradually, I became more and more attracted to this fair slim lady. I instinctively sensed that she was also attracted to me. Her name was Miss Edna Johnson.

I owned a bicycle at the time. Frequently when I was going home for lunch in the afternoon, I would visit all the young ladies at the dressmaker's shop. But my intent was to converse with Edna Johnson. Gradually, we both fell madly in love.

Edna and I eventually married at St Anthony Roman Catholic Church at Brookfields, Freetown, on 9 February 1956. The marriage ceremony was a very modest one, and we are still happily married as of this writing.

chapter 2

JOINING THE POLICE FORCE

BECOMING A POLICE OFFICER

In 1956, I was already a second-class customs officer and was in charge of the correspondence section (chief clerk) at HM Customs.

In those days, Sierra Leoneans were precluded by the British colonial administrators from the higher ranks in the civil service. Nevertheless, it had always been my burning desire to be a senior official in the civil service one day. Sometime in February 1956, I saw an advertisement in the *Sierra Leone Royal Gazette* for sub-inspectors (chief clerk) and cadet sub-inspectors. I had all the criteria for both posts.

As I was already a chief clerk at the customs department, I applied for post of sub-inspector (chief clerk) together with several others. Eventually, ten of us who had applied for the position were successful in the interview, and we were sent for medical examinations. Four of us passed the medical examination and we were enlisted into the Sierra Leone Police Force as sub-inspectors (chief clerks). Among those who had applied for the post of cadet sub-inspector, about twenty were successful at the interview. They were also sent to undergo medical examinations, and five passed. But only four were enlisted in the police force. The other was placed on the waiting list.

Another cadet sub-inspector of police was enlisted in Britain and joined us later on, whilst we were already undergoing training at the Police Training School at Hastings near Freetown.

According to the conditions, sub-inspectors (chief clerks) were not to be promoted above the rank of chief inspector. But cadet sub-inspectors were being groomed for higher ranks, starting from the rank of assistant superintendent of police (ASP). Later the policy was changed by the commissioner of police to enable sub-inspectors (chief clerks) to be promoted to senior ranks.

To Police Training School, Hastings

Sometime in May 1956, all of us recruits entered the Police Training School at Hastings, where we were lodged during our training. The fifth recruit cadet sub-inspector who was recruited in Britain[1] joined us a few days later.

The training school's commandant was Captain D. Dale-Smith, an ex-paratrooper in the British Army. During the Second World War, he and others were parachuted into then occupied Europe with the intention of securing certain key points ahead of the advancing Allied Forces. But Captain Dale-Smith, together with a few others, was captured by German soldiers. He spent the rest of the war as a prisoner of war in Germany. On his release after the war ended in 1945, he was enlisted as a senior officer in the British Colonial Police Force and posted to the Sierra Leone Police Force. He was a strict disciplinarian, and he instilled discipline in us. As recruit police officers, we were all subjected to very strict discipline.

---

[1] There may be doubt how this recruit cadet sub-inspector happened to have been recruited in Britain instead of in Sierra Leone. In 1956, Sierra Leone was still a colony of Britain and had not yet been granted independence. Independence would be granted five years later in April 1961. So in 1956, Britain was still responsible for the administration of Sierra Leone. Personnel for senior posts in the civil service of Sierra Leone were recruited in Britain. Since cadet sub-inspectors were considered to be in training for higher posts in the police force, vacancies for the posts of cadet sub-inspectors were also advertised in Britain, and the colonial office in London selected this recruit.

At 5.00 a.m., we would be awakened by the sound of a bugle and made to perform physical exercises, which included running to and from a section at Hastings called Robangbah, a round distance of about two miles. After that, we would shower and get dressed in our uniforms within a relatively short time and would assemble, after which we were marched in formation from our billet to the dining hall. In the dining hall, we had a limited amount of time to take breakfast. Then we would be marched to go either on parade or to lectures.

**Cadet Sub-Inspectors and Sub-Inspectors (Chief Clerk)
who were enlisted in the Sierra Leone Police Force in April 1956
seen here with the Commandant and two of their lecturers
at Police Training School, Hastings, Sierra Leone**

Cadet Sub-Inspectors and Sub-Inspectors (Chief Clerk) who were enlisted in April 1956, seen here with the Commandant, Police Training School, Hastings and two members of staff of the Training School.

Front Row (seated) – from Left to Right: Gerald Williams, Sub-Inspector (Chief Clerk); Melvin Macauley, Cadet Sub-Inspector; Inspector Salieu Bangura, Lecturer; Capt. D. Dale-Smith, Deputy Supt. of Police, Commandant; Chief Inspector E.M. Speck, Lecturer; Ezekiel A. Coker, Sub-Inspector (Chief Clerk); Cyril S. Grant, Cadet Sub-Inspector.

Rear Row (standing) – from left to right: Darlington W. Quee, Cadet Sub-Inspector; Maurice Rotobah-During, Cadet Sub-Inspector; Frank A. Jalloh, Sub-Inspector (Chief Clerk); J.S.F. Williams, Sub-Inspector (Chief Clerk); Abdul O. Bangura, Cadet Sub-Inspector.

**Cadet Sub-Inspectors of Police and
Sub-Inspectors (Chief Clerks)**

Cadet sub-inspectors including myself in 1956

About three weeks into the training at the Police Training School, the cadet sub-inspector who had been enlisted while he was in Britain resigned. He said that the food was not palatable to him. He called the rice as "granite."

Cyril Grant, who was already on the waiting list, filled his place. Cyril was a teacher at the Methodist Boy's High School. Fate was stalking him. We had all passed successfully through training and posted to various police divisions in the country. In 1965, Cyril was transferred to the anti-diamond smuggling squad in the CID. One Saturday in 1966 or thereabouts, he was escorting a known diamond smuggler to a ship berthed alongside the QE II Quay to be deported. The deportee, called Kurubally, was a Malian citizen who had been convicted in the court for the smuggling of diamonds and sentenced to a short term of imprisonment, after which he was ordered to be deported.

Kurubally was secretly resentful for his conviction and deportation. While he and Cyril were waiting at the QE II Quay before Kurubally was escorted on board the vessel, his handcuffs were taken off. Meanwhile, Kurubally found a heavy piece of metal which was lying on the ground. He hit Cyril on the head with the metal, crushing Cyril's skull. He died in hospital the following day.

On completion of recruit training, I was posted to the then colony division as chief clerk to the chief police officer, Mr Leslie William Leigh (commonly called William Leigh). In December 1958, I was transferred to divisional police headquarters at Kenema in the Eastern Province of Sierra Leone as chief clerk to the chief police officer, eastern division for a few months. In April 1959, I was transferred to police headquarters, Freetown as chief clerk. At this post, I worked under the eyes of the commissioner of police, the deputy commissioner of police, and the assistant commissioner, who were all British. The commissioner was W.G. Syer, the deputy commissioner was Anthony Sherriff Keeling, and the assistant commissioner was D.V. Noot. After serving as chief clerk at police headquarters, I was transferred to the CID as chief clerk in about June 1960. In November 1960, I was selected, together with Chief Inspector Albert Brown, to be sent to Glasgow Police (now Strathclyde Police) in Scotland for training in the examination of handwriting and typewriting in documents that were exhibits in cases being investigated by the CID.

On the successful completion of the training, both Albert and myself returned to Freetown. We were again posted to the CID and mandated to establish a questioned documents examination section in the CID. This we did with enthusiasm and expeditiously.

On 1 July 1962, I was promoted to the rank of assistant superintendent of police (ASP) – in other words, the first rank of senior officers from the bottom in the senior hierarchy of the police force.

I then purchased my first car – a Vauxhall Victor saloon of British manufacture – with a loan from the accountant general in accordance with the provisions in the general orders of the civil service. No interest was paid on the loan. That provision in the general orders for loans to be given to senior civil servants to purchase cars of British manufacture but without paying interest on such loans was a legacy of the British colonial rule.

MY TRANSFER TO THE SPECIAL BRANCH

Sometime in March 1963, I was transferred from the questioned document examination section at the CID to the Special Branch. This was the only intelligence service in the country apart from the Military Intelligence Bureau that dealt only with matters relating to the military.

The next day, I reported officially to the head of the Special Branch, Assistant Commissioner of Police John Ellen. John, a British national, had wide experience in the intelligence service. He was in the Special Branch in the British colony of Malaya when that colony was gripped by bloody insurgency.

After the serious riots in Freetown, followed by the uprising against some of the chiefs in the then protectorate in 1955 and 1956, the Sierra Leone colonial government set up a commission of inquiry to look into all the causes for these serious civil disorders in the country and to make recommendations to prevent the recurrence of such serious civil unrests in the future. One of the findings of the commission of inquiry was that the government lacked an intelligence service, which could have had foreknowledge of the causes for the disorders. It was suggested that such a service might have forewarned the government and suggested appropriate action to forestall the serious disturbances that had erupted in the country.

Through the colonial office in Britain, John Ellen, who was a senior officer in the Malaya Special Branch, was then transferred from Malaya to Sierra Leone in 1956 and given the task of creating a Special Branch in Sierra Leone, similar to the Special Branch in Britain. On arrival, Assistant Commissioner John Ellen started to organise a Special Branch in the police force. Thus was born the Special Branch in Sierra Leone in 1956 with John Ellen as its head.

Sierra Leone had gained independence from Britain in 1961. Yet two years later in 1963, a substantial number of British expatriates still occupied senior ranks in the civil service, as well as in the army and the police force. The commissioner of police at that time was Anthony S. Keeling, also British. Most of the other senior police officers were also British.

The second in command in the Special Branch was Anthony Hall, who was also British and held the rank of a superintendent of police. Unlike John Ellen, who was a trained and experienced intelligence officer, Tony Hall had no vast experience in intelligence, apart from a very short spell in intelligence whilst he was enlisted in the British Army before he was appointed as assistant superintendent of police (ASP) and posted to the Sierra Leone Police Force.

The next senior officer was Alpha Kamara, who was a Sierra Leonean. Two other senior officers in the Special Branch were Bill Quee, deputy superintendent of police (DSP), and Alfred Koroma, assistant superintendent of police (ASP). Both were Sierra Leoneans.

John Ellen welcomed me and intimated me that I had good credentials for work in the Special Branch. He then briefly explained to me what went on in the Special Branch, including the importance of extreme secrecy. I was also informed of the section in the Special Branch to which I would be attached. John then informed me that I would be sent to London, England, in a few weeks for training in the British Special Branch training school for commonwealth police officers.

John introduced me to the senior members of staff, including a British woman who was the head of the registry section. The next senior staff in the registry was a young Sierra Leonean named Sarah Shears, who had recently arrived from Britain, where she had received training as a secretary.

My transfer to the Special Branch (the police intelligence service) opened my eyes to a vast array of knowledge I had previously not been privy to. And this knowledge was to facilitate my future advancement in the police force.

My orientation into the Special Branch included lectures by the second in command, Tony Hall. In his lectures to me, he strongly emphasised loyalty to the government, as well as total secrecy. It was also impressed upon me that I should not tell anyone outside Special Branch what went on in there. Nor was I to disclose to anyone the contents of reports I had seen. Different aspects of security were explained to me, including the importance of always securing all reports, files, and keys. I found all this secrecy somewhat strange at first. But very soon, I came to understand both its importance and the need for security in the Special Branch.

When I had been in the Special Branch for about two weeks, one day I left my office and went upstairs to the registry. I left my office open and the keys for the office door and the filing cabinet in my office on my desk. On my return, I did not see the keys. I searched everywhere, but still the keys could not be located. I asked my colleagues in the opposite office whether they had seen my keys. They said they had not gone into my office. I became very worried and uneasy. Late in the afternoon, the head of the Special Branch called me to his office and enquired whether I had seen my keys. I replied that I had not.

He then produced the keys and gave me a stern lecture on keeping my keys secure. He said he'd casually gone into my office whilst I was upstairs in the registry and had found the office door open and the keys lying on the desk. He had, therefore, picked up the keys. He lectured me, pointing out that a stranger who was intent on stealing secrets could have easily walked into my office and picked up secret files along with the keys. He added that the stranger could have made quick impressions of the keys, and duplicate keys could have been made for unauthorised entry into the office to steal secrets. I apologised for these lapses.

He could have caused an adverse entry to be made in my records. But instead, he warned me very strictly against such lapses in security. From that day on, I was never careless in the handling of keys, not even my personal keys. And so I was indoctrinated into the intelligence service. And I soon "fell in love" with it.

At first, I was placed under the tutelage of Alfred Koroma, one of the original personnel who had started the Special Branch along with John Ellen. Alfred, as he was fondly called, was an average educated officer. Nevertheless, he was quite proficient in the collection of intelligence. He was, without doubt, a talented officer in intelligence collection. Through his efforts, the Special Branch succeeded in acquiring vital intelligence on many delicate matters. But he seemed jealous of his role in the Special Branch and was not enthusiastic about introducing me to all the secrets of the Special Branch.

Nevertheless, apart from this minor kink in his character, Alfred was quite a nice guy and someone who was easy to get along with. Under the circumstances, I had to learn about intelligence duties in the hard way, until I proceeded to London for a short course of training in intelligence.

After returning from training in London, I was again posted to the Special Branch, where I was to serve for a long time.

POLICE TRAINING IN AMERICA

In April 1965, I was sent to the United States of America for training at the then International Police Academy in Washington DC. I arrived in Washington DC early in the evening of Saturday, 17 April 1965. On Monday, 19 April, I reported at the International Police Academy in

Washington DC. There were police officers from different countries, including Liberia, Nigeria, Ethiopia, Iran, Iraq, the Philippines, Syria, and Vietnam, as well as a few from countries in South America.

We received training in various aspects of police administration and operations. It was at this academy that I was taught properly how to shoot a pistol. This aspect of police training in America was taken very seriously, as many police officers in America were (and still are) being shot while on duty. During this training, each of us in the class was asked by our lecturer how many policemen had been shot in our respective countries during the last three years. When I replied that no policeman had ever been shot during that period, the lecturer could hardly believe me. Finally, we also received a short course in counter-insurgency at the large military base in Fort Bragg, North Carolina.

RACIAL PREJUDICE EXPERIENCED IN AMERICA

I had been to Britain twice before my training in America. In Britain, I had sometimes seen racial prejudice demonstrated in a subtle manner and I'd always ignored it. During this training in America, we trainees were taken on official sightseeing tours by bus to other states in America. When on such trips, we students from Africa tended to adhere to the principle "birds of a feather flock together" – those of us from Nigeria, Liberia, and Ethiopia traveling in a group. At that time, racial prejudice was still rampant in America.

During one such tour, we passed through Madison, the capital of the state of Wisconsin. It was lunchtime, and our official guide took the entire group to a restaurant, which apparently had been booked in advance of our arrival. Each of us had displayed prominently on the front our jackets a tag, indicating that we were official guests of the government of the United States of America. It was during the time that Martin Luther King, Jr was in the midst of his campaign for racial equality in America. Unfortunately, the campaign had not yet taken root in many Americans. A certain amount of prejudice against blacks was still in practice.

At the restaurant, each of us ordered, and the waiters said we would be served soon. After several minutes of waiting, we Africans observed that, whereas all the white and Asian students, as well as those from the Middle East, had been served, we had not been. We called the attention of the waiters several times, and we were told that we would be served soon. We waited indefinitely.

All the white students had completed their meals, but still we black students had not been served. It was then that we realised that we were not going to be served, as we were black. I had twice been to Britain to receive training, and I had never experienced open racial prejudice. The racial prejudice there was subtle. But this glaring show of prejudice in the United States of America greatly surprised me.

We protested vehemently to our official guide, who was quite embarrassed. He had a lengthy conversion with the manager of the restaurant. It was then that we were assured that we would be served almost immediately. We refused the promised service and stormed out of the restaurant, saying that we would be poisoned. Instead, we headed to a nearby Chinese restaurant, where we had our lunch.

We told our guide that we would make an official complaint to the director of the International Police Academy when we returned to Washington DC. But he pleaded with us not to submit a report and confessed with embarrassment that, unfortunately, racial prejudice lingered in some parts in America. We therefore relented. But on our return to Washington, our guide made an official report to the director of the International Police Academy, who apologised to us, explaining again that, unfortunately, lingering prejudice against blacks remained in some parts of America.

On the other hand, A.J. Brown, another police officer from Sierra Leone – who had arrived in America a few weeks earlier for handwriting analysis in questioned and disputed documents training with another institution – was being taken care of by a Jewish couple, the Gaitlemans. When I later arrived in DC, Mr Gaitleman arranged for A.J. and I to reside in a newly constructed apartment complex

(Park Monroe Apartment) on Sixteenth Street. Mr Gaitleman also arranged for the apartment to be furnished with rental furniture. At the end of every month, A.J. and I split the rent for both the apartment and the furniture. In addition, the Gaitlemans regularly invited A.J. and I to dinner at their residence in Maryland on the weekends. They would also drive us to see places of interest in DC, Maryland, and Virginia. They were truly a wonderful couple to us, despite being white.

chapter 3

MY IMPRISONMENT

OMINOUS POLITICAL STORM GATHERING OVER SIERRA LEONE

On returning to Freetown, I was again posted to the Special Branch. Dr Milton Margai, the chairman of the Sierra Leone People's Party (SLPP) and first prime minister of Sierra Leone after the country gained independence in April 1961, died on 28 April 1964. He was succeeded as prime minister by his younger brother, Albert Margai, a lawyer. There followed a growing political struggle between the SLPP and the All People's Congress (APC) under the leadership of the very crafty and charismatic Siaka Stevens, a former trade union leader. Very soon, the dark and ominous clouds of political problems, which had not occurred under the British colonial administration or under the short rule of Dr Milton Margai, darkened the country.

In March 1967, Sierra Leone saw its first military coup. A few days later, a counter-coup followed. This second coup was led by young military officers, who formed the National Reformation Council (NRC) under the leadership of then Major (later Brigadier) Andrew Juxon-Smith. They ruled the country relatively well, except for a slight kink in the character of Brig. Juxon-Smith, who tended to be an extreme martinet.

MUTINY BY SOLDIERS IN THE ARMY

Agitation for the overthrow of the NRC soon followed. As the agitation continued, the Special Branch received a flow of reliable information pertaining to the diabolical plans being made by some politicians for the violent overthrow of the NRC, if its members were reluctant to hand over power to the APC. Eventually, beginning on the evening of Wednesday, 17 April 1968, a group of army NCOs staged a military coup. This resulted in almost all senior police and army officers being arrested and detained at Pademba Road Prison. I was among them.

Chronicled below are the events that took place during the military coup. Around 10.00 p.m. on that fateful night, Commissioner of Police William Leigh, together with his family, arrived unexpectedly at my residence at the top of the Central Police Station in the old Elder Dempster building along Water Street, Freetown. The commissioner informed me that soldiers in Murray Town barracks, not too far from his Murray Town residence, had started to revolt. Sporadic gunshots had been fired in the barracks. He and his wife had fled quickly from their residence. The commissioner of police was the deputy chairman of the National Reformation Council (NRC).

Leaving his wife at my residence with my family, the commissioner and I rushed downstairs to the station, where a few officers had already assembled as per prearranged instructions for any emergency. Among the officers was Alpha Kamara, assistant commissioner of police. He and Commissioner Leigh were the only two police officers in the NRC.

The commissioner ordered Alpha Kamara and myself to go up to Special Branch. We were to collect another officer there and drive together up to Wilberforce, where we were to pass through the main public road in front of the military barracks and assess the situation there. Under the circumstances, this was a potentially dangerous assignment. But an order, especially one from the commissioner himself, could not be disobeyed.

Alpha Kamara and I drove up to the Special Branch office at State Avenue. There we met Ira Manley, who resided at Wilberforce Village not far from the military barracks. He said that, when he'd heard unusual commotion and sporadic gunfire at the barracks, he'd driven down to the Special Branch to find out what was happening. Alpha Kamara conveyed the commissioner's order. We decided to take one of the Special Branch vehicles, a Volkswagen Beetle with no police identification. We summoned one of the drivers and ordered him to drive us up to the main road, which passed through Wilberforce Military Barracks. Before setting on our journey, I took an Uzi sub-machine gun and loaded about thirty bullets in the magazine. The three of us, together with the driver, set off in the unmarked Volkswagen Beetle car towards Wilberforce.

The night was quiet. The military barracks was located on a hill which could be approached through Hill Cot Road, part of which was in a valley. From the lower part of Hill Cot Road, we could see from the distance to the right that the barracks were illuminated, and we couldn't hear any gunfire from the barracks. We became complacent. Reaching the top of Hill Cut Road, we turned right towards the main public road, which went through the barracks. A few hundred yards down the road, as soon as we turned a slight bend, we saw through the headlights of the car a large roadblock manned by soldiers, who we could see were in an agitated mood. The driver dared not stop the car abruptly to allow us to try and escape. That might have resulted in a hail of oncoming bullets. So he was told to continue slowly towards the roadblock.

Before the car had come to a halt, soldiers had already surrounded it. Some were shouting words mixed with expletives, upset that another group of officers were inside the car. As they saw men in civilian clothes inside the car, they thought we were army officers trying to escape. There was a wild rush by some of the soldiers to open the door of the Volkswagen. At the same time, we were shouting that we were not army officers but police officers on night patrol to catch burglars.

During the ongoing commotion, a military sergeant forced his way through the throng of agitated soldiers and rushed towards the car. Fortunately, there were bright lights around that area of the barracks. Alpha Kamara had, by this time, been dragged out of the front seat.

Ira Manley and I were in the back seat and, as is well known, the only way to exit the Volkswagen was through either of the front doors. My heart was already pounding. I was thinking about the loaded Uzi sub-machine gun on the floor of the car and what would happen when the soldiers saw it. I guessed that would be our end.

Fortunately, the military sergeant recognised Alpha Kamara. He shouted above the din and confusion that "Kortor Kamara" ("**Kotor**" *is an expression in the Temne language meaning someone of his status or someone for whom you have high respect*) was a police officer and that the other people in the car were not army officers but police officers. He instructed the soldiers to open the roadblock and let us drive through. The roadblock was partially opened, and we were allowed to drive through. We drove down the road, and fortunately, we did not encounter any other road blocks.

We thanked our stars at having escaped from what might have almost certainly been our death, had the soldiers discovered the loaded Uzi inside the car. We drove as fast as we could down to Central Police Station, where we informed the commissioner what had transpired between us and the mutinous soldiers at Wilberforce and how out of control the situation was. The commissioner ordered us, along with the few uniformed officers who had arrived at Central Police Station, to proceed to our respective police formations in Freetown and take charge of the police personnel there but not to offer any resistance to the military.

Ira Manley and I headed to the Special Branch. Whilst we were in the compound there, we heard vehicles rushing along the streets and soldiers shouting and firing sporadically, we believed in the air. About half an hour later, we started hearing automatic gunfire coming from the direction of Central Police Station at Water Street. My apartment was located on the top floor of the old Elder Dempster building at

Water Street nearby. My family had been left in the apartment since the commissioner had ordered all officers to report to our respective formations. From the duration of the automatic gunfire, I concluded that my family had been massacred by rampaging soldiers. I wanted revenge.

Tom Kessebeh, who was then the head of the Special Branch, had already arrived at headquarters. I told him that I believed my family had all been massacred, as volleys of automatic gunshots could be heard coming from the direction of Central Police Station. I further told Tom that I was going to avenge the massacre of my family. I took out the Uzi sub-machinegun, concealed myself behind a concrete pillar, and readied myself to shoot soldiers who would attempt to enter the compound of the Special Branch. Had I carried out my intention, it would have been suicidal and might have resulted in the killing of the other Special Branch officers.

But I was then, for a very brief period, temporarily insane. Tom Kessebeh advised me not to act impulsively and precipitately because my family might not have been killed. He ordered me to put away the Uzi and go inside the Special Branch. I complied.

I tried to contact the police information room, which was at the time located in another section above the Central Police Station, over the radio. But all the police radios had become silent. Nervously, I telephoned my apartment. Fortunately, the phone to the apartment was still working. The voice of Jenkins Smith, then deputy commissioner, answered the phone. He recognised my voice. I enquired what was going on there. He replied in a trembling whisper that soldiers had shot their way into my apartment where his own family and the family of the commissioner had sought refuge together with my family. He added that, fortunately, no one had been killed or injured. He had been in hiding somewhere in the station, but the soldiers had arrested the commissioner and a few other police officers and taken them away. Alpha Kamara had escaped from the agitated soldiers. The conversation was abruptly cut short when he whispered that soldiers were again about to enter the apartment; he could hear the sounds of boots approaching the apartment. I was, thus, temporarily assured that my family had not been massacred.

The other officers and I remained in the Special Branch compound till daybreak the next day, by which time swarms of soldiers were all over the city, firing wildly and sporadically. We were quite afraid, not knowing exactly what was going on. Around 10.00 or 11.00 a.m. some soldiers, led by a sergeant, came to the compound in a military Land Rover and seized all the arms and ammunition at the Special Branch headquarters. The sergeant singled me out and told me to enter the Land Rover, which I did nervously. He drove down to Central Police Station and ordered me to alight. He asked me in an aggressive manner where the other police officers were. I told him that I earnestly did not know. He pointed the muzzle of his rifle menacingly towards me and said he was going to shoot me if I did not disclose the whereabouts of the other officers. I was petrified and responded nervously again that I did not know where the other officers were. He then lowered the muzzle of the rifle and said he was not going to shoot me.

After searching around Central Police Station and having seen no officers, the sergeant again ordered me to board the Land Rover, after which he drove the vehicle to Special Branch headquarters, where he left me. I joined the other Special Branch officers and personnel and told them what transpired between the sergeant and myself. We were all scared and wondering what our fate would be.

Meanwhile, we were made to understand that many army and police officers had been arrested and detained at the military guardroom at Wilberforce Military Barracks. Around 4.00 p.m., a small group of policemen headed by a police sergeant arrived at the compound in a police Land Rover. They told us officers that we were invited to attend a conference at Wilberforce Barracks. The sergeant was armed with a revolver, and the other policemen carried rifles. Of course we were not fools. We understood that the sergeant had been sent to arrest us. We knew that "invited" was a euphemism for arrest. We had no option but to comply with the "invitation" to go to the "conference." But we were not in any way molested. Tom

Kessebeh, Ira Manley, Alfred Koroma, and I climbed into the Land Rover, which was then driven to the barracks guardroom.

There, military sergeant majors and sergeants welcomed us with kicks, after which they asked us our names and ranks. These were then recorded in a register. Next, we were shoved into a large cell that was already holding many police officers including Commissioner Leigh, who had been arrested during the night when the mutiny had commenced. Some had slight wounds and torn clothes as a result of the beatings they had suffered at the hands of the soldiers who had arrested them. Many of the officers appeared dejected and despondent, although a few appeared to be in a feigned buoyant mood. Otherwise, there were no reports of any officers having been shot. This reassured those of us who had just been arrested.

Whilst we were in the cell, I saw what appeared to be water in a corner. Some of our colleagues told us that all pleas with the soldiers who were guarding the cell to be allowed to use the toilet had fallen on deaf ears. As such, they had been compelled to use the corner as an emergency urinal. Urine was flowing around some parts of the large cell. In an adjacent large cell were many military officers, including Brig. Andrew Juxon-Smith, Col. Charles Blake, and several others who had also been arrested at different locations during the night.

Around 5.00 p.m. on the evening of 18 April 18, both the military officers and the police officers so far arrested were again documented by NCOs in the army. Next, we were handcuffed in pairs and ordered to mount two large military trucks, which had been driven to the entrance of the guardroom. Any officers who were not able to mount the trucks quickly were assisted by kicks from the soldiers. We were made to sit down on the floor of each truck, obscuring our view of the road. We were then driven in a convoy under armed escorts. With the recent military coups of Ghana and Nigeria in mind, during which it was reported that some officers had been shot, I was apprehensive at first. I thought we were being conveyed to a secret location to be shot. But soon we glanced the tops of few buildings we recognised, and we guessed we were being conveyed to Pademba Road Prison in Freetown.

On arrival at the entrance of the prison, we met some armed soldiers. They shouted at us to alight from the trucks quickly. Still handcuffed in pairs, we were led into the "processing room" for prisoners. In this room, the handcuffs were unlocked and the individual "processing" of each of us began. Everyone was ordered to undress completely. We were each weighed naked and our individual weight recorded in a register by a prison officer. Next, we were ordered to surrender all items in our possession, including watches, trousers belts, money, shoes and socks, and the like. These articles were recorded by a prison officer and deposited in separate bags. The prison officer informed us that if and when we were released, these personal belongings would be returned to us.

Following this "processing", we were lined up in twos and ordered to march barefoot into the inner part of the prison compound. The path was enclosed in thick chicken wire, interspersed with coils of barbed wires, on top of which were additional coils of barbed wire. We encountered three gates, each of which had to be unlocked by a prison officer before we could proceed to the other compartment.

At last, we arrived in front of a large two-storey building that was to be our "guest house" during the period of our detention. This was Clarkson House. Each block of buildings containing cells in Pademba Road Prison was named after one of the former British governors of the colony of Sierra Leone.

About 120 military and police officers from the rank of lieutenant in the army (assistant superintendent in the police force) and above were detained in Clarkson House in the maximum security prison at Pademba Road. My rank at the time was deputy superintendent of police (DSP), the equivalent of captain in the military.

We were led to the upstairs floor of Clarkson House, and three of us (a mixture of army and police officers) were shoved into a cell of approximately 10 foot by 10 feet. I was placed in cell B-2-2, together with Chris Thomas, another police officer, and an army lieutenant, Larry Lightfoot-Boston. Larry was the youngest of the three of us. As we were being placed into the cell, the prison officer in charge of that cell listed our names. Then the thick wooden cell door was shut with a loud bang, and the three of us were left in the cell. So commenced what, for most us, would be four months of twenty-four-hour-a-day confinement with three meals a day as "guests" of the new Sierra Leone government.

A few minutes after we'd been locked in the cells, the prison officer in charge of each row of the cells distributed six blankets to each cell, as well as a bucket containing water and three metal cups. The prison guard in charge of our cell explained that two of the blankets were intended for each of us. There were no mattresses or pillows. After this, each cell door was, as usual thereafter, shut with a heavy bang, and we were left to ourselves for a short period. Each of us then spread one blanket on the bare concrete floor and folded the top to serve as a pillow. The other blanket would serve as cover. After this, Chris and Larry began to talk about how and where they were each arrested.

Chris Thomas and Larry Lightfoot-Boston shared stories about their individual experiences from the night through the afternoon. Chris and Larry did not seem very concerned about our fate. Their chatter was lively. But I was morose. Being in the Special Branch (in other words, the police intelligence service) I had been privy to grim information prior to our arrest – information suggesting that, for our perceived support of Brig. Juxon-Smith and his NRC regime, vengeance was going to be brought on us. Therefore, I was rather apprehensive and not inclined to talk.

After about an hour (around 9.00 p.m.) three plates of rice and stew, each with a small piece of fish, were supplied to each cell. Chris Thomas and Larry Lightfoot-Boston took plates, leaving one plate for me. No spoons were supplied, leaving us to eat the meal with our bare hands. I had eaten rice with a spoon since I was young, so eating with my bare hand was somewhat awkward. But I was soon to learn how to eat with the naked hand (*mondor* in Creole). Chris Thomas and Larry, on the other hand, quickly gobbled their own rice with their bare hands. As for me, I only took two or three handfuls of the rice with my bare hand. But before I could put the rice into my mouth, nearly half of what I'd scooped up would drop back into the plate. After several attempts, I became frustrated and abandoned the plate of rice, shoving it to one corner on the floor. On seeing this, Chris eagerly asked me whether I did not want to eat. I replied that I had no appetite. He made fun of me. He said that I was thinking of Edna (my wife). He said that, if I did not eat, I would die. We laughed over his humorous comments. Then he quickly drew my plate of rice from the corner, and within a short time, he had devoured the contents.

At 10.00 or 11.00 p.m., the bright lights along the corridor that illuminated each of the cells were turned off, leaving only dim lighting. That was a signal for us to go to sleep.

Imprisonment was traumatic. Suddenly, we found that we were confined to a small cell with no beds and made to suffer degradation, lying on the bare floor with only a thin sheet of blanket. This made me more and more dejected, and I could not sleep.

My mind was wild. I pondered our ultimate fate and the fate that might have befallen my wife, mother, and children, who I had left in my apartment above Central Police Station soon after the coup had started the previous evening. Occasionally as I lay down on the floor of the cell, I could detect someone peeping on us through the peephole on the cell door. After a long time, I fell asleep. But I was soon startled by the sounds of heavy boots along the corridor in front of our cell. I realised that I was not in my comfortable bed at home but on the floor of a cell I could not leave. I heard low whispers, after which the sounds of the boots moved towards other cells. After a few minutes, I got up from my "bed" on the floor and watched through the peephole. I saw on the opposite corridor of our block a few soldiers with guns, together with some prison officers going from one cell door to another to view us detainees.

My mind began to play tricks on me. I started to think that we were being inspected prior to being led out of our cells to be shot. I awoke my two cellmates and informed them of the goings-on. They seemed not to be particularly concerned, and they soon fell asleep again.

Morning was rather slow in coming, and I'd had few fitful hours of sleep. I thanked God silently for letting me see another day. At about 6.00 a.m., each cell was opened, we were allowed to congregate outside the corridor along the top floor. We were also permitted to wash our faces and use the toilet. We chatted, our voices lively. Following this, we were each served a hot cup of coffee and two thin slices of bread with a thin layer of butter between the slices. We voraciously devoured the "breakfast" that was provided for us. We conversed for about half an hour, after which we were ordered to return to our respective cells. Then each of the cell doors was shut with the now familiar loud bang.

In the afternoon, around 1.00 or 2.00 p.m., lunch was distributed to each cell. Each of us received a plate of rice, on top of which was either *plassas* soup or stew with very few pieces of fish. After lunch, we were left in peace to relax. In the evening, around 7.00 p.m., supper was served. The meal consisted of a cup of coffee and two slices of bread with a thin layer of butter between. At about 10.00 p.m., the lights along the corridors of the cells were turned off, and only a few dim lights remained. This was to be the routine whilst we were in detention at Pademba Road Prison.

When any of us wanted to use the toilet, we had to knock on the cell door, after which the prison officer on duty would approach the cell and enquire what we wanted. When informed that one of us wanted to use the toilet, he would summon another colleague, and the two of them would position themselves vigilantly by the cell door before opening the door and allowing the individual detainee to go to the toilet on the far end of the block. Only a few of us were let out to use the toilet at a time, after which another group would be allowed to go. As restrictive as the practice was, it was not too bad.

This relaxed atmosphere continued for about three or four days. All of us thought that our detention was not too hard after all. But we were soon proved wrong by the consequent deplorable conditions under which we were compelled to live and the harassment and humiliations we were to suffer at the hands of prison officers.

The toilet at the far end of the block was filthy; urine covered part of the uneven floor. Urine would pool in the slight depressions in the floor, about a quarter of an inch deep in some spots. Thin layers of faeces were also scattered on various parts of the floor. One had to tiptoe to avoid the faeces on the floor in order to get to the toilet seat, which also was soiled. The stench was nauseating. I had been used to a flawlessly clean toilet devoid of any offensive odour. Now there I was, taking very good care not to step on thin layers of faeces. All these conditions demoralised me further.

After about a week, we were in for a shock. One afternoon, prison officers started distributing a second bucket to each cell. Some of us enquired what the extra buckets were intended for. We were told that, henceforth, we would no longer be allowed to use the toilet at the far end of the block. Rather, we would have to use the extra bucket for our toilet needs. We protested that this would be most unhygienic.

From then onwards, whenever any of us wanted to go to the toilet and knocked on the cell door, the prison guard on duty would simply say, "Use your *poh.*"

One of the prison sergeants was particularly heartless. He was in no way sympathetic to any of us. Even when any of us became ill, which was quite common given the unhygienic conditions in the cells, all he would do was upbraid us for knocking on the cell door and threaten us with punishment. Consequently, since none of us could get any redress, we could not help but to use the extra bucket for all our toilet needs.

There were two buckets in each cell, one of which contained fresh water, which the ordinary prisoners would replenish daily in the morning. The other bucket was where the three of us in each cell would urinate and defecate. We had to do everything inside our respective cells. We had to wash our faces and clean our teeth with the water in the other bucket. We had no soap, no toothpaste, and no toothbrushes. We had to go to the toilet in front of each other. When any of us wanted to expel intestinal gas, we would inform the two others, who would then cover their nostrils with their blankets until the odour was gone. There was nothing that could be done. In our cell, we would each cover ourselves with our blankets whilst defecating. But the odour could not be masked. We learnt to be most tolerant towards each other.

At first, one toilet roll was supplied to each cell. But those were exhausted within a few days. No additional toilet rolls were supplied. The attention of the prison guards was called. But still no additional toilet rolls were supplied. So we officers were compelled to use bits and pieces of our underwear. When our underwear was completely used up, each of us turned to using parts of our trousers, starting with one leg. When that leg was short, we would go to the other leg of the trousers. It was after several weeks of this humiliation that a roll of toilet tissue was again supplied to each cell. But before long, that roll was exhausted, and we had to resort again to tearing part of our clothes to clean up.

One afternoon, we were reshuffled and transferred to different cells. I was placed in cell B-2-16 with another police officer, Jed Jackson, and an army captain, Ben Kargbo. This was to be my permanent cell until I was released. One of the adjacent cells contained Col. Charles Blake of the army and a former member of the NRC, Supt. Pelham of the police force, and another officer who I cannot now remember. Very occasionally I would get the opportunity to go along the corridor and peep into the adjacent cell (B-2-14) where Blake, Pelham, and the other officer were detained. I was full of admiration for Col. Charles Blake. He was optimistic. Not only that, he would neatly fold his own blankets when he was not lying down. He would, at times, offer words of encouragement to other inmates.

We were sequestered and kept incommunicado. We were forbidden to have any contact with anyone outside, not even with ordinary prisoners, who were given more laxity than us. We were forbidden to have in our possession razor blades to shave, newspapers or any other reading material (except the Holy Bible or the Holy Koran). Money, matches, soap, and the like were also forbidden. We were not permitted to bathe or shave. We were subjected to severe punishments if any of us was found with any of the contraband articles in our possession. No radio was available. If any of us was caught making contact with any of the other normal prisoners or with any contraband articles, we would be subjected to punishments, which included being placed in an isolation cell; being supplied half rations for several days; and, sometimes, beatings by prison guards.

Each cell was subjected to surprise searches at any time during the day or night. We were informed that, if any contraband articles were discovered in a cell and none of us would admit possession of the banned articles, then all three of us would be given collective punishment. But in spite of all these precautions by the prison authorities, some of us managed to outwit them. We had a way of concealing cigarettes, matches, and soap in the cell. Occasionally, newspapers, as well as money, would be smuggled in to us with the connivance of prison officers who were in the pay of some of our relatives in town.

In spite of the fact that we were kept in isolation with no news from the outside world, some prison guards who were given the right incentives would occasionally secretly give us titbits of news about what was going on around Freetown. Thus, we learnt that desperate efforts were being made by some of our relatives and others to secure our release.

Newspapers and money were difficult to conceal. But we managed to conceal these even when surprise searches of our cells were carried out. Later on, after our release, we learnt that not all the money our relatives were giving to the prison officers was delivered to us. The prison officers helped themselves to a large part of the money.

Meanwhile, we continued to be subjected to degrading and humiliating treatment by prison guards. On one Saturday, during about the third or fourth week of our detention, the guards supplying our lunch put the plates of rice on the floor and then kicked them into the cells, commenting all the while that, when we had taken our girlfriends to Lumley Beach, we had not invited them. Such comments were ludicrous. However, we had no recourse, we were forced to bear these unnecessary harassments and humiliation.

Detention was traumatic. The sudden loss of one's freedom and the degradation, as well as the restrictions we were subjected to, transformed our lives.

Some humorous incidents occurred while we were in prison. One evening, C.V. Roques, a police officer, was sick, I believe with the usual diarrhoea. He had knocked on his cell door incessantly to gain the attention of the prison guards. But none had turned up. Roques started to shout that, if he were allowed to die in cell, he would not agree but instead would protest. His comments incited lots of laughter from the rest of us. Some of us shouted to him that, if he were dead, how then could he protest?

To show how wicked some prison officers were, on one occasion, the prison officers were supplying lunch when one of the plates of rice accidentally capsized onto the filthy floor. Through the peephole on the door, we could see the prison officers collecting the rice from the filthy floor. We shouted to those on the opposite cell not to accept the plate of rice. It happened that it was Ivan R. Golley-Morgan, a police officer, who was supplied that plate of dirty rice collected from the filthy floor. He refused to accept the plate of rice. This resulted in the prison officers punishing him by beating him severely and dragging him to solitary confinement. He sustained serious injuries as result of the beatings.

I understand that, after we were eventually released from detention, he sued the prison officers who were responsible for assaulting him. But I don't know what became of the case. Golley-Morgan, who was a wireless engineer, resigned from the police force immediately after our release from detention.

THE ONLY VISIT TO US IN PRISON BY MEMBERS OF OUR FAMILIES

After we had been in detention for about six weeks without any shaving and bathing, each of us was requested to name any member of our family we would like to visit us. Eventually the day came when members of our families (one visitor for each detained officer) were allowed to visit. From Clarkson House, where all of us were detained, to the main building containing the administrative headquarters of the prison, the entire short distance was lined with armed soldiers. And we were called in very small groups to go see our relatives.

The visits were conducted in a large hall in the administrative building of the prison. We detainees sat on chairs along one side of a line of double tables. On the other side, opposite each detainee, sat the detainee's relative. The double tables were intended to prevent physical contact. They also required us to shout during the conversation. Armed soldiers, as well as armed policemen, were placed around the hall. Both the acting deputy commissioner of police and the director of prisons were there, listening intently to our conversations with our relatives.

Since none of us had been permitted to shave during the past month, we had grown beards. Some of our relatives burst into tears when they saw us – unkempt unshaven apparitions of our former selves. Anyhow, some good came out of the visits. I would later learn that, after the brief visit, our wives protested very seriously about the deplorable conditions in which we were being held. A few days later, we were allowed to take our first baths since our detention.

One morning, we were marched in small groups outside. When we arrived at a shed, we saw several buckets filled with water, along with a few small cakes of soap. Small groups of officers were allowed to use each bucket of water, and getting that water was a rush. Within a short time, the water in each of the buckets had been coated with human fat. And after a few minutes, the whistle was blown indicating that our time to bathe was over. We had no towels, and we air-dried our naked before re-donning the clothes we had worn since the beginning of our detention.

But after this "privilege" we were still subjected to strict restrictions and humiliations.

RECKLESS AND DANGEROUS INTENTIONS OF ARMY OFFICERS

After several weeks in detention, news spread among us detainees that some of the detained military officers were planning a revolt. They would seize the keys from the prison officers and make a break for it.

The senior police officers quickly circulated instructions through clandestine means that none of us police officers should get involved in the reckless and crazy plan. We police officers let it be known to the military officers that we were not going to join them in their reckless and dangerous plan. We added that, if they persisted, we would inform the prison officials because, if any attempt were made to stage a revolt in prison with the intention of escaping, soldiers would be called in. And they would massacre both military and police officers indiscriminately. After that warning, nothing further was heard about the reckless and dangerous plan to revolt and stage a mass escape.

Some rather surprising aspects of this mutiny or coup should be brought to light. Military coups or mutinies are usually followed by anarchy and mayhem. Some junior personnel typically seize the opportunity to pursue personal revenge against officers who might have imposed severe discipline on them. Army coups had recently occurred in Nigeria and Ghana, and these coups were accompanied by collateral fatalities among officers. There was absolutely no reason the coup in Sierra Leone should be different. The absence of any fatalities among officers did not happen by chance. It was later revealed, by secret and reliable sources, that the hidden hands secretly directing the mutiny behind the scene had strictly warned the leaders (the NCOs) who were carrying out the coup that, if no resistance was put up by the officers, then the operation should be carried out without bloodshed among them. Therefore, the NCOs carried out the entire operation in a humane manner.

RELEASE FROM PRISON AND SACKINGS
FROM THE POLICE FORCE

The humiliating treatment and harassment soon became "normal." After several weeks, we started to hear from secret sources that efforts were being made by the government for the release and reinstatement of some of us (both police and army officers). A few weeks later, on 23 August 1968, the majority of army and police officers were released from prison. I was among them. Only former NCR members were not released.

We had been in detention for four months. And we were glad to be once again free, to see people walking along the streets, and to enjoy the other benefits of freedom that we had hitherto missed. No one knows the value of freedom, which is taken for granted, until it is taken away.

I headed to 3 Clarence Street, not too far from the prisons. There I met Edna and the children, along with my mother. They had been given temporary shelter there by my brother Olu after my arrest.

Many army and police officers, mainly those who were Mendes[2], were prematurely retired. However, some of the released police officers were recalled to duty and reinstated in their former ranks. But a few police officers, including me, were not recalled, and we were kept in abeyance.

After about two weeks, I received a letter from the establishment secretary saying that I had been retired from the police force and that my retirement would be after the expiration of few weeks leave which I had already earned had expired..

I was stunned. I was forty-two years old. I later learnt from secret sources that my "sin" was that certain persons who harboured malice against me (and who most likely were police personnel) had informed political leaders then in power that, during the days when the SLPP

---

[2] The two largest ethnic groups in Sierra Leone are the Mende people and the Temne people.

and the NRC had been in power, I was overzealous in keeping track of the activities of APC members.

I accepted reality with fortitude and turned my attention to what I would do to support my immediate family. As I'd become a trained photographer whilst in the Special Branch, I decided that I would set up a professional photo studio. I also intended to purchase vehicles with the money for the gratuity I expected to be paid to me for my service in the government of Sierra Leone and set up a small transport company. At the same time, I tried to find a suitable job with one of the few British commercial companies in the country.

chapter 4

BACK WITH THE FORCE

MY REINSTATEMENT TO THE POLICE FORCE

All of a sudden, a miracle happened. Fortune seemed to smile on me. On a Friday in November 1968, a few days before my retirement from the police force, I received another letter from the establishment secretary saying that my retirement from the police force had been cancelled and that I would be reinstated to my former rank.

The following Monday, I reported to Commissioner of Police Malcom Parker. He welcomed me profusely and said that I would be posted to my previous formation in the police force – the Special Branch.

I reported to Kessebeh, the head of the Special Branch, who posted me to the section where I had been before we were arrested in April. I was in the Special Branch until early the next year when I was transferred.

TRANSFER TO HARBOUR DIVISION AS CHIEF POLICE OFFICER

In January 1969, I was transferred from the Special Branch to Harbour Division as chief police officer. That was my first independent command. By then, the brazen thefts of cargo from the Queen

Elizabeth II Quay (QE II Quay) had become widespread and had almost gone out of control. Sometimes lorry loads of cargo from the quay would go unaccounted for. They would just "vanish" into thin air.

In their desperate effort to improve the security situation at the quay, the government disbanded the entire Ports Security Force, which had hitherto been responsible for security. In its place, the police force was put in charge of security at the quay. I was appointed Chief Police Officer, Harbour Division, and I was mandated to reorganise the division and implement appropriate measures to stop the widespread thefts of cargo from the QE II Quay. This was not an easy task. But with the full cooperation and loyalty of several police personnel – including Woman Police Constable Conteh and Police Constable Kandeh Bangura, who was later to become acting inspector general of police – the task was greatly facilitated. The hitherto rampant thefts of bulk cargo from the quay were soon significantly reduced to petty thefts or pilfering of cargo.

TRANSFER TO KONO DIVISION AS CHIEF POLICE OFFICER

In April 1970, the Commissioner of Police Jenkins Smith transferred me to Kono Division as chief police officer. My transfer was quite a surprise to me because – apart from a short spell of a few months when, from December 1958 to April 1959, I was temporarily transferred to Kenema as chief clerk to the chief police officer – I had never worked in any other provincial division.

In Kono Division, I relieved Walter Wray, who was then chief police officer. I was accompanied to Kono by Edna. The headquarters of the police division in Kono District was located in a small town called Motema, about three miles from the capital, Tankoro, and a short distance from Sefadu, where the headquarters of the mining company Sierra Leone Selection Trust (SLST) was located.

I found out that, unlike the QE II Quay in Freetown, which was a very limited area whose problems consisted mainly of cargo thefts, Kono District had a quite different set of problems. First, Kono

District occupied an area of many hundred square miles, most of which was rich in alluvial diamonds. These diamonds did not require heavy or sophisticated machinery to mine. They could be found by digging a few feet in the ground, especially in areas near streams and rivers. This encouraged widespread and illicit diamond mining and smuggling. Consequently, a large influx of people – both Sierra Leoneans and foreigners, including Lebanese and other West African nationals who were termed "strangers"[3] – was flocking to the area. And they were there mainly to engage in illicit diamond mining and smuggling. Whilst the police had to prevent these illicit activities, they also had to control the large illegal influx. At the same time, certain unscrupulous bona fide residents in Kono were secretly aiding and abetting the illicit mining and smuggling of diamonds.

During Britain's rule of Sierra Leone, the colonial government had given the Sierra Leone Selection Trust (SLST), a British-owned mining company, a sole lease of 100 years and rights to mine diamonds in Kono since 1933. Knowing that almost the whole of Kono was blessed with diamonds, the British colonial government had enacted laws giving the SLST legal authority to mine diamonds even inside the compounds of citizens, whereas the owners of such land had no legal right to mine diamonds even inside their own property. The people in Sierra Leone were never consulted before such iniquitous laws were enacted. The colonial government acted unilaterally and arbitrarily. This was brazen exploitation.

The SLST had, therefore, been exploiting the country by mining and exporting thousands of carats of diamonds since 1933, whilst paying a pittance of revenue to the Sierra Leone government. Even the district from which the diamonds were being mined had been left in a dilapidated condition, and the SLST had made no effort to develop it. Roads were most deplorable. They were simply the paths that bulldozers and other machinery had cleared and made into crude passageways simply to gain access to diamond mining sites. There was no public water system and no electricity, except when the Sierra

---

[3] People who were not born in Kono were officially referred to as "strangers."

Leone government constructed electricity-generating station in the seventies. There were very few schools, and these lacked basic items, such as furniture and books.

The only area in Kono District that might be considered "developed" was in Sefadu, where the headquarters of the SLST were located, along with most of the bungalows of the expatriate staff of the company. There was a first-class hospital, equipped with modern equipment and staffed by doctors and professional nurses from Britain. There was also a shop stocked with various consumer goods for the expatriate staff. SLST generated its own electricity using private generators and supplied electricity to all of the company' buildings and the staff bungalows. Some time later, a few Sierra Leoneans were appointed to senior positions in the company as engineers, doctors, female nurses, and so on. The company even had two passenger planes to ferry its employees between Freetown and Kono. It also had two or three helicopters that were used to carry out aerial patrols of diamond mining sites and to prevent illicit diamond mining. These helicopters functioned as aerial observation posts to detect illicit diamond mining and also served as escorts to vehicles transporting diamonds.

I mentioned the foregoing to show that there was some justification for the people in Kono to carry out what was considered to be illicit diamond mining. After all, the diamonds were their natural wealth, which was being "stolen" by the SLST for the benefit of Britain.

Some old people in Kono told humorous stories about the days prior to the colonial government leasing SLST the sole right to mine diamonds in the district. Whenever the locals, mostly illiterate and highly superstitious, found diamonds along the footpaths after heavy rains, they did not know what they were. They only considered diamonds shining stones. According to the stories, when this was brought to the attention of the British district commissioner or other British colonial officials in Kono, these officials would exploit the locals' superstitions, telling them the shining stones were the eyes of devils and that they (the Europeans) alone knew how to close the eyes of the devil. They would then rush up to the site where the shining stones had been found and perform some mock cabalistic ceremonies while the locals watched. During this " ceremony", the shining stones would eventually be placed inside envelopes or other containers. And that would be the last the people would see of what they had no way of knowing were valuable minerals.

"ALL DI MARAKAS MUST GO" (ALL THE MARAKAS MUST DEPART)

By the fifties, both Sierra Leoneans as well as foreigners had become aware of the large quantities of diamonds in Kono and of the immense value of the "shining stones". They were also aware of the relative ease with which the diamonds could be mined. Therefore, large numbers of people from other parts of the country, as well as many foreigners, started flocking into Kono by the droves to illicitly mine and smuggle this valuable resource.

Consequently, the then colonial governor in Sierra Leone, Sir Beresford Stookes, ordered the first expulsion of foreigners from Kono. The address over the radio to the nation included an order stating that all Marakas (in other words, citizens from Mali and other countries in neighbouring countries) who had flocked into Kono must depart from the country. The governor ended the address to the nation over the radio by saying in not too perfect Creole, "All di Marakas must go."

This became a popular ditty in Creole in the fifties throughout the country – "All den Marakas must go."

But the influx of people could not be prevented, as many roads from surrounding areas led into Kono District. The British colonial government got the Sierra Leone Police Force to establish a large presence in Kono to help prevent both the migration into the area and the illicit mining and smuggling.

But still the influx of people into Kono could not be stopped entirely. Furthermore, some of the bona fide residents of Kono were secretly aiding and abetting the illicit diamond miners. Some of them used various types of subterfuge to deceive the police and auxiliary security force of the SLST. A common subterfuge was to declare certain areas where illicit diamond mining would take place as Poro (pronounced Poror) "sacred bush" – in other words, an area designated for the performance of the rites of the secret indigenous Poro society. Formerly, the Poro society was held in awe, and non-members dared not enter the genuine Poro bush. Non-members who dared violate the sacred bush of the Poro society would face dire retributions.

But some of the residents in Kono had no qualms about using fake Poro societies as a subterfuge to mine diamonds illicitly. Previous chief police officers (CPOs) in Kono (especially former British police officers) had been confronted with this problem. And at first, they'd had total respect for the Poro society and had hesitated to send police detachments into the areas that had been declared Poro bush. But later the deception was discovered – many of the sites were labelled as Poro bush to deter police officers from going into the areas and arresting the illicit diamond miners. Detachments of police would then be sent to the "Poro bush" to make the arrests. Serious confrontations between the police and the illicit diamond miners inside the so-called Poro bush erupted. The police officers were compelled to use force to disperse the illicit miners. Whilst I was chief police officer in Kono, I was confronted with the same problem.

It is most unfortunate that some people would desecrate one of Sierra Leone's traditional societies in order to engage in illicit diamond mining. The other unfortunate aspect of this whole affair was that foreigners would derive most of the benefit from this illicit diamond mining. The Sierra Leoneans, apart from being tricked by foreigners into selling the diamonds at very low prices, received very little. And the money they did receive was not put to fruitful purpose. Some took delight in purchasing expensive Mercedes Benzes, which broke down in no time. The main cause for the very short span of life of the vehicles was the deplorable condition of the roads in Kono.

ONE OF OUR MEN IS MISSING

In Kono, both regular police officers and the auxiliary security forces of the SLST were tasked with two primary mandates. They were to carry out patrols to prevent the illicit mining of diamonds. These patrols were termed IDM patrols. (IDM is the acronym for Illict Diamond Mining). And they were to arrest strangers (persons residing in Kono without permits).

Officers in both forces were frequently warned that none of them should be separated from the main body of personnel whenever they were engaged in these activities. But either through bravado or overenthusiasm, a few police personnel would chase illicit diamond miners far into the forest, thereby becoming separated from the main body of their colleagues. And so it happened that, one day, a detachment of security personnel under the command of one of the expatriate auxiliary officers was on IDM patrol (Illicit Diamond Mining Patrol) to apprehend illicit diamond miners in a certain area.

At the end of the operation, it was discovered that one of the auxiliary policemen was missing. A thorough search in the forest by the other members of the patrol, as well as by the senior expatriate officer who was in charge of that patrol, failed to locate the missing security personnel. The search resumed the following day. Late in the afternoon, the corpse of the missing auxiliary policeman was discovered deep inside the forest. He had been bludgeoned to death. Apparently, he had become separated from the main body of the patrol and was captured by illicit miners, who might have gagged him, tied him with bush ropes, and dragged him inside the forest where he was killed.

On receiving the sad news, I rushed into the forest with a few policemen. I examined the corpse of the unfortunate auxiliary policeman. His body was covered with bruises, and his head was swollen. The corpse was conveyed to the man's residence, accompanied by a convoy of trucks filled with auxiliary policemen who were singing indigenous dirges. That was the only fatal casualty among police personnel in Kono Division due to hostile action of illicit diamond miners during my tenure in office as CPO, Kono Division.

DRAMATIC RESCUE BY HELICOPTER

When a senior police officer is posted to a provincial division as commander (CPO) of that division, all the inhabitants in that province expect him to be their protector, rendering any and every assistance necessary. The CPO may be called upon by local residents to assist in driving away wild animals, such as elephants, bush cows, and the like, destroying their crops. He may be called upon to render assistance to people involved in serious road accidents, to rescue people from any form of danger, and so on.

And so it was that, one late afternoon in 1970 during the rainy season, I received a radio message to the effect that a launch that had been plying along the Bafi River had wrecked on a rock near a village called Dogboy, about forty-five minutes' drive by road from Motema. There were reported to be about ten passengers and crew members on board, including women, one with a baby. The message added that the boat and all its passengers were likely to be swept away at any moment by the swift-flowing river unless help was immediately rendered.

Without wasting any time, I ordered one of my officers to rush to the scene with a handful of policemen and see what could be done to rescue the passengers and crew.

I may add that, during those days, there was no telephone service in Kono. The police force depended on wireless radios to communicate with each station or post, as well as with the SLST.

The Bafi River was navigable in some sections to small launches and boats when the water level was normal, and so a few launches and boats would ply along that river from village to village along the riverbanks. The "captains" of the boats and launches knew how to manoeuvre their vessels to avoid the large rocks in certain areas in the river. But on this occasion, it had been raining very heavily since the previous day, and so the river had risen to an exceptionally high level and was flowing more swiftly than usual.

The officer I had detailed to go to the scene reported that it was impossible to rescue the people in the wrecked launch, which was leaning precariously on the rock in the middle of the river. He added that some villagers in the nearby village of Dogboy, assisted by a few police personnel, had made desperate efforts to rescue the stranded passengers and crew in vain.

I got in touch with the chief security officer of SLST, explained the grim situation to him, and requested his help by making available one of the company's helicopters to fly me to the scene so I could have a look myself. He agreed. But as it was already dark, he said the helicopter would be ready the following morning.

Early the following morning, about 7.00 a.m., I went to the SLST airfield. I climbed into the bird, together with Assistant Superintendent of Police Jabba and the pilot, a Swiss national, and we took off. The helicopter was rather small and could only accommodate two passengers in addition to the pilot, all of whom would sit abreast. It also had no hoisting mechanism, which would have greatly facilitated the rescuing of the stranded people. We arrived over the scene after a few minutes.

That particular morning was overcast and dull, which made the atmosphere somewhat depressing. The river was flowing along a slight valley. On either side was thick forest.

We were filled with awe by the scene below us. The Bafi River had risen to an unusually high level, foaming as it swirled swiftly among the rocks in the river. The launch was not a conventional launch. It was, more or less, a simple large canoe, powered by an outboard engine attached to the rear end. People in that part of the country called such vessels "launches".

The craft on the Baffi River that day was not the conventional launch. A canopy or awning had been erected on the middle of that boat to serve as a shelter. But a substantial part of the bow, as well as the stern, was open with no covering.

On the previous evening, the outboard motor had malfunctioned whilst the craft was in the middle of the swiftly flowing river. And so it had drifted uncontrollably along the river until it had become wrecked on one of the huge rocks in the river. The craft was tilting precariously on the rock, whilst the swiftly flowing river was buffeting it constantly. It lurched frequently, and it appeared that, at any moment, it would be dislodged from the rock by the rough and fast-flowing water. The passengers and crew must have spent a harrowing night in that craft, leaning on one side on the rock and fearing that, at any moment, they might have been swept away. Rescuing the stranded passengers and crew seemed impossible.

Amidst the noise being made by the rotating blades of the helicopter, the pilot shouted to Jabba and I that he would land the helicopter in the nearby Dogboy village. On landing, the pilot requested that we scout around the village for a thick rope. The villagers, fortunately, had few cattle. But most of the men in the village had gone to the riverbank, where they were assisting vainly in the rescue attempt.

A few men were still around in the village. With their help, a length of thick manila rope was located. The pilot explained that one end of the rope should be tied firmly to one of the skids of the helicopter, and the other should be made into a slip knot, which would not become loose when a heavy weight, such as that of an adult, was on it. With the assistance of the few men who had remained in the village, these instructions were followed. Jabba then drew the end with the slip knot into the helicopter, and the pilot examined the helicopter before taking off. Whilst the pilot was examining his helicopter, the other senior police officer and I rushed down the hill leading from the village to the riverside. There were already some policemen along the bank of the river.

A vast crowd of agitated men and women from the nearby Dogboy village had already gathered along the riverbank, and they were shouting confusing instructions to the people in the wrecked craft. Some were trying in vain to hurl the ends of ropes towards the crew and passengers. But as the river was wide in this area, the ropes could not reach their mark but would fall into the swiftly flowing river short of the craft.

With luck, the end of one rope hurled towards the craft reached it. One of the male passengers in the launch quickly grabbed the end of the rope. Amid the confusion among the agitated people on the shore, some of the people shouted that he should tie the rope around his waist and hold firmly to it so that he would be pulled to safety. The man held onto the rope and leapt into the swiftly flowing river, where he was almost completely submerged with only part of his head above the water. And some of the people on the shore started to pull the rope towards the shore.

All a sudden, on account of the swift current of the river, the rope slipped completely out of the man's hands. Immediately, the helpless man started to thrash his hands frantically as he was swept away by the swift current. Gasps of horror, screams, wails, and shouts of panic erupted along the riverbank. The gathered crowd could only watch the man hands thrashing frantically and pitifully above the water until he was inexorably swept away. The last sight of him was part of the loose garment he'd worn, which floated momentarily in the water, whilst the unfortunate man was being dragged under the water by the current.

Amid the noise, confusion, and agitation, we told the people to stop all efforts to rescue the passengers and crew. Meanwhile, the helicopter was already hovering overhead again. On seeing the helicopter overhead, some of the passengers and crew in the open ends of the wrecked craft struggled to maintain their balance, as the craft was leaning sideways and being constantly buffeted. They waved their hands frantically in the air, pleading for help.

Jabba, who was held firmly by straps in the helicopter, leaned out of the helicopter. He gesticulated to the stranded passengers and crew that they were to slide the slip knot at the end of the rope over the head of a passenger and push the knot down to his or her arm pits. He or she should then hold on firmly to the rope. This was rather risky. But under the existing circumstances, it was better to take the risk than to do nothing at all.

The slightest mistake by the helicopter pilot or by Jabba, who was held firmly by the strap on his seat in the helicopter, would have sent the helicopter plummeting into the swiftly flowing river. The first to try was a male passenger, who wore a large gown, which was the common dress for males in that area. He wrapped the slip knot around his armpits and held firmly to the top of the rope. Jabba, straining greatly, slowly hoisted the man, until he was finally pulled into the helicopter, amid rapturous applause and shouts of joy by the crowd. The pilot then flew the helicopter to Dogboy village, to the loud acclamation and applause of the people.

After the passenger had alighted, the pilot and Jabba returned to hover over the wrecked launch.

The next passenger was a woman, together with her baby. Jabba leaned over the helicopter and gestured to her to first tie the baby tightly to her chest, instead of her back with her *lappa* (cloth wrapped about the middle part of the body to hold a baby tightly on the mother's back). The woman could hardly keep her balance inside the craft, which tilted partly on the rock and strained against the continuous buffeting of the river. After great strain, in view of the craft's condition, the slip knot at the end of the rope was passed under the arm pits of the woman and drawn tightly. It was clear that she was terrified.

Jabba again slowly hoisted the rope. Soon, both woman and baby were in the helicopter, and another round of excitement and loud applause erupted from the crowd below. The pilot again flew the helicopter to the village, where the woman and the baby were dropped off.

This exercise was repeated several times until all the remaining passengers and crew members had been successfully rescued. The entire crowd was rapturous and full of praise for the bravery of the helicopter pilot and ASP Jabba. Fortunately, not many passengers were aboard the wrecked craft, and the distance from the village to the river was not great. Otherwise, the helicopter would have run out of fuel before the operation was completed.

I later sent a full report to the commissioner of police in Freetown, explaining the extremely brave roles the helicopter pilot and ASP Jabba had played in the rescue. As a result of my report, the commissioner wrote to the general manager of SLST, thanking him for consenting to make the helicopter available to rescue the stranded passengers and crew. He also recommended to Prime Minister Siaka Stevens that both the helicopter pilot and ASP Jabba receive the insignia of the Member of the British Empire (MBE).

At that time in 1970, Sierra Leone was not yet a republic. Although it had become an independent nation in April 1961, Her Majesty the Queen of England was still considered Queen of Sierra Leone. Therefore, citizens of Sierra Leone or residents in Sierra Leone were entitled to receive British national awards.

So ended the saga of what would have almost certainly been a serious disaster, which might have resulted in the drowning of all the crew members and the remaining passengers.

POLITICAL UNRESTS – ABORTIVE MILITARY COUP

In 1971, Sierra Leone was plagued by constant political problems, resulting in frequent unrest throughout the entire country. The political situation grew more and more tense with a political party formed by Dr John Karefa-Smart, stiffly opposing the APC and creating instability. During this period, there were frequent rumours of a coup being planned.

One morning in April 1971, the police wireless operators at divisional police headquarters in Motema reported to me that, despite persistent efforts, contact could not be established with police headquarters in Freetown. They said that was unusual. I told them to keep trying and said that the temporary breakdown in communication might be due to atmospheric disturbance.

I should add for the edification of readers who do not know Sierra Leone that, in the seventies, there were no telephone communication between Kono and Freetown. Nor were telephones used in most parts of the country. Communication had, therefore, to be made by wireless Morse code.

After about half an hour had elapsed, a senior official at SLST arrived at my office in a hurry. He stated that there had been a coup in Freetown overnight and that many people had been killed. He further explained that the message had been received from the wireless operator at their headquarters in Freetown.

Immediately after the SLST official had left my office, I summoned my senior officers, including the expatriate officers in the auxiliary police force and informed them of the news. I told them that police officers should not become involved in any attempt to overthrow the government. However, I instructed them to arrange for the control of any disturbance by civilians that might erupt. I told the expatriate officers (three of them were attached to the auxiliary police) that, in case of serious disturbances, they should not get directly involved in controlling such disturbances. They should remain in the background.

As news spread regarding the attempted coup, the atmosphere in Kono was filled with tension.

Army Commander Brigadier John Bangura had previously posted a few military men to the police compound at Motema, on the pretext of providing any necessary assistance in case of any serious disturbances. I understood that detachments of soldiers had also been posted to the other major towns in the country on the same pretext. After hearing news about the abortive coup, it dawned on me that these detachments had been stealthily deployed in strategic points around the country as part of the army commander's secret and diabolical plan to stage a coup.

After I received a report about the coup in Freetown, I went to the army staff sergeant in charge of the detachment of soldiers in Motema to find out what was happening. He was evasive to my questions. I therefore left him. But within an hour, the detachment of soldiers, including their staff sergeant who had been posted to Kono, quietly disappeared from Motema.

By afternoon, news of the coup had spread all throughout Kono. Meanwhile, it was learnt that, following the attempt on his life, Prime

Minister Siaka Stevens had disappeared. It later turned out that he had escaped to neighbouring Guinea to seek refuge and to request the assistance of President Sheku Toure of Guinea to put down the revolt of the army in Sierra Leone.

The following morning, the situation was quite volatile. Gangs of bellicose youths and others who were armed with various types of offensive and dangerous weapons were on the rampage. A large and boisterous crowd of hooligans uttering profanities and in a bellicose mood had gathered and were advancing aggressively towards Motema Police Station. Rocks and other offensive missiles were already being thrown at the station. Police personnel in riot gear had earlier been deployed to defend the police station, and they were keeping the riotous mob at bay.

About a week later, the situation in the country had returned to normal. I then requested my transfer from Kono Division. In the latter part of April 1971, I was transferred to traffic division headquarters in Freetown as chief police officer.

APPOINTED PRINCIPAL IMMIGRATION OFFICER

On my return to Freetown, I was first posted to traffic division as chief police officer. My stay there did not last long. In June, I was transferred to the Department of Immigration and appointed principal immigration officer.

The Department of Immigration/Passport Control was formerly an integral part of the police force. But after Sierra Leone became independent in April 1961, the then government decided that the immigration department should preferably come under the control of the Ministry of Foreign Affairs. And so in 1962 or thereabouts, the change was made.

By 1970, that department had not been functioning quite well. So the government decided to return the immigration to the police force. This was done, and I was appointed principal immigration officer. During my service in that department, I carried out fundamental reorganisation, which resulted in substantial improvement in the administration and effectiveness of that department.

TRANSFERRED TO THE SPECIAL BRANCH
HEADQUARTERS AS HEAD

In 1974, after three years heading the Department of Immigration, I moved again. Commissioner of Police Prince Kaetu-Smith transferred me from that department to the Special Branch and appointed me head of that important branch in the police force. I was head of Special Branch when the Students Revolt erupted in 1977. During my service in the Department of Immigration, I was promoted to the rank of senior assistant commissioner of police in 1975, making me third in the hierarchy of the police force. But I remained head of the Special Branch.

TRANSFERRED TO POLICE HEADQUARTERS AS SENIOR
ASSISTANT COMMISSIONER (POLICE OPERATIONS)

A little after taking over the helm of the Special Branch, I was transferred to police headquarters in late 1977 as senior assistant commissioner of police in charge of all police operations.

chapter 5

UNEXPECTED APPOINTMENTS

BECOMING ACTING COMMISSIONER OF POLICE, MEMBER OF PARLIAMENT, AND CABINET MINISTER

In quite unexpected circumstances, I was suddenly appointed acting commissioner of police by His Excellency the president, Dr Siaka Stevens, from my number three position in the hierarchy of the police force. Commissioner of Police Kaetu-Smith and Deputy Commissioner of Police Gbassay Kamara had serious differences with each other over matters regarding the administration of the police force. The issue had gone to the president. But instead of summoning the commissioner and the deputy commissioner and warning them to cooperate with each other, President Stevens decided to relieve the two of them of their duties and appointed me acting commissioner of police on Friday, 29 September 1978.

On the following Monday, 2 October 1978, I was sworn in as acting commissioner of police and minister of state before His Excellency the president and took the oath of allegiance.

A few weeks later in November 1978, I was also appointed Member of Parliament in accordance with a provision then in the Sierra Leone constitution. The whole situation was like being in a dream.

Edna and two of our children, Tunde and Yamede, witnessed me being sworn in as acting commissioner of police and as a member of cabinet by His Excellency the president. The ceremony took place in Freetown. During that period, an unspoken undercurrent flowed in my brain: Had all this really happened to "Borbor", who had grown up under poor conditions and who had resided in a thatched house by the steps at number 4 Highlane Street in Gloucester Village?

I suddenly found myself heading the national police force, then comprised of 5,000 male and female personnel, from constables to senior officers. I continued to have misgivings about the difficult and colossal task confronting me. But there was nothing I could do under the existing circumstances.

I immediately commenced to perform my duties as head of the police force. At first, everything went smoothly, and I would occasionally receive the commendation of the president. But by the latter part of 1979, I began to encounter problems related to the administration of the police force. Some came from the president himself, who would give certain orders that were in conflict with the efficient administration of the police force. Others were from politicians who would pretend to be strong adherents of the governing APC party but who, in actual fact, were trying to serve their own selfish motives and to feather their own nests.

Another photograph showing
Hon. Ezekiel Alfred Coker, Ag. Commissioner of Police
(holding a paper while giving his vote of thanks)
during his swearing-in by President Siaka Stevens (standing with back to camera)
as Minister of State and Cabinet Minister in October 1978
On Ezekiel's left is his wife Edna Coker
On Ezekiel's rear right is his daughter Sarah Yamede Coker

Me being sworn in as acting commissioner of police

chapter 6

THE WELL-OILED BICYCLE

WHY THE EFFECTIVENESS OF THE SIERRA LEONE POLICE FORCE REMAINED ELUSIVE

When I was a young boy, I did not personally witness the incident I am about to narrate. But it was most probably true. The story is about a man who had acquired a brand-new bicycle. He was desirous of keeping the bicycle spotlessly clean and shining always. One day, he washed the bicycle; dried it; and polished every part of it, including the rims and the sprocket of the wheels, with oil. He was satisfied that the bicycle looked new and shiny.

He jumped on the bicycle, proud of the sparkling frames and wheels. He was proceeding down a hill, and when he applied the brakes, the bicycle would not stop. Rather, the bicycle continued to accelerate down the hill. In a panic, he shouted, "Hold me coat; hold me coat." But no one could hold his coat, as the bicycle picked up speed as it rushed down the hill. The bicycle consequently crashed in a gutter, leaving the man badly injured and the bicycle seriously damaged.

In his ignorance, the man did not know that the bicycle could be braked on account of friction between the rotating rims of the wheels and the brake pads when the brake pads were allowed to get in contact with the rotating rims. Therefore, any oil or grease applied to the rims of the rotating wheels will reduce the friction between the brake pads and the rims of the rotating wheels. Consequently, the bicycle's brakes could not work.

The British colonial administrators handed Sierra Leone a set of proper, functional, smooth, and efficient machinery for running the administration of the country, including the civil service, the judiciary, the army, and the police force. The machinery they left us was exactly the same as that in existence in Britain, which had, over the years, steadfastly withstood the test of time.

The bicycle analogy may well be applied to the administration of the country after the British colonial administrators had left. Most unfortunately, not too long after Sierra Leone became independent from British colonial rule, the flawless machinery left in the country was being tinkered with by political leaders, as well as by others who pretended to be strong adherents of the governing political party but whose real aims were their own selfish ends.

Party politics – which emerged soon after Sierra Leone had become an independent state – instead of benefiting the country, indirectly contributed to the malfunctioning of the flawless machinery the British had handed over to us. Consequently efficiency and effectiveness in the administration of the country as a whole gradually began to decrease. Discipline, morality, probity, and law and order began to crumble gradually as a result of tinkering with the machinery by some who were ignorant of the machinery's functionality.

Some formerly mediocre and ill-motivated people soon found out that, by pretending to be strong adherents of the party in power, they would be able to wield power everywhere. Most unfortunately, they would have the support of leaders of the party in power. But when there happened to be any change in the government and another party came to power, the same people who had formerly pretended to be strong supporters of the previous ruling party soon became chameleons and gradually switched their allegiance to the present party in power.

On the other hand, some of the political leaders who, prior to gaining political power, were more or less mediocre people soon found out that their new-found political power could make them powerful figures in the country.

Some of us who had been in the civil service of Sierra Leone's government since pre-independence suffered frustration under the new government that emerged. We witnessed the unnecessary tampering with the machinery of administration until the machinery (that is, the administration of all the public services) started to malfunction seriously. The effectiveness of the government as a whole thus became illusive.

During the colonial era, there had been no need to set up administrative machinery to maintain probity and discipline in the public service, the educational institutions, and other public services. The heads of departments exhibited responsibility and honesty, and they were emulated by us junior personnel in the civil service.

I will now give a few examples of unnecessary tampering and meddling with the machinery of administration that contributed to its malfunctioning. Some of these examples even involved me when I was acting commissioner of police.

When the APC government came to power in 1968 after the NRC military government had been overthrown, either to show the citizens that they were in sympathy with imagined errors of the previous military regime or perhaps in an effort to gain popularity with the citizens, the then commissioner of police was pressured to reinstate into the police force some personnel who had previously been dismissed from the force as result of serious violations of police rules and code of conduct. When this happened, some of the reinstated personnel continued to manifest their irresponsible conduct. They became truculent to officers, sometimes hinting that they had the support of politicians.

Even some police personnel who had not be put on any disciplinary charge for violation of the disciplinary code of conduct were prone to exhibit a certain amount of truculence to some officers. Others would intentionally refuse to comply with police rules and regulations.

One glaring example was a police personnel who happened to have been enlisted in the police force through political influence. That personnel was posted to one of the divisions in the country. The wearing of a uniform by all police personnel in the uniformed branches, as well as proper grooming, was compulsory. But this particular personnel refused to shave his beard or even to wear a police uniform. The rather flimsy excuse he gave was that his doctor had advised him not to shave. In support of his irresponsible excuse, he even produced a medical certificate from a doctor of questionable character. The divisional commander under whom this police personnel was serving persistently ordered him to shave his beard and put on a uniform. But he consistently refused.

After persistent prodding by his commander, this recalcitrant officer eventually agreed to wear a uniform but still refused to shave his beard. Now, he looked like a scruffy unkempt thick-bearded apparition. Neither his boots nor the buttons on his uniform were polished; his uniform was not pressed. The humorous commanding officer caused this officer to be marched before the then commissioner of police so the commissioner could see him for himself. The commissioner ordered the officer again to comply with police rules and regulations or else face dismissal from the police force. Eventually the policeman got his beard shaven and wore his uniform. But even then, he did not look smart in uniform. After a few years, he voluntarily resigned from the police.

In another instance of gross indiscipline, certain cadets, police JPOs (junior police officers), were in training at the Police Training School. They had recently returned from studying abroad, and they pretended to be staunch members of the APC, always mingling with the top brass in the party. Whilst these JPOs in training were at the training school, they refused to comply with certain police rules, which forbade recruits from leaving the school's compound without permission. The commandant warned them on several occasions that they were violating the rules of the training school and failing to demonstrate exemplary leadership, an essential quality for officers. But still these cadet JPOs did not desist from the flagrant violation of police rules. The commandant then reported the matter to the commissioner of police, who threatened to bring them up on disciplinary charges and have them dismissed from the police force. It was only then that the cadets reluctantly began to comply with rules and regulations.

Incidents like these demonstrated that discipline in the police force deteriorated – to such an extent that even a divisional commander and the commandant of the training school could no longer exercise authority over junior personnel. In 1956 when I was at the training school for training as a sub-inspector, none of us trainees would have dared behave so irresponsibly; we would have considered doing so conduct unbecoming of officers in training. And if we'd tried, the commandant of the training school would have had us arrested for insubordination and locked up in a cell for a few days, after which we might have been dismissed from the police force, in accordance with the force's rules and regulations. But by twenty years later, when the country was newly independent from Britain, gross indiscipline was perpetrated due to politics.

Other unnecessary interference in police affairs by politicians caused a serious drop in discipline. During pre-independence days and a little after independence – up to the time Sir Milton Margai was prime minister – one had to have no adverse criminal records and a relatively high standard of literacy in order to enlist in the police force. The British colonial administrators left Sierra Leone with an efficient and effective police force, which continued to be efficient and effective until Dr Margai, the country's first prime minister, died in 1964. But soon thereafter, a gradual and imperceptible drop in discipline began as political party functionaries began to meddle in the administration of the force. However, the situation was not too bad then. This was, perhaps, due to the fact that the political party then in power did not last long before they were ousted from power by a military coup three years later.

Prior to Sierra Leone being granted independence, illiteracy had almost been swept away from the police force. The few illiterate and semi-literate personnel were older and had been recruited many years previously; they had only a few years of service left before their retirement. But soon after a certain political party came to power, recruits who were illiterate and semi-literate, as well as some with adverse criminal records joined the force.

The commissioner of police soon found himself unable to exercise the supreme authority over his personnel previous commissioners had had during pre-independence. The ability to award promotions and make transfers, which had formerly been at the discretion of the commissioner, in consultation with his senior officers, and by which he had wielded complete authority over his personnel, had been gradually taken away from him by politicians.

Shortly after the country had gained independence, the process of awarding promotions changed. Before doing so, the commissioner would have to consult senior politicians, who would list those who were to be promoted. During pre-independence days under British colonial administration, such irregularity never existed. Of course, there were no political parties then. The commissioner of police was responsible only to the colonial governor for the effective administration of the police force.

The British colonialists left the police force with rules for the proper administration of the force. These were the Force Standing Orders, the Police Rules and Regulations, and the laws of the state. In addition, the colonialists left behind a set of criteria a candidate should meet before he or she would be considered for promotion.

But on account of politics, a few years after the country had gained independence, the emerging governments quietly dispensed with the criteria, on the pretext that "not everything that the British left with us should be copied and that "we must adapt to our own African methods."

There was a certain very senior politician who was fond of saying that the police force did not require what he termed "bookmen". His diatribe went on to suggest that, in fact, were educated young men recruited into the police force, they would be inclined to question the orders of their senior officers. But with semi-literates, when an officer gave orders, they would not question but rather would promptly obey. What a fallacy!

Other personnel who were enlisted into the police force long after independence made derisive comments about the older personnel who had been enlisted long before the country gained independence. Some of the new personnel termed the older personnel "bookmen," indoctrinated by colonial leadership, whilst they younger folks were "republican policemen".

The consequence is obvious today. These changes have resulted in the organisation becoming completely out of control. And when "our own African methods" ("republican methods") did not work, the very people who were shouting the loudest that not everything British should be copied were the same people who, when things went completely wrong, were vociferously advocating that an expatriate police officer should be hired as commissioner of police.

That said, I will disclose some of my experiences whilst I was head of the Special Branch and during the short time I was acting commissioner of police. I'll give only a few examples of the unnecessary tinkering with the machinery of the police force that has damaged its efficiency, effectiveness, and discipline.

PROMOTIONS

Promotions were formerly the sole prerogative of the commissioner, in consultation with his senior officers. Thereby, the Commissioner and his officers maintained effective control over personnel. But soon after the country had gained its independence from Britain and Sierra Leone politicians took over the administration of the country, things became very different. Politicians started tinkering with the administration of the police force and other public services. In the police force, promotions could only be made after consulting with senior politicians. Even transferring officers from one formation to another required first consulting senior politicians. And this was not the only method of unnecessary interference in the police force.

HOW MANY ARE "SEVERAL"?

During the 1977 Students Revolt in Sierra Leone, which very nearly toppled the APC from power, I was the head of the Special Branch. As such, it was my responsibility to report all activities of security interest, thereby ensuring the president was aware of goings-on and enabling him to react properly and respond adequately to accusations from the public. And this I did. Special Branch reports had frequently contained information on simmering discontent among the public and students. The members of the Fourah Bay College Students Union were reportedly planning to demonstrate against the alleged corruption in the government.

In the days leading up to the revolt, the Special Branch's Daily Intelligence Reports had continually detailed the unrest among students, as well as among the public. The reports were ignored. The demonstration eventually took place on Saturday, 29 January 1977. It then spiralled out of control to something quite unexpected and resulted in widespread countrywide revolt by students, as well as riots. It took several days before the police force was able to bring the situation under control.

On Tuesday, 1 February 1977, the ISU (Internal Security Unit) of the police force battled with hooligans who had by now joined the general riots, with the main intention of looting. During the ensuing skirmishes in Freetown, several rioters and looters were killed and wounded before the situation was brought under control.

On the following day, part of the Special Branch Daily Intelligence Report included a summary of the events of the previous day. A portion of the report contained the following:

> The rioting was very serious and quickly spread to almost all over the city; but through the determination and courage of the ISU personnel, the situation was eventually brought under control in the evening. However, several persons were killed during the riots.

On receiving the report, the president became enraged, and he sent for me to appear before him. As soon as I entered his office, the president began to rant and rave, lambasting me. He accused me of being an agent of the BBC, whereby that broadcasting organisation in Britain was able to broadcast what he termed "false news" over worldwide media outlets. The BBC had, on the previous day, broadcast reports on the students revolting in Sierra Leone. The report was based on an eyewitness representative of the BBC who was actually in Freetown and had personally witnessed some of the scenes where the rioting and looting took place.

I was both shocked and astounded at the false and unnecessary accusations by the president.

Thereupon, he took the report which I had prepared from inside one of the drawers in his desk and read aloud the following part:

> The rioting and looting were very serious and quickly spread to almost all over the city; but through the determination and courage of the ISU personnel, the situation was eventually brought under control in the evening. However, several persons were killed during the riots.

The president was livid with rage. "How many are several?" "Who killed the people?" he demanded. "If we were in a court of law, I would give you serious *whahala*" – serious embarrassment – "for submitting such a distorted and vague report." He then summoned into his office G.L.V. Williams, who was then the secretary to the president. On arrival of G.L.V. Williams, the president again read the same part of the report.

Upon finishing, the President spoke to Mr Williams in Creole. "GLV" (this is how he typically fondly addressed his secretary) "you are a bookman. How would you interpret the portion of the report I have just read?"

Before GLV could respond, the president craftily continued, "Does it not infer that it was the ISU personnel who killed the people?"

Mr Williams had no option but to concur.

The president then turned to me and asked, "Did you personally type the report?"

I replied that I had not.

The president hurriedly stated that it was by such means that the BBC correspondent got his material to broadcast nonsense. The president continued, suggesting that, after the girl who'd typed the report had completed it, she must have surreptitiously inserted a copy of the report within her underwear. He continued to excoriate me seriously.

When he paused, I tried to explain that I felt I ought to let him know exactly what had happened during the riot and looting the previous day. I noted that the report did not exactly say it was the ISU who'd killed the people. That explanation would not appease the president. After he had exhausted himself by castigating me, he then asked the commissioner and myself to leave his office, which we quickly did.

I was quite annoyed because, as far as I was aware, I had done my job in reporting fully all that had transpired during the previous day. The report had been marked "Secret", which meant that it was meant for limited circulation among a few officials – namely, the president and the two vice presidents. I had been lambasted for doing my job. If I had not reported all that had transpired to keep the president fully informed, I might have still been lambasted for failing to report in detail.

"Poyoh Tong Wahalah"

Before telling this story, I should explain the meaning of the Creole expression, "Poyoh Tong Wahalah." *Poyoh* is an alcoholic drink extracted from the palm tree. *Tong* is the Creole word for "town". *Wahalah* is the Creole expression of a problem or trouble or disaster or an embarrassment, depending on the gravity of the situation.

Another incident that made the president angry with me involved an amateur performance group called the Freetong Players. The group, which staged plays for the entertainment of the public, had for several weeks been staging a play called *Poyoh Tong Wahalah*. This was a satirical play. It was quite innocuous and humorous and had been staged several times in public. I had even attended one of the shows. It depicted the head of a fictional government who took to the pleasure of drinking "poyoh" and neglected his duties and responsibilities to the country. This consequently led to the soldiers becoming seriously disgruntled, and they eventually staged a coup, overthrowing the government. It was quite a humorous play, and everybody enjoyed it.

The Daily Intelligence Report on the day after its premier included a summary of the play. As always, the report was shown to the president by the commissioner of police. And after reading it, the president had scrawled his initials in red ink, indicating he had seen the report. He had not then made any adverse comments about anything in it.

I had forgotten about that play when, several weeks later, Commissioner of Police Kaetu Smith came to my office in a hurry. He had just been briefing the president on daily security matters. "We are in trouble," the commissioner said, adding that the president wanted to see both of us in his office right away. Kaetu Smith was notorious for not saying much when it involved matters with His Excellency the president.

I quickly accompanied him to the State House, and we were ushered into the president's office. The president peremptorily began to comment, his tone angry, that I had not been performing my duties satisfactorily. He continued that he'd heard that a group of irresponsible people had been teaching the public how to stage a coup and that I had never reported it. I became alarmed by his comments. I did not know what he was referring to. After he had lambasted me, I assured him I would find out what this was all about. I hurriedly returned to Special Branch headquarters. I told both my second in command and the head of registry, Sarah Shears, what the president had said and noted that no mention of the group teaching the public how to stage a coup had made it into the Daily Intelligence Report. We were baffled.

After some time, Sarah suggested that, perhaps, the president was referring to the play *Poyoh Tong Wahalah*, which was still running and which had already been reported on in one of the Daily Intelligence Reports. She quickly traced the original copy of the report in the registry. The report contained the president's initials in red ink.

I rushed to State House with the report. I was ushered into the president's office. I explained to the president that I thought he may have been referring to a satirical play that had been publicly staged several times. I showed him the Daily Intelligence Report in which the play had been mentioned. He did not take the report from me but said that the report had not emphasised the delicate nature of the play in terms of security. He said that someone else had informed him of the rather delicate nature of the play.

I tried to explain that the play was purely fictional and that it was a satire. This infuriated the president all the more, and he would hear none of it. He continued to berate me. After he had expended his anger, I apologised and assured him that I would make sure future reports contained all delicate aspects relating to security. After this, he asked me to leave his presence.

What I suspect was the cause for this "storm" was a pseudo informant or politician who went to the president to beg for money. That informant or party activist must have completely distorted the nature of the satirical play and convinced the president that it was wilfully teaching the public how to stage a coup. Because the president listened to this interpretation, he viewed the Special Branch in a very bad light, imagining that we had not been reporting everything related to intelligence. But in this instance, whoever it was who'd distorted the play's intentions had ignored the fact that civilians do not stage military coups. It is military personnel who stage coups.

EMERGENCY DRILL IN CASE OF THE
ACCIDENTAL CRASH OF AN AIRCRAFT

As far as I was aware, no emergency drill had ever been carried out to test the reaction of the security forces, airport emergency arrangements, medical and communication teams, and the like in the event of an accidental air crash. It is quite necessary for emergency drills to be carried out occasionally, to test the readiness of all organisations that would be involved in a rescue operation. Therefore, whilst I was acting commissioner of police, I consulted the director of civil aviation on the need to carry out an emergency drill in case of an accidental air crash. He gave his wholehearted consent to such a drill.

Thereafter, I consulted the management of the major airlines then operating in Sierra Leone – British Caledonian Airways, KLM, and UTA. They all agreed that an emergency drill simulating an accidental air crash was necessary and that all organisations that would be involved in the rescue should be included. The airlines were not only in favour of such a drill but also promised to provide some modest financial assistance and other forms of support that might be necessary. The British government had hitherto provided training for police officers on airport security.

I briefed His Excellency the president, noting that British Caledonian and KLM were entirely in support of such a drill and had promised to provide support, including modest financial support. The president wholeheartedly agreed the emergency drill was a good idea.

About a week later, I was in the president's office for the usual morning security briefing. After the army commander and I had briefed him, the president suddenly turned to me, his demeanour serious. He said that he understood I was planning for the accidental crash of an aircraft. He added that at no time hitherto had there been an air crash in the country and suggested I wanted to bring the country "bad luck".

I was completely surprised and taken aback; but I suppressed my amazement and indignation. I explained that I had previously briefed him on the need for such an emergency drill. I added that conducting such drills was what prevailed in other countries and that he had given his prior approval to the operation. The president pretended that I had not briefed him on the planned drill. He berated me again for my intentions of "bringing bad luck into the country". I had no alternative but to apologise and stated that I would cancel the intended drill.

What I guessed might have happened was that, as usual, someone or a group of people who presented themselves as informants but whose ulterior motive was self-interest might have heard about the intended emergency drill. Such person or persons might have gone to the president to try and curry favour, with the intention of receiving some money from him. The individual or individuals might have intentionally distorted the intention of the drill, convincing the president it would bring "bad luck". Perhaps for political reasons, the president acquiesced to this abominable distortion of the facts and, consequently, made me a sacrificial lamb.

THE SEMI-LITERATE WHO WANTED TO BE HELICOPTER PILOT

During pre-independence days, anyone who intended to join the police force as a recruit had to first pass an examination. Failing the exam would result in disqualification. Furthermore, after successfully passing the exam, the intended recruit would have his or her fingerprint taken to ascertain whether he or she had had any criminal convictions.

The Chinese government wanted the APC government to be self-sufficient in the internal defence of Sierra Leone. Therefore, the Chinese government offered scholarships to several young men, some of whom would be trained as sailors to operate small, armed patrol vessels. Others were to be trained as helicopter pilots and so on. The APC government sent to China several boys who presumably pretended to be party adherents regardless of the boys' educational qualifications and aptitudes.

One such boy was a young man who I will call Mr Ceesay (this is not his real name). Mr Ceesay was to be trained as a helicopter pilot in China. After he had been training for a short period, the Chinese found out that his education was not up to the standard required for helicopter pilots. He was, therefore, returned to Sierra Leone.

A senior functionary of the APC wanted this young man to gain employment. He therefore appealed to me to enlist Mr Ceesay in the police force as a motor mechanic. I eventually agreed but with the proviso that this chap would first sit for the basic examination given to all those who intended to join the police force as recruits. The answers to the test indicated that this chap did not possess the minimum basic standard of education. He was, in fact, semi-literate.

This was pointed out to the senior party functionary, who then insisted that, even though the chap seemed semi-literate, he had certain "talents" that would make him a suitable apprentice motor mechanic.

Despite my great reluctance to enlist this chap, the party functionary prevailed on me to employ him. Eventually, with reluctance, I allowed Mr Ceesay to enlist as a recruit constable and sent him to Police Training School in Hastings to undergo basic police recruit training, together with other recruits.

The Hastings Airfield, where a few light aircraft were parked, was adjacent to the school. Whilst this chap was at the school, one day, he surreptitiously left the school and boarded one of the aircraft. Apparently using the scanty knowledge he'd gained, he started the plane's engine. He was reportedly taxing the aircraft around the airfield when he lost control of it, and the plane crashed into a tree, causing extensive damage to the aircraft. That was the end of his career in the police force. I do not know how the damaged aircraft was repaired.

THE IRRESPONSIBLE MOTOR MECHANIC

For those of us who were trained during pre-independence days, any serious indiscretion or reckless or irresponsible behaviour by any police personnel would result in severe penalty. This was intended to act as a deterrent to others.

The case I am about to mention demonstrates how certain people who pretended to be staunch APC party adherents used their positions to encourage the spread of indiscipline in the police force. This case involved a motor mechanic who was a sergeant in the transport section. On one Sunday morning, this sergeant mechanic caused false entry to be made in the station diary, stating that he was going to tow a police vehicle, which allegedly had a mechanical breakdown. He then drove a brand-new Fiat tow vehicle all the way to Port Loko, about 80 miles from Freetown. He was suspected to have become intoxicated whilst in Port Loko. On his return to Freetown in the evening, the brand-new vehicle was involved in a very serious accident; it somersaulted and became a total wreck.

This sergeant was placed on a disciplinary status in accordance with the provisions of Force Standing Orders. He was also suspended from duty until the verdict in the disciplinary case had been reached. After hearing all the evidence, the adjudicating officer recommended that the sergeant be dismissed from the force. When the proceedings reached me for final approval, I endorsed this recommendation. Action was accordingly initiated.

Later on, several politicians who claimed to be strong adherents of the APC approached me, pleading for the recommended dismissal of the sergeant to be reversed. The grounds on which their pleas were based were, firstly, that the sergeant had an old and ailing mother to support and, secondly, that he was a strong APC party supporter. The additional most flimsy, irresponsible, and ridiculous plea was that the sergeant had "made a mistake" and that he would not repeat the same mistake.

I pointed out the sergeant's grossly irresponsible and reckless conduct of this had resulted in the destruction of the force's sole tow truck and cost millions of leones (the country's currency). I later learned that these people had stated behind my back that I wanted to impose "colonial discipline" in the police force. Eventually, despite the serious nature of the case, due to strong political pressure exerted on me, I had to relent. It was another case of the unnecessary and irresponsible tinkering with the "machinery."

SPECIAL NUMBER PLATES FOR VEHICLES

The vehicle licensing laws in force at the time contained a provision for special registration number plates to be issued to owners of vehicles with the prior approval of the commissioner of police and upon payment of the stipulated special fee.

This was partly intended for vehicle owners who wished to display flamboyance in the number plate of their vehicles. Previously, relatively few owners of motor vehicles would apply for the issue of special vehicle registration number plates.

But soon after I was appointed acting commissioner of police, some dishonest persons saw this provision as a loophole, whereby they could circumvent the payment of customs duties on vehicles, particularly those imported by road from Liberia. The subterfuge involved importing the vehicle from neighbouring Liberia by road on the pretext that it was a temporary importation and that the vehicle would be returned to Liberia within the time specified for temporary importation.

Owing to lax documentation, as well as some other factors, neither the customs department nor the police force were able to keep track of all vehicles imported for temporary use and to ensure that all such vehicles were either returned to Liberia after a few weeks in Sierra Leone or the necessary customs duty due on such vehicles were paid.

The dishonest person would approach the police department and give a fictitious story that he had assembled the vehicle from two or more old vehicles and that a special number plate was intended for the allegedly reassembled vehicle. The engine number, as well as the chassis number, would have been obliterated before such applications were made to the police.

When I eventually discovered this subterfuge, which defrauded the government, depriving it of revenue, I refused to give further approval for the issue of special registration number plates for vehicles.

Some persons with strong connections to certain highly placed politicians complained that the acting commissioner of police was "not cooperating" with them and that he wanted to preserve the former rigid colonial service procedures.

I stood my ground against such irresponsible utterances and subterfuge. The topmost politicians apparently recognised why I was refusing to grant further approval. But to appear not to offend the so-called party adherents, as well as to absolve themselves from the wrath of the dishonest party members, they told the persons concerned that such matters were left to the discretion of the commissioner of police.

I later wrote a memo to the secretary to the president, pointing out the dishonest intentions of some applicants for the issue of special registration number plates. I informed the secretary that I would no longer give approval for said number plates.

I thought that this was the end of this problem. But it was not. A certain cabinet minister was determined to use another method to force the hands of the commissioner. The minister, who was also a member of cabinet, prepared a cabinet paper recommending that the commissioner of police should issue special number plates with the initial letters of the names of the registered owner. One of the specious reasons given in support of this irresponsible proposal was that it would generate quite a lot of revenue to government.

I was then also a cabinet minister. I vehemently opposed this proposal. I first pointed out the vehicle licensing laws contained provision for the issue by the police of special registration number plates. Therefore, it was not necessary for cabinet to make any decision on the matter.

I noted that I had discovered the privilege was being abused by dishonest persons, to the detriment of the collection of customs duty. I explained the subterfuge involving alleged temporarily imported vehicles from Liberia. After the vehicles had been in the country for several weeks, the individuals would approach the police licensing section to request the issue of a special number plate for a vehicle that had allegedly been rebuilt from two or more old vehicles. Meanwhile, before such requests were made, these people would have obliterated the serial numbers from the chassis and engine.

I emphasised that, if the minister's proposal was to be adopted, the systematic registration of vehicles in the vehicle licensing section of police force would be seriously disrupted. Moreover, the recommendation would facilitate further dishonest and fraudulent activities. This, I explained, would far outweigh whatever benefits in revenue might result, which would only be minimal. I ended by emphasising that, if the proposal was approved, I would be unable to implement such flawed decision, and furthermore, I should not be held responsible for any undesirable consequences.

The proposal was debated in cabinet with no definite decision reached. It was eventually shelved. That was the end of this particular problem for me during my relatively short time as acting commissioner of police.

THE FERRY IN DISTRESS THAT NEVER WAS

On another occasion, the army commander and I were in the morning security briefings with the president when the army commander made an alarming report. He had been informed that a very dangerous situation had developed the previous evening with one of the ferries. Loaded with passengers, the ferry had been traveling from Lungi to the Kissy Ferry Terminal at Kissy Dockyard, Freetown, during a storm. He added that the incident had almost ended in a calamity. According to the report he had received, the ferry had lost power whilst in midstream and was drifting out of control towards Cape Sierra and heading for the open Atlantic Ocean. According to the army commander, the many passengers who were on board the ferry were screaming in panic for their lives.

The president turned to me and asked why I had not informed him of the alleged near disaster. I said that I had not received any such report. This infuriated the president, who continued to excoriate me. I was quietly angry at this unnecessary accusation. The president then ordered me to request that the general manager of the Ports Authority report to him immediately.

I hurried to a nearby office in the State House and called the general manager, informing him that His Excellency the president wanted to see him in connection with an alleged serious ferry incident the previous evening. I informed the general manager of the information that the president had received. The general manager said that, although there had been a strong storm the previous evening, as far as he was aware, no ferry had been reported to be in distress.

Armed with the information, the general manager, who was a Sierra Leonean, quickly arrived, together with the operations manager, who was British, as well as the Sierra Leonean ferries manager. They brought along the logbook of incidents affecting any ferries or vessels within the territorial waters of Sierra Leone.

They were all ushered in to the president together with me. The president's tone towards the Ports Authority officials was not the angry one he had displayed towards me. He simply mentioned that he had received information about a very dangerous situation, wherein a ferry had allegedly lost power in midstream and drifted out of control towards Cape Sierra and the Atlantic Ocean, its passengers in a panic and shouting for their dear lives.

After he had expressed his concern, the general manager told the president what he had told me – that no distress call by the captain of the ferry conveying passengers from Lungi to Freetown had been received. He further pointed out that the captain of the ferry that was at sea when the storm had occurred had simply complied with standard operational procedure by not attempting to land the ferry during a storm but riding the storm at sea till the storm subsided before landing. The general manager then requested that the operations manager add his own explanation. The operations manager concurred with the general manager. In addition, he produced the ferry's logbook, as well as the log book in the ferries manager's office to corroborate the general manager's explanation. The operations manager added that the ferry was not out of control. Neither was it drifting helplessly towards the open Atlantic Ocean.

He said that, after the storm had subsided, the ferry was landed safely at Kissy Ferry Terminal. The general manager assuaged the president's concern further by requesting that the operations manager explain all the precautions in place in case any distress call from a passenger ferry or any other vessel in the territorial waters of Sierra Leone was made.

With those explanations, the president's anger subsided. He was placated. He playfully apologised to the three officials of the Ports Authority for "dragging" all of them into his office. He added that, given the alarming report he had received, they should understand his concern.

By then the army commander had gone away, and he was not present to hear the explanations. And as far as I was aware, the president never scolded the army commander for making such an alarming and baseless report.

MY RETIREMENT FROM THE POLICE FORCE

In April 1981, after serving in the Sierra Leone Police Force for a total of twenty-five years, in addition to my previous nine years of service in the Customs Department, I retired from the police force.

chapter 7

THE PARISH COUNCIL

APPOINTED A MEMBER OF THE PARISH COUNCIL OF THE ROMAN CATHOLIC SACRED HEART CATHEDRAL

I am a Catholic. And, in 1985, a few years after my retirement from the force in 1981, I was appointed a member of the Parish Council of Sacred Heart Cathedral, Freetown. I was later elected to the post of chairman of the Parish Council. During the period of my chairmanship, Sacred Heart Cathedral celebrated 150 years since the establishment of the parish. I endeavoured to enhance the parish's finances, which I found in an unhealthy state.

ABORTIVE VISIT OF POPE JOHN PAUL II

In 1992, the Vatican had wanted Pope John Paul II to visit many countries in West Africa. The trip was to include a three-day visit to Sierra Leone. During that period, the civil war in Sierra Leone had just commenced. The rebel army of the Revolutionary United Front (RUF) was making rapid advances in the eastern parts of the country, wreaking devastation and committing horrendous atrocities.

Nevertheless, tentative plans were being made in Sierra Leone for His Holiness the Pope's intended visit. I was appointed to the security section of the Central Planning Committee, the committee was responsible for the planning of the Holy Father's visit. The security section would be responsible for all aspects of security during the visit, including the security of His Holiness, in liaison with the Vatican's own security officials.

Draft programmes had been drawn up, and subcommittees had already been formed in Bo and Kenema, the two provincial towns the Pope was to visit. In fact, the Central Planning Committee had already made a number of plans. But suddenly, we received notice that the Pope would no longer be visiting Sierra Leone. We learnt that senior Vatican officials were apprehensive about the Pope's security whilst in Sierra Leone, particularly with the civil war raging. Many towns in the provinces had already been overrun by RUF rebels, who were committing heinous atrocities against hapless civilians. Catholics in general were dismayed, as they had eagerly looked forward to seeing the Holy Father. No Pope had ever visited the country before.

MY RE-EMPLOYMENT ON CONTRACT IN THE POLICE FORCE

A few years after I had retired from the police force, the then police inspector general requested my help in training a few middle cadre officers (JPOs and NCOs) in the CID. The training would focus on the examination of handwriting and typewriting on documents that were exhibits in cases CID was investigating. I was also asked to train JPOs in the Special Branch. I gladly consented, and I was re-enlisted in the police force with the rank of senior assistant commissioner of police (on contract).

chapter 8

ESCAPE

ANOTHER SERIOUS POLITICAL TURMOIL IN SIERRA LEONE: YET ANOTHER MILITARY COUP AND MY ESCAPE TO THE USA

During the time when Teddy Williams was police inspector general and I was still training JPOs in the Special, there was another military coup. On 25 May 1997, the coup ousted then President Ahmed Tejan Kabbah. Meanwhile, the civil war perpetuated by the RUF rebels war raged relentlessly. President Tejan Kabbah escaped to Conakry, the capital of neighbouring Guinea. After the rebellious soldiers of the Sierra Leone Military had staged the coup, they released from prison ex-Major Johnny Paul Koroma, whom the soldiers appointed to head of the interim military government. Koroma had previously been an officer in the Sierra Leone Military. He was alleged to have been involved in the planning of a coup several months previously. But the alleged plot was discovered, and Koroma and other alleged conspirators were arrested and detained at Pademba Road Prison whilst investigations were carried out.

When the mutinous soldiers staged the coup, the RUF rebels then joined forces with the mutinous soldiers who then invited the RUF rebels to enter Freetown. It was believed in some circles that the mutinous soldiers hoped the invitation would compel the rebels to agree to stop the war and make peace. But the rebels were in no mood for peace-making, and after a lull that lasted only a few weeks, the fighting continued. On one occasion, the RUF rebels along with the mutinous soldiers they had now joined forces with captured a sizeable number of Nigerian troops. Those troops, based in Aberdeen, a suburb about seven miles from Freetown, had been fighting alongside troops loyal to the Sierra Leone government.

While President Tejan Kabbah was in refuge in Conakry, he began to broadcast messages to the citizens of Sierra Leone. In one of his broadcasts, he said that Nigeria should bomb Freetown in order to drive the RUF rebels and mutinous soldiers out of the city. He added that bombing was the price Sierra Leonean citizens had to pay for democracy. But while he was in a safe haven in Conakry, it was the citizens of Sierra Leone who would suffer as result of the bombing for what he termed "democracy".

SHELLING OF FREETOWN

A few days after the coup – as a result of either Tejan Kabbah's insensitive broadcast or the capture of the Nigerian soldiers by the RUF rebels and the AFRC[4] soldiers or both – Nigerian air force jets soon engaged in intensive bombing. They targeted specific areas in Freetown where it was suspected that the RUF rebels and the AFRC soldiers were deployed. Then one morning in June 1997 (I have now forgotten which day it was) two Nigerian frigates that had entered Freetown harbour a few days earlier started shelling the military headquarters at Cockerill on Wilkinson Road and the military barracks at Wilberforce. The former was not far from my house – only about 300 yards as the crow flies. Given the proximity, almost every hostile activity in the military headquarters adversely affected mine and my neighbours' houses.

When the shelling became too intense, Edna and I decided to vacate the house temporarily and seek shelter at our son's (Alfred's)

---

[4] The Sierra Leonean soldiers who aligned themselves with the RUF forces called themselves the Armed Forces Revolutionary Council (AFRC).

residence in Lumley, about a mile away. Edna, my sister Sarah, who was then residing with us together with Frederica, our adopted daughter, hurriedly climbed into my small Mazda 323. I drove up towards Alfred's residence at Lumley. We passed a few RUF rebels along Wilkinson Road. Fortunately at that time – and this was the case for a few days after they had entered Freetown – they were not in a belligerent mood, and they did not even stop us. We breathed a sigh of relief when we eventually arrived at Alfred's residence in Lumley.

International radio and TV stations started to broadcast reports on the shelling of Freetown. On hearing the news, Eddie, one of our daughters in America, telephoned us in a panic and urged us to escape from Freetown. She said we should try to sail to Conakry. I told her straightway I thought it too precarious a journey to undertake. I told her about several boats that had capsized due to overloading on their way to Conakry; most of the passengers had drowned. Still Eddie persisted, urging us to escape.

Meanwhile, I heard about a small rusty motor vessel that was conveying citizens from Freetown to Banjul, the capital of the Gambia at exorbitant fares. Many Freetown residents who could afford the fares rushed to board this vessel, which was anchored at the old government wharf. I resisted the temptation to follow. Edna had stoutly refused to travel by boat to Conakry or to travel by the small vessel to Banjul, Gambia. She said, and I entirely agreed, that we did not have any relatives in Conakry or Banjul. Where would we reside if we reached either of those places?

Even though I agreed with her, I was now focused on figuring out how we could escape from the panic that had overtaken the citizens of Freetown and from what appeared to be oncoming doom.

Meanwhile, Eddie (Edna Jr) in America continued to urge us, almost daily, to escape from Freetown. She informed me that she had contacted a Mr George in the Sierra Leone Embassy in Conakry, who had promised her that he would arrange accommodation in Conakry for all of us if we were able to escape to Conakry. She also gave us of the name of the consular officer at the US Embassy in Conakry who we should contact upon arrival.

The die was now cast. I had no more evasive comments I could make to Eddie. I told Edna we had no option but to escape to Conakry. I also informed both my sons, Tunde and Alfred; my sister Sarah; and our adopted daughter Frederica. Freetown was in a panic, and all government departments had closed. Fortunately, we all had passports that had not yet expired. In fact, Sarah was working in America, and she had just been in Freetown on leave a few days before she was caught up in this very dangerous situation. A minibus was chartered to convey the six of us to Conakry. On Monday, 30 June 1997, Edna, Sarah, Tunde and Alfred, Frederica, and I left home early in the morning, about 8.00 a.m. Samuel, our ward, was left in charge of the house.

After one of the most eventful journeys in my life from Freetown to Conakry by road, during which Frederica was temporarily seized by RUF rebels/mutinous Sierra Leonean soldiers, we finally arrived at the Sierra Leone Embassy in Conakry late in the night. We were welcomed by a chorus of "Johnny Paul, Johnny Paul, Johnny Paul" sung by the vast crowd of Sierra Leonean refugees inside the embassy compound, as well as inside the embassy lounge.

It was raining lightly. I had never before witnessed a scene like the one we faced. The place was crowded with refugees, and no one was in control. There were hundreds of people both outside the compound and inside the building. Utter confusion prevailed. In two open garages in the compound, people were sitting or lying down on anything they could find. Many lay on the bare concrete floor of the main room inside the building.

None of us had expected to find such a chaotic and dysfunctional situation. There was no embassy staff responsible for establishing any form of organisation among the vast, disorganised crowd. We met some refugees in the compound and enquired about the embassy staff. We were informed that the staff didn't work during the night, and they had all long gone home.

This is quite contrary to what Eddie had told me over the phone. She had been informed that the embassy staff was on duty twenty-four hours a day, in view of the unexpected emergency and so many Sierra Leoneans escaping and seeking refuge in Conakry.

I asked a woman who seemed to be attempting to control the situation about Mr George, whom Eddie had said would arrange accommodation for us. The woman said that George was not employed at the embassy. She added that he was a private individual who only went to the embassy to contact refugees who might be in need of accommodation, which he would arrange for a fee in addition to the rent. This left me flabbergasted. The six of us were all very tired, and we couldn't believe the predicament in which we found ourselves. The utter confusion that prevailed in the embassy unnerved us and filled us with dismay.

We had no choice but to wait outside the embassy compound. Edna, Sarah, and Frederica sat on our luggage, whilst Tunde, Alfred, and myself stood by a window on the side of the building. Whilst we waited, confused by the unexpected scene, the woman who appeared to be helping refugees called Edna and Sarah and said they could enter the lounge. She showed them two chairs, which she had managed to provide for them. As for Frederica, being that, at the time, she was very small, the woman told her to try and squeeze somewhere among the many people lying on the floor inside the lounge.

Now only Tunde, Alfred, and myself remained outside. It was still raining slightly. Around 1.00 a.m. on Tuesday morning 1 July, the woman called me inside the lounge. She asked me to tiptoe among the many people already asleep on the floor and make my way to a small chair perched in a corner of the lounge. There was hardly any empty space on the floor. People were lying down, some in grotesque positions, on every inch of space available on the concrete floor. By tiptoeing very carefully, I finally reached the chair. There, I made myself as comfortable as I could. But I could not sleep.

Hordes of mosquitoes filled the room, and those who were not asleep could be heard slapping their faces and bodies to drive them away. I had to do the same when the mosquitoes sensed they had a new prey. I carried all six of our passports in a small handbag I had. In addition, this handbag contained all the money we had, both in

US dollars and leones. I dared not fall asleep, for fear someone might stealthily snatch the handbag from me.

Morning was slow in coming, and when it came, it was welcomed by all of us. Many people, men, women, and children, were swarming all over the compound, and the embassy was abuzz with the conversations. I found a water tap by the side of the building. There, after queuing for about half an hour, I washed my face and mouth.

It was not until around 10.00 a.m. that some of the embassy staff, including the ambassador, arrived, almost unconcerned with the situation. The situation in Sierra Leone seemed to have overwhelmed the embassy staff.

At about 10.30, the woman who seemed to be helping refugees sought me out among the many people now milling around both inside the building and outside on the street, and she pointed out Mr George. I was glad that at last I would get in touch with Mr George. I approached him, greeted him enthusiastically, and introduced myself. Alfred and Tunde were nearby. I mentioned to Mr George that my daughter in America had assured me that he would make arrangements for our temporary accommodation. This chap said that no one had spoken to him. He seemed most uncooperative. And so saying, he departed abruptly. I was totally annoyed.

After Mr George had disappeared, Tunde, Alfred, and I mingled among the large crowd of Sierra Leonean refugees congregated in the street in front of the embassy. Some Guinean boys were trying to get customers to rent houses. One or two approached us. But we were warned very strongly by other Sierra Leoneans not to accept any of the boys' offers to find accommodation for us. We were informed that the accommodations were located in areas notorious for criminal activity and that we would be robbed of all our properties. On hearing this advice, we declined the offers.

RELIEF AT LAST

As Tunde, Alfred, and I contemplated where we could find decent accommodation, I saw a gentleman who had visited me in Freetown a few weeks previously. He said he was on his way to America and would depart the next week. I eagerly enquired where he resided. He replied that he stayed at Hotel de Golf. I further enquired whether the hotel had any vacant rooms. He said that many rooms were vacant.

I immediately requested that he take us to the hotel, which he did. I booked two rooms, and then Tunde, Alfred, and I hailed a taxi and returned to the embassy. We gladly informed Edna, Sarah, and Frederica that we had succeeded in reserving two rooms at Hotel de Golf.

We wasted no time in boarding two taxis, which conveyed the six of us, together with our luggage, to Hotel de Golf. Edna, Sarah, and Frederica occupied one of the rooms, whilst Tunde, Alfred, and I occupied the other. We quickly took a bath, which was utterly refreshing after having travelled from Freetown to Conakry on the previous day through mostly dusty roads.

OBTAINING VISAS FOR THE USA

A few days later, we all except Sarah went to the American Embassy to apply for visas. Sarah had a re-entry visa for America. After we had queued for about one hour, the consular section was opened, and all of us who had been waiting outside the building entered. After each of us had filled out the appropriate forms, the consular officer asked each of us some questions. We were soon informed that all our visas had been approved and that we should send someone on a certain date mentioned by the consular officer to collect all our passports. On the date mentioned, Alfred collected the passports from the embassy after paying the fees for the visas.

A few days later, Eddie remitted a few hundred dollars to us. And after about a week, she sent tickets for the six of us to travel to America.

RENTING A HOUSE IN CONAKRY

As it was too expensive for the six of us to stay in the hotel, we did not stay for long. After about two weeks, we rented a vacant house in Conakry for one month. We would prepare breakfast and supper by ourselves. But lunch was brought to us daily by a Sierra Leonean who was a resident in Conakry.

chapter 9

A New Life

Arrival in the USA

Late on the evening of 4 August 1997, we left Conakry via Dakar for New York, where we arrived late in the morning on 5 August 1997. After the completion of immigration and customs formalities, we boarded another flight in New York for Raleigh-Durham International Airport in North Carolina.

On our arrival at Raleigh-Durham Airport, we were met by some of our daughters, together with their children. They were very glad to see us. We were conveyed to Eddie and Hilary's house at 1413 Dutch Garden Court, Raleigh, where we were entertained, after which we were separated into groups of two. Each group was allocated to reside with one of our daughters who were already residing in Raleigh, Durham, and Garner respectively.

Unfolding events prevent our return to Sierra Leone

Edna and I did not intend to stay in America for long. We expected that the situation in Sierra Leone would very soon return to normal and that we would then return to Freetown. But subsequent events

91

that were to unfold in Freetown prevented our departure. During the early hours of 6 January 1999, news came from Freetown that the RUF rebels, together with some rebellious Sierra Leonean soldiers, had invaded Freetown, spreading widespread mayhem by destroying houses and killing and maiming many helpless citizens.

In view of the forgoing events, Edna and I had to postpone our planned return to Freetown indefinitely. In due course, Edna and I became naturalized US citizens, and we remain in the United States of America as of this writing.

MY EMPLOYMENT IN THE UNITED STATES

In 2000, I obtained a North Carolina driver's license. I then applied to Burns Security Services for a position as a security officer in June 2000.

With my application, I included my résumé, which showed that I had been commander of the national police force in Sierra Leone and that I had extensive training and experience in various aspects of security. I thought the management of Burns Security Services might consider my experience in determining the post in which I should be placed, as well as the salary I should receive. But I suspect that the management thought I was lying and did not have the qualifications and experience I claimed to have. I was employed as an ordinary security officer and posted on normal security duties in the North Carolina Department of Transportation (NC DOT) off Poole Road in Raleigh, North Carolina.

There I met another security officer who was a few years older than I was. The older security officer was a white American who was a veteran of the Second World War. He informed me that he had taken part in the Allied invasion of France in 1944 to free Europe from German occupation. This chap was very troublesome. He seemed to me to be a Negrophobe. But I learnt that he was not harassing me alone; he was also harassing other NC DOT staff. I suspected that, when he was young, he was rather truculent and troublesome.

I reported his harassment of me to my supervisor. But nothing came out of it. Eventually, the security officer with abrasive attitude changed his comportment and appeared to be friendly. On one occasion, he told me the story of when he and thousands of American soldiers were landed in Normandy Beach in France in 1944 during the Second World War to free Europe from German occupation. A young captain was his commanding officer. When they landed, there were many bodies of soldiers lying on the beach. These soldiers had been killed by German machine guns and mines. He was driving an armoured car, and the young captain ordered him not to drive over the dead bodies. Bullets were flying all around. He told the captain he should drive the vehicle himself and show him how he could avoid driving over the many dead bodies lying all around.

Unfortunately, this man died at his residence suddenly in 2002, apparently after suffering a heart attack.

I served as security officer for four and a half years, until I suffered from very high blood pressure. I was admitted at WakeMed Hospital. On 29 January 2004, I resigned from the post of security officer.

It was fortunate that I had done so. A few months later, I suffered from a stroke. I was again admitted at WakeMed. Although I recovered, the stroke left me with a slight impairment in my speech, which now made me to stutter. Due to the timely intervention of my daughter Eddie, who quickly rushed me to WakeMed emergency, I received prompt medical treatment. Thus, the stroke did not have a much more devastating effect on me.

PART 2

A BYGONE ERA IN SIERRA LEONE

chapter 10

A Profile of Colonial Sierra Leone

Activities and customs in Sierra Leone, especially in Freetown, from the thirties to present

In the thirties, when I was young, Sierra Leone was under British colonial control. In this chapter, I have endeavoured to recapture what I term the halcyon days of Sierra Leone. I will detail the system of government in the country, activities during the Second World War (1939–1945), and other activities and customs in Sierra Leone, particularly in Freetown.

The administration of the country

Of the four British colonies in West Africa – the Gambia, Sierra Leone, the Gold Coast (now Ghana), and Nigeria – Sierra Leone was unique. The British divided the country into two administrative regions. Freetown and the surrounding areas were termed the colony. This area was populated mainly by the Creoles (Krios). The other area, which is by far the larger, was termed a protectorate. That meant that the British were only "protecting" the inhabitants of that area. But the entire country, both colony and protectorate, was being effectively ruled by the British, mainly as one entity.

The British colonial government was headed by a British governor, who was based at Fort Thornton in Freetown. From there, assisted by other British administrative officials, he administered the entire country.

LEGISLATIVE COUNCIL

During the British colonial period, Sierra Leone had no parliament and no elections by the citizens, whereby they could choose their own representatives to enact laws. Rather, what was known as the Legislative Council (LEGCO) enacted laws for both the colony and the protectorate. The laws were then termed *ordinances*. The members of the Legislative Council were predominantly heads of departments who were all British officials, plus few local prominent citizens in the colony and few paramount chiefs from the protectorate. These Sierra Leoneans were specially selected by the governor to be in the Legislative Council as representatives of the people in both the colony and protectorate.

The meeting place of the Legislative Council was an annex to the old Secretariat Building along George Street in Freetown. The Legislative Council was the "Parliament". There, legislations were tabled, read, debated, and passed (or should it be said "rubber-stamped").

EXECUTIVE COUNCIL

The "cabinet" was termed the Executive Council (EXCO), over which the governor himself presided. The other members of the Executive Council were the colonial secretary, who was the deputy governor, and selected heads of some of the more important departments. The Executive Council proposed laws for the entire country and made very important plans, which were then approved by the Legislative Council. But then there were two sets of laws – one for the colony and the other for the protectorate. Laws that were applicable to the colony were not applicable to the protectorate, except when any law had been specifically declared applicable to both colony and protectorate.

The general public could sometimes give their views about certain proposed legislations (or ordinances) by writing letters to the governor or by articles published in the very few daily newspapers in Freetown at the time.

THE PROTECTORATE ASSEMBLY

In 1946, the British colonial government created a separate government for the protectorate. This was called the Protectorate Assembly. This assembly was composed of prominent paramount chiefs from each of the provinces in the protectorate and other prominent citizens of the protectorate. Some of the members of that assembly were Dr Milton Margai, Albert Margai, Siaka Stevens, Doyle Sumner, Rev. Dr Fitz-John, Abu Magba Kamara, and several others who I cannot now remember. The meeting place of the Protectorate Assembly was at Bo, the capital of the Southern Province.

Such an assembly was only a farce and an attempt to prolong the divide-and-rule policy – in other words, to divide the people of the protectorate from those in the colony. The latter were predominantly Creoles who were most vociferous in their demands for greater control of government to be left in the hands of Sierra Leoneans. The Protectorate Assembly gradually faded into oblivion just before Sierra Leone gained its independence from Britain on 27 April 1961.

THE MAIN ADMINISTRATIVE BUILDING IN FREETOWN

Situated along the middle section of George Street in Freetown was a majestic concrete building. It was formerly called the Secretariat Building. The main departments of the government, including the office of the colonial secretary, who was the deputy governor, were originally located in this building.

During colonial days, there were no "ministries" in the country. All the administrative units were termed *departments*. Most of the government departments were then located in the Secretariat Building. This building was at the time well respected. Civil servants therein were well dressed at work, and there was decorum in all the offices. Persons who had no legitimate business in any of the offices in that building would not have the temerity to enter the building. No peddlers, newspaper vendors, or anyone else dared enter this building. The building was not a free-for-all, as it would later become, several years after Sierra Leone had been an independent nation. Then hordes of unemployed men and women, itinerant fishmongers, sellers of cakes, and so on would be seen roaming in and out of that building.

The building opposite the old Secretariat Building also on George Street was named the Ministerial Building. It wasn't built till after independence, sometime in the mid-sixties. It was constructed by the Israeli-owned construction company National Construction Company (a branch of the Israeli commercial company Dizengoff) and funded by what was termed soft loans by the Israeli government. The same construction company had constructed the House of Parliament building at Tower Hill, the new general post office (SALPOST) building at Gloucester Street and Siaka Stevens Street (formerly named Westmoreland Street).

After the Second World War had ended in 1945, some government offices were moved from the Secretariat Building to prefabricated buildings in New England, Freetown. Before the Second World War, the entire area now known as New England had been forest. During the war, the British military cleared the forest and constructed prefabricated buildings, which were at that time used for war purposes. The RAF communication centre in Freetown was located in some of these prefab buildings.

THE LAW COURTS

Seated along Westmoreland Street (now called Siaka Stevens Street) in the centre of Freetown, adjacent to the historic Cotton Tree, is a majestic concrete building. On top of the front entrance are statutes of two old men in a reclining position. This is the Law Courts building of Sierra Leone. I do not know what the symbolism of the statues is. But I am sure legal practitioners can explain the symbolism.

The foundation stone of this great building was laid by Field Marshall His Royal Highness Arthur W.P.A. Duke of Connaught and Strathearn on 15 December 1910.

Part of the basement of the Law Courts formerly housed the headquarters of the Sierra Leone Police Force. But in 1949, the headquarters was moved to the building that had previously housed the headquarters of the Sierra Leone government railway, located on George Street and Westmoreland Street (now known as Siaka Stevens Street). It served as police headquarters until it was torn down in the early eighties for the construction of a large new building that now houses police headquarters.

Front entrance of The Law Courts building

Law Courts Building, Freetown, Sierra Leone

RESIDENCES OF BRITISH ADMINISTRATORS IN FREETOWN

The permanent official residence and office of the colonial governor was at Fort Thornton at the foot of Tower Hill in the centre of Freetown near the historic Cotton Tree. Fort Thornton was constructed as far back as 1796, during the very early stages of colonialism. That building was reconstructed sometime in the fifties by the Public Works Department (PWD) and given its modern look. It is now officially called the State House, but it is no longer the residence of the president of Sierra Leone. Rather, it's used solely as offices for the president.

As this building had originally contained the official representative of the king (or queen) of England, a ceremonial guard – a contingent of the First Battalion of the Sierra Leone Regiment of the Royal West African Frontier Force (WESTAFF) – was a constant figure at the entrance. These ceremonial guards were changed after a few hours on duty. The changing of the guards at Fort Thornton was a ceremonial parade similar to the ceremonial changing of the guards at Buckingham Palace in London, England. The ceremonial uniform worn by these soldiers consisted of a red monkey jacket, a red cummerbund, khaki short trousers, and a red Fez cap with a tassel. They also wore khaki puttees wrapped around their legs from below the knee to a little above the ankle.

RESIDENCES OF OTHER SENIOR OFFICIALS

Up to the late fifties, some of the British administrators occupying top positions in the colonial civil service in Sierra Leone resided in bungalows inside Freetown along Charlotte Street and Gloucester Street. Some other residences were located at Brookfields along Kingharman Road. The vast majority of the British colonial servants resided up at the reservation at Hill Station, a suburb of Freetown. All the houses at Hill Station at that time were reserved for British administrators. No Sierra Leone citizens resided at Hill Station. It was a reservation for whites only. The British senior staff of the Sierra Leone Railway resided in bungalows at Cline Town by Ross Road and along Race Course Road.

Each of the bungalows that housed British administrators, engineers, and other personnel – whether at Hill Station, Brookfields, downtown Freetown, or Cline Town – had Sierra Leonean staff. These included servant, cooks, and gardeners. The staff cleaned the houses and compounds and prepared meals for the British administrators and engineers. Each house also had a watchman at night. The salaries of all these ancillary staff were a pittance. They were paid out of public funds, which were included in the annual budget of the colonial government of Sierra Leone.

Each of these areas where British senior civil servants resided – Hill Station, Brookfields and Cline Town – had its own club, where the staff and members of their families would go in the evening to relax; have drinks; and play table tennis, lawn tennis, bingo, and so on.

Since local citizens were not permitted to reside at Hill Station, Sierra Leonean domestic staff who were working in these houses had to travel to and from Hill Station every day. Some travelled by buses up to Wilberforce and walked the short distance to the nearby Hill Station, whilst others walked all the way to and from Freetown.

Newly arrived British administrators, engineers and other technical staff who were bound for the protectorate were accommodated temporarily in buildings at Brookfields. This area was termed "Transit Camp." There were facilities for the newly arrived British staff to have their meals. After the arrival of British administrators ended, the Transit Camp was converted to a hotel called Brookfields Hotel. Some of the buildings in that facility were constructed in 1980 for the hosting of officials during the OAU Summit in 1980.

THE FREETOWN CITY COUNCIL

In regard to the municipality of the capital, Freetown, the British colonial government permitted the municipality to have its own local government, known as the Freetown City Council, since Freetown was incorporated as a municipality in 1893 with its own mayor. But the Freetown City Council was under the watchful eyes of the central colonial government. Candidates for mayor, as well as candidates for the Freetown City Council election, had to be literate. They also had to be holders of properties in Freetown valued at certain minimum amounts. In addition, candidates had to be paying annual rates for their property. There was then no universal adult suffrage as there is now. There were also no political parties. The organisations in place at the time were Rate Payers Associations in each ward in Freetown.

SECURITY: WEST AFRICAN FRONTIER FORCE (WESTAFF)

Prior to the Second World War, the Sierra Leone army was called the First Battalion of the West African Frontier Force. The popular name in Sierra Leone was WESTAFF. The British colonial government termed the armies in each of their West African territories the "West African Frontier Force." The uniform of the soldiers in each of these territories was the same. They wore khaki shorts and shirts and wrapped their legs in khaki puttees. Originally, these soldiers did not wear boots. But later boots were issued to them.

ENFORCEMENT OF LAW AND ORDER

As has already been mentioned, there were separate laws for the colony and the protectorate. Consequently, the organisation responsible for the maintenance of law and order in the colony was quite different from that responsible for the maintenance of law and order in the protectorate.

In the colony area, the responsibility of enforcing law and order fell to the Sierra Leone Police Force. Up until the early fifties, the Sierra Leone Police Force in Freetown consisted of only a few hundred constables, NCOs, and inspectors. These few carried out normal law enforcement and crime prevention duties in Freetown and around the other areas of the colony (the peninsular area). They patrolled the streets, investigated crimes, and made arrests whenever necessary. The police force was, at that time, viewed in awe, and the mere threat by a parent to call the police would bring unruly and errant kids under control.

The Sierra Leone Police Force, despite its name, was not responsible for the enforcement of law and order throughout the then protectorate. The body that was responsible there was the Court Messenger Force, which was under the command of the district commissioner in each district in each province.

Some of the personnel in the Court Messenger Force were semi-literate, and some were completely illiterate. But there were also some literate personnel in this force. These personnel were highly disciplined and extremely loyal to the colonial administrators in the protectorate. Allegedly, they acted like robots. Orders from the district commissioners were carried out strictly and promptly without any questions being asked. Some of the members of the Court Messenger Force reportedly took illegal and brutal actions towards citizens in the protectorate.

It was not until 1 September 1954, after long delays and protracted debates, that the Legislative Council eventually enacted a law giving the Sierra Leone Police Force jurisdiction throughout the country. The Court Messenger Force was disbanded, and detachments of the Sierra Leone Police Force were sent to all the large towns in the protectorate (now called provinces). This was a timely move because, about a year later, sometime in 1955, there were serious revolts against the paramount chiefs in the protectorate, mainly in the northern province. The revolts lasted until early 1956.

SENIOR ADMINISTRATIVE STAFF IN THE CIVIL SERVICE

All senior administrative posts and all technical posts – engineering posts, for example – in the civil service were occupied by British graduates from Oxford or Cambridge or other colleges in Britain. It was sometime in the fifties that the British colonial government gradually began to promote a few Sierra Leoneans to senior posts.

SIERRA LEONEAN PERSONNEL IN THE CIVIL SERVICE

Up to about the mid-fifties, only males had posts in the Sierra Leone civil service. In the medical field, there were many female nurses. And in the teaching profession, there were female teachers long ago.

APPOINTMENTS COMMITTEE

Prior to independence, entry into the civil service by Sierra Leoneans was a process. One would first have to pass the Cambridge School Certificate (known as the GCE) or an equivalent examination and then undergo an interview with a panel of top civil servants, including the director of education, and a few prominent members of the public who had distinguished themselves. That committee was known as the Appointments Committee. It was replaced by the Public Service Commission after Sierra Leone had gained her independence from Britain in 1961.

DISCIPLINE IN THE CIVIL SERVICE

Discipline in the civil service was very strict. Since all the heads of government departments were British expatriates, they imposed the same very high standard of discipline in the British civil service upon the Sierra Leone civil service. Civil servants were to report for work promptly before 8.00 a.m. Latecomers were allowed only fifteen minutes. After 8.15, the staff supervisor or staff superintendent in each office would draw a red line in the attendance register underneath the last name of the person who reported for duty. Any staff who made a habit of going to work after 8.15 a.m. would be issued a query to explain why he was persistently late for duty. Such queries, together with the explanation as well as the decision taken by the head of department would be placed in that person's personal file (PF). This mark might likely adversely affect the individual's chances for further promotion to higher ranks. Even the heads of departments, who were all British expatriates, would generally go to work within the time stipulated in general orders.

Three manuals outlined the various regulations with which all civil servants were obliged to comply. These were the General Orders, the Financial Regulations, and the Store Rules and Regulations. It was the direct responsibility of each head of a department to ensure that his subordinate staff complied with all these regulations. No deviation or violation whatsoever was tolerated. Infraction or violation of any of the rules and regulations would result in a query being issued to the defaulter. And queries would have to be responded to within a certain time. Penalty was issued on the defaulter depending on the gravity of the violation. Punishment varied from admonishment to reprimand or serious reprimand, temporary withholding of the defaulter's increment or deferment of his increment altogether, temporary suspension or termination of employment. Very serious lapses or irregularities of a criminal nature were referred to the Criminal Investigation Department (CID) of the police force. And, depending on the evidence, the civil servant could be charged to court. If found guilty, penalty would be issued in accordance with the civil laws.

Civil servants were not allowed to hold second jobs or to engage in any commercial enterprise. Also, unlike now, no civil servant was permitted to be involved actively in politics. Any deviations would be subject to disciplinary action.

GOVERNMENT FINANCE

Unlike the present, when there is lose supervision of disbursements of government finances, very strict control was exercised over government finances in colonial days. The provisions of the general orders and financial orders had to be strictly complied with. Any deviations or discrepancies, however minor, would be subject to very severe disciplinary action, which at times would result in the person facing criminal charges for embezzlement or other appropriate charges.

When I was a young boy, I learnt of an instance involving a postal clerk at the central post office at Gloucester Street in Freetown. The clerk was reported to have been charged criminally for a shortage of only one shilling (now equivalent to about one leone). The unfortunate civil servant was convicted and imprisoned.

All these possible penalties, and the resultant opprobrium to the individual as well as his family, acted as strong deterrents and prevented civil servants from misappropriating government funds and property. In those days, no one would had dared approach the British head of a department or the governor to "plead" for leniency – a situation that is now normal in Sierra Leone, due to politics.

EDUCATIONAL STANDARDS AND SALARIES OF SIERRA LEONEAN CIVIL SERVANTS

Before someone was appointed as a third-grade clerk to work as a civil servant in any government office, that person (mainly males) must have passed the Cambridge Senior School Certificate or attained an equivalent educational standard. The British colonial government made no compromise when it came to this rule.

However, after the Second World War ended, as compensation, a very small number of literate personnel who had served in the armed services in various capacities were absorbed into the civil service as third-grade clerks.

Civil servants were paid salaries commensurate with their responsibilities and sufficient for them to live normal lives. A young man joining the civil service as a third-grade clerk received a basic monthly salary of £3.15s.[5]

However, in 1946 and 1947, the colonial government had a senior official from the British civil service come to Sierra Leone to review the conditions of service of Sierra Leone civil servants. That official was named Harragin. The Harragin Commission of Inquiry into the salaries and conditions in the civil service in Sierra Leone in resulted in a hefty hike in the commencement of monthly salaries. For third-grade clerks or the equivalent, the monthly salary more than doubled, from £3.15s to £7.0s. Other grades in the civil service also received increases in their monthly salaries.

BRITISH DISCRIMINATION

During British colonial days, recruitment into the senior ranks of the civil service was open only to British expatriates. The British practiced racial discrimination. Sierra Leoneans were prevented from being promoted to senior ranks. It was not until the fifties, and only after long and persistent demands by Sierra Leoneans, that the British colonial government relented and began to promote Sierra Leoneans to senior ranks. But the salaries and other amenities of these high-ranked Sierra Leoneans civil servants were lower than those of similarly ranked British officials.

The British created two categories of senior civil servants – "British expatriate" senior civil servants and "African" senior civil servants.

---

[5] I cannot give the equivalent now in the Sierra Leone currency, the leone.

The salaries and amenities of the former were higher than those of the letter.

In the judiciary system, Ernest Beoku-Betts (a Sierra Leonean) was quite a brilliant legal practitioner. When the colonial administration wanted to appoint him as a judge in the Supreme Court, the British judges in Sierra Leone threatened to resign. They did not want an African appointed as a judge of equal status to them. Confronted with these protests, the colonial government had to compromise and, instead, appointed Justice Ernest Beoku-Betts as puisne judge (that is a judge of lower status than the British judges).

The British colonial government had a slightly different policy for Sierra Leoneans who had qualified abroad as doctors, either in Britain or in Europe or America. These Sierra Leonean doctors were appointed to senior positions in the medical department before the fifties. But their salaries and amenities were lower than those of British doctors.

It was after a long struggle by Sierra Leoneans that the British eventually instilled a unified senior civil service, wherein both British and Sierra Leonean senior civil servants and professionals received equal salaries and amenities. That was towards the end of colonial rule.

SIERRA LEONEANS WHO BECAME THE FIRST
HEADS OF GOVERNMENT DEPARTMENTS

The first Sierra Leonean who became assistant colonial secretary was Mr T.C. Luke. Other Sierra Leoneans who first became the heads of departments and military divisions included Brig. David Lansana, who was appointed brigadier of the Sierra Leone Armed Forces; Lloyd Beckley, who was appointed accountant-general; and Christo Davies, who was appointed postmaster-general and later became the director of posts and telecommunications. Leslie G. Thompson was appointed comptroller of customs, Ade Hyde was appointed secretary to the cabinet, Mitchell Johnson was appointed director of civil aviation, and Leslie William Leigh was appointed commissioner of police. A.J. Momoh was appointed head of a certain department, which I have now forgotten. George Sulaiman Panda was appointed Commissioner of Labour and would later become the first secretary to the prime minister after Sierra Leone became independent in April 1961.

EDUCATION

Citizens who were born after the British colonial government had been replaced by a democratic system of government consisting of Sierra Leoneans may like to know something about the system and quality of education that existed through the thirties up to the fifties whilst Sierra Leone was under British colonial rule. I will try my best to throw some light on this very important aspect of Sierra Leone.

During British colonial days, education was neither compulsory nor free. But every child was free to attend school, subject to the payment of a small monthly fee by each pupil. For the most part, the various Christian religious bodies provided education. Most of the elementary schools and secondary schools were in the colony area (Freetown and its environs). There were only very few schools in the protectorate. Most of the secondary and primary schools in Freetown were owned by one of the various Christian denominations – Anglican, Catholic, Methodist, and the American UBC mission. There were one or two Muslim primary schools but no Muslim secondary school.

All primary schools, with the exception of St Edward's Primary School (boys), Cathedral Boys' Primary School, Cathedral Girls' Primary School, and St Anne's Primary School (girls) were co-ed. That is male and female pupils attending the same school and sitting in the same classes.

There were two government-owned schools. One was the Model Primary School at Circular Road and Berry Street in Freetown. The other was the Prince of Wales Boys Secondary School at Kingtom, also in Freetown. There was a government-owned secondary school in Bo, the capital of the Southern Province. That was the Bo Secondary

School, which was constructed by the colonial government in 1906, mainly for the sons of chiefs in the provinces.

These religion-owned schools were closely supervised by the colonial government's Department of Education. Starting in the late twenties, the colonial government became more actively involved in the administration of all schools and exercised a strict supervisory role over all educational activities. All the primary schools, with the exception of one or two private schools, were amalgamated, and the Department of Education ensured that schools maintained consistent standards.

Pupils in primary schools paid token fees on a sliding scale. These fees ranged from 6d for those in infant classes to 1s.0d for pupils in standards 1 to 3 and 1s.6d for those in standard 4. Students in standards 5 and 6 paid 2s.6d. Any pupil who defaulted in the payment of his or her monthly school fee was sent home for the day and told to inform his or her parents or guardians that, unless the monthly fee was paid, he or she would not be allowed back in class. The monthly school fees might seem like relatively small amounts. Nevertheless, not every parent could afford to pay the fees regularly. The fees collected in each primary school were paid to the government's accountant general by the headmaster or headmistress of each primary school.

Primary school pupils of priests of the Anglican churches were exempt from the payment of the monthly fees. Also, students who came from large families with many children by the same parents paid only half the monthly fees.

Apart from school fees, no extra charges were levied on pupils by teachers. In comparison, pupils are currently compelled to pay a variety of "fees" to teachers for questionable purposes. Back then, if any teacher had been so dishonest as to levy unofficial charges on pupils, apart from losing his or her job, such teacher and his or her family would have faced great shame. This would have acted as a strong deterrent to any teacher being involved in dishonest or immoral activities.

The Department of Education was responsible for supplying to all primary schools free of charge schoolbooks; various furniture and equipment, including desks; blackboards; and items like chalk, pens, pencils, ink, nibs, erasers, slates, and the like. The textbooks were the same as those used by pupils in schools in Britain. That was why primary school pupils in Sierra Leone learnt about the London Bridge in the song "London Bridge Is Falling Down" without having seen the Bridge. The Department of Education also paid the salaries of all primary school teachers.

Primary school pupils needing to acquire their own small desks and benches, which they would convey to and from school, was completely unheard of. Nor would any pupils be made to sit on stones on account of the absence of benches or chairs, desks, and other furniture. The manifestation of such situations in Sierra Leone recently is a completely disgraceful spectacle and an adverse reflection on the competence of those responsible for the administration of education in the country. Specious reasons were advanced for these rather disgraceful spectacles, among them that more and more children are attending schools. But the real cause is to be found in the lack of competence among administrators.

Students in secondary schools paid school fees quarterly. Each secondary school was responsible for the provision of furniture. But students had to purchase text and exercise books . Each secondary school paid its own principal and teachers. But the Department of Education exercised strict supervision over all secondary schools.

In British colonial days pupils in primary schools did not wear uniforms. Rather, they would wear ordinary clean and tidy dresses. The teacher in each class ensured that his or her pupils were properly dressed and groomed. Pupils who were untidy, unkempt, and not dressed properly were sometimes caned or sent home to be properly dressed.

With the exception of the Prince of Wales Secondary School and all the girls' secondary schools, the boys in secondary schools did not wear uniforms.

The following is a list of all the secondary schools that existed in Freetown up to the fifties:

Boys' Secondary Schools

1. Albert Academy
2. CMS Grammar School
3. Collegiate School
4. Methodist Boys' High School
5. Prince of Wales School
6. St Edward's Secondary School

Girls' Secondary Schools

1. Annie Walsh Memorial School
2. A.M.E. Girls Industrial Institute
3. Methodist Girls' High School
4. Roosevelt Secondary School for Girls (established in the early fifties by Mrs Constance Cummings-John)
5. St. Joseph's Secondary School for Girls (known as Convent).

Some accuse the British colonialists of providing a very limited and narrow education for children in the colony during colonial days, focused mainly on providing future clerks and the like to serve in government offices and keep the colonial machinery running properly. Perhaps to a certain extent this may be true.

In addition, the British colonial government did not appear too keen to provide widespread education in the protectorate. Rather, the Christian denominations, which followed very closely behind the heels of British administrators, provided education. But the Christian organisations were handicapped by lack of sufficient funds and were unable to build schools throughout most of the protectorate.

Discipline in all schools was very strict. It was unheard of for pupils to riot or manifest the other forms of indiscipline and unruly conduct that presently prevails. In those days, it was not necessary for the government to set up the quasi-government organisation known as Organisation for Attitudinal and Behavioural Change (ABC). Even with today's ABC, there seems to be no significant improvement in the comportment of pupils.

NO GHOST SCHOOLS OR GHOST TEACHERS

In British colonial days, there were absolutely no ghost schools or ghost teachers. Such a concept was unheard of. Any officials who would have been dishonest enough to include ghost schools or ghost teachers in the official lists of schools would automatically have found themselves facing serious criminal charges. Convictions would have resulted in severe penalties.

ORIGINAL SITES OF THREE GREAT EDUCATIONAL INSTITUTIONS IN FREETOWN

No history of Freetown would be complete without noting the original sites of three great educational institutions, which were to play very important roles in education in Sierra Leone.

First is the Fourah Bay College. This great educational institution in Sierra Leone was first established at the mountain village of Leicester, a few miles from Freetown. It was later transferred to Fourah Bay, a suburb in Freetown's east end – hence, the name Fourah Bay College.

Next is the CMS Grammar School. This school was originally established in the mountain village of Regent, several miles from Freetown. After several years, the CMS Grammar School was relocated to Oxford Street between Bathurst Street and Wellington Street. That is why students in CM.S Grammar School are still known as "Regentonians".

The Annie Walsh Memorial School, for girls, is the third great educational institution. It was originally established by Christian missionaries in another mountain village, Charlotte, about seven miles from Freetown. That school was later relocated to its present site along Kissy Street, Mountain Cut, and Elk Street in Freetown.

PRINCIPALS, HEADMASTERS, AND HEADMISTRESSES

The principals of all the male secondary schools except the Prince of Wales, St Edward's Secondary, and Albert Academy were Sierra Leoneans. The principal of Prince of Wales was a British national. A Catholic priest, usually Irish, took the helm at St Edward's. One prominent, renowned, and widely revered principal was the Rev. Father Cornelius Mulchy of St Edward's Secondary School. The principal at Albert Academy was an American national.

As for the girls' secondary schools in Freetown, the Annie Walsh Memorial School, as well as the Methodist Girls High School and the St Joseph's Girls Secondary School each had a female expatriate as principal. The principal of St Joseph's Secondary was a Roman Catholic nun. The Freetown Secondary School for Girls (FSSG) has always had a Sierra Leonean principal. In the forties the principal was Mrs Hannah Benka-Coker.

The secondary schools that previously had expatriate principals had Sierra Leonean principals after independence.

All the primary schools in Freetown except the Roman Catholic St Edward's Primary School, St Anne's Primary School, and St Anthony Primary School had Sierra Leonean headmasters or headmistresses.

PUBLIC EXAMINATIONS IN SECONDARY SCHOOLS

In colonial days, pupils in secondary schools sat two compulsory public examinations. One was the Cambridge Junior School Certificate Examination, taken by secondary school pupils in standard 3. The other was the Cambridge Senior School Certificate (the Cambridge GCE), which was taken by students in standard 5. The Cambridge Senior School certificate was the "passport" to finding jobs, in the civil service, as well as in any other field.

Mail vessels from Britain delivered the examination papers in sealed envelopes to Freetown. During the examinations, at each examination centre, the senior supervisor would break the seal on the envelope containing the examination papers in front of all the pupils sitting the examinations before distributing them.

During the examination, there was strict silence in the examination hall, and no pupil was permitted to leave, not even to go to the bathroom. If any pupil wanted to use the bathroom during the exam, he or she had to surrender his or her written answers and would no longer be permitted to continue the examination.

While today, exam questions are rampantly leaked ahead of time, no such leakages occurred in colonial times. This reflected the high integrity of the principals and teachers during pre-independence days.

The written answers, also in sealed envelopes, were conveyed to Britain by mail vessels. The answer papers were then marked and graded in Britain. All this went on smoothly without interruptions. As far as I am aware, despite the fact that many British and Allied vessels were being torpedoed and sunk in the Atlantic Ocean by German U-boats, no question papers or answer papers were ever lost at sea owing to hostile enemy action. I think this was a tribute to the effectiveness of the British Royal Navy and its heroic crew, who risked their lives to protect merchant vessels plying the Atlantic Ocean.

LONDON MATRICULATION CERTIFICATE

The other examination, which relatively few students sat for after having passed the Cambridge Senior School Certificate, was the London Matriculation Certificate. Only students in advanced form five (known as upper five) or sixth form sat for this examination. Very few secondary schools then had form six. The question papers were also sent to Freetown from London by London University. Passing this examination would entitle a student to be admitted at Fourah Bay College in Freetown or enter into any university in Britain.

Up to the early sixties, only one university existed in the whole of Sierra Leone – the Fourah Bay College in Freetown. Fourah Bay College was the major college in British West Africa at the time. Students from other British West African colonies – Nigeria, Gold Coast (now Ghana), and the Gambia came to Freetown to attend Fourah Bay College. Almost all the leading politicians in each of these colonies prior to independence from Britain attended Fourah Bay College. Those were the glorious days when Freetown was given the accolade "The Athens of Africa," radiating intellectual light to all black Africa.

FOURAH BAY COLLEGE

Fourah Bay College was originally established in 1827 as an affiliate of Durham University in England to train Sierra Leoneans as priests for the Church of England and as teachers. Students who graduated from this college were awarded the degrees of the University of Durham. This college was the first higher educational institution in the whole of British West Africa.

Not too long after the Second World War commenced, the British military acquired certain buildings in Freetown to be used for war purposes. Fourah Bay College building, which was then located near the sea at Cline in the East end of Freetown, was soon taken over by the British War Office. The staff and students were moved to a town in the protectorate called Mabang. There stood large vacant buildings that had formerly been used as accommodation for students of an old agricultural college.

Mabang is about forty miles from Freetown and situated along the railroad, which ran from Freetown to the extreme east of the country, ending at a town called Pendembu. It was not too difficult in those days to travel from Freetown to the new location of this famous college. Fourah Bay College remained in Mabang throughout the war. But it seemed from information received that the students and staff were given a hostile reception by hordes of mosquitoes, which reportedly relentlessly harassed everyone. Because of its new location, this prestigious college, which had once turned out many luminaries from both Sierra Leone and the other British West African colonies, became inhospitable.

The British colonial government was experimenting with the education of students in all the West African Colonies. In 1944, the government decided that it was not necessary for Sierra Leone to have a university. It planned to remove Fourah Bay College from Freetown and relocate it in Nigeria, which was a far larger British colony. Instead, Sierra Leone would have a technical college.

Never before had there been such unanimous and vociferous outcry among Sierra Leoneans, particularly among Creole intellectuals. They banded together to prevent this college from being removed from Sierra Leone. Vigorous and widespread protests against the British government were mounted. Groups of citizens sent written protests to the governor in Freetown, as well as petitions to the Secretary of State for the Colonies in Britain. The opposition to the proposal to remove Fourah Bay College was so widespread, determined, and fierce that the British colonial government eventually had to relent and agreed to let Fourah Bay College remain in Sierra Leone.

That's how Sierra Leone retained its prestigious educational institution, through which many of the former leaders of other British colonies in West Africa as well as leaders in Sierra Leone had passed.

Several years later, on account of the inhospitable environment in Mabang, a vigorous search was launched – its aim to find an ideal location for the college in Freetown. After the end of the Second World War, the buildings at Mount Aureol were chosen. The location, on a hill overlooking Freetown, had many large vacant buildings. The British military had formerly used the buildings as a hospital and accompanying facilities for sick and injured British soldiers based in Freetown. And so Freetown is fortunate to have, high above the hills overlooking the city, Fourah Bay College.

No College Education for the Majority of Students

In my day, the vast majority of students in Sierra Leone did not receive any college education. The prohibitive cost was the primary obstacle that prevented them from attending Fourah Bay College. Only the very affluent were able to send their children to Fourah Bay College. And only a very few others sent their children overseas (mainly to Britain or the United States) for further studies in any profession.

The highest standard of education in Sierra Leone for the average student, both male and female, up to the fifties was the Cambridge University Senior School Certificate. Nevertheless, the standard of education in secondary schools was very high at the time.

It was only from during the mid-fifties that government scholarships were liberally available to students, enabling them to attend Fourah Bay College. By then, the British colonial government wanted to accelerate higher education, especially among young male Sierra Leoneans. Britain was then on the verge of granting independence to Sierra Leone. The British colonial government wanted young male Sierra Leoneans to replace British administrators then in senior positions in the civil service. Therefore, a substantial number of male students who had passed the Cambridge Senior School Certificate Examination were granted scholarships to attend Fourah Bay College. A few others were sent to Britain on scholarships to study in British universities.

Acquisition of Secondary School Buildings by the War Office during the War and Relocation of the Schools to Other Areas in Freetown

A few months after the Second World War began, the British War Department acquired several large buildings, including secondary school buildings. The following four secondary schools were affected by this forced acquisition of buildings:

1. **Albert Academy** – The school was relocated from Berry Street to some private houses on Garrison Street by Howe Street in Freetown.

2. **CMS Grammar School** – Removed from its century-old building along Oxford Street by Liverpool and Wellington Streets. CMS Grammar School was relocated to some of the buildings housing Cathedral Boys' Primary School on Howe Street opposite Victoria Park.

3. **Prince of Wales School (POW)** – Removed from its premises at King Tom, POW was relocated to the buildings previously occupied by Government Model School. Government Model School was relocated to the school at Bathurst Street. The Prince of Wales School building was taken over by the British Royal Navy and served as headquarters of the commanding officer of the British Royal Navy in Freetown.

4. **Freetown Secondary School for Girls (FSSG)** – FSSG formerly occupied buildings at the lower end of Tower Hill, near Paramount Hotel's current location. Those buildings had been War Office buildings during the First World War (1914–1918). Those buildings were taken over by the British War Department, and FSSG was relocated to the CMS Cathedral Church building along Oxford Street (now Lightfoot Boston Street), and which was occupied by the CMS Diocesan Bookshop.[6]

During the Second World War, as a result of the acquisition of school buildings for war purposes, six secondary schools were crowded around central Freetown. They were FSSG at Oxford Street and Gloucester Street; St Joseph's Convent and St Edward's Secondary Schools both at Howe Street; CMS Grammar School at the upper part of Howe Street, not too far from the St Joseph's Girls' Secondary School; and the Albert Academy, which had been relocated to buildings at Garrison Street and Howe Street. The Methodist Boys'

---

[6] CMS is an abbreviation for Church Missionary Society.

High Secondary School was at Soldier Street. But it was not relocated to any other building. Fortunately, Freetown was never bombed by hostile aircraft during the Second World War. If it had been bombed during the day, in view of the number of schools in central Freetown, there might have been very heavy casualties amongst students.

RUSH OF YOUNG MEN AND WOMEN
TO BRITAIN IN THE FIFTIES

In the fifties, a few years after the end of the Second World War in 1945, young men and women flocked to Britain to gain further education. The prevailing circumstances encouraged this rush to Britain. First, many British men and boys had lost their lives during the war; therefore, Britain wanted people who would do the menial jobs young British men and women were rather reluctant to do. Second, there was no need to obtain a visa to enter Britain. Sierra Leoneans and all the nationals of the other British colonies in West Africa, as well as those in the West Indies, were considered British subjects. (Or, in the case of Sierra Leone, the citizens in the protectorate were British-protected citizens.) Each student simply had to produce a British passport on landing in any port in Britain and he or she was granted free entrance.

British shipping companies in West Africa were making lots of money transporting passengers from West Africa to Britain. Elder Dempster Lines, one of the major shipping companies in Sierra Leone, had a large passenger vessel called the SS *Almanzora*. This vessel would call in Freetown and the ports of the other British West African colonies (Lagos, Accra, and Banjul) once a month to collect passengers for Britain. The third class fare for passengers was relatively low – about £40.0s one way. (This was equivalent to about six months salary of third-grade clerks in the civil service). Later on, Elder Dempster Lines added to its fleet three passenger vessels—MV *Accra*, MV *Apapa,* and MV *Aureol*. Elder Dempster had had passenger vessels named MV *Apapa* and MV *Accra* before the Second World War. But both had been torpedoed and sunk by German U-boats during the war.

Unfortunately, once the young men and women arrived in Britain, most of them found the environment less than conducive to the enhancement of their education, which they had hoped for. Their plans to work during the day and attend college in the evening soon evaporated. The jobs they could get were, for the most part, menial jobs. And the wages were barely sufficient to pay for a room in an apartment, cooking gas and electricity, food and clothes, and transport fares to and from work. Consequently, almost all the young men and women who had rushed to Britain in the fifties and sixties with the intention of enhancing their education eventually became disillusioned. Most of them were never heard from again. Some of them existed on doles under the British welfare scheme.

Some women fared better than the men. These women were able to enter the nursing field, where they qualified as state-registered nurses. And on their return to Sierra Leone, they were able to secure lucrative employment in hospitals.

BOOKSHOPS IN FREETOWN

From the thirties up to even the sixties, Freetown posted only two bookshops – The CMS Bookshop and Mrs Smith's Bookshop. The former was located along Oxford Street (now Lightfoot Boston Street). It was the larger of the two, and it was well stocked with stationery, exercise books, textbooks, literature, and various other books.

Mrs Smith's Bookshop was located in the ground floor of a three-storey wooden dwelling house at the junction of Howe Street and Westmoreland Street (now Siaka Stevens Street) directly opposite the side of the Catholic Sacred Heart Cathedral.

MINI LIBRARY IN THE WILBERFORCE MEMORIAL HALL

Freetown was also home to a public library. The library was located in the basement of the Wilberforce Memorial Hall at the junction of

Gloucester Street and Water Street (now Wallace Johnson Street). This hall was built in the early 1900s, in memory of William Wilberforce, a philanthropist and one of those Englishmen who fought strenuously for the abolition of the slave trade. Wilberforce Memorial Hall was unfortunately burnt down in 1959. It is believed the fire was accidental.

J.T. THOMAS MINI LIBRARY

There was also a private library located at Howe Street in Freetown. The building was diagonal to and on the opposite side of the street from the St Edward's Schools (the site now occupied by Santano House at Howe Street). This library was financed by funds provided by the late J.T. Thomas, who was a philanthropist. I do not know what eventually became of this library, but it appears to have faded into oblivion.

PUBLIC HEALTH

Hospitals

During the colonial period, Sierra Leone, particularly Freetown, had what could be described as virtually a free national health service. Hospitals included the Connaught Hospital and the Princes Christian Mission Hospital in Freetown and the government hospital at Hill Station, which was then reserved for British expatriates. The PCM Hospital was only for pregnant women. There was also a hospital at Cline Town, which was then a suburb of Freetown. But that hospital had no facility for admitting patients. All these hospitals, with the exception of the Cline Town Hospital, were staffed with regular doctors throughout the day and night. The hospital at Cline Town only had a doctor during the day. In addition, the large villages around Freetown had health centres, which were also called hospitals. Health centres were located in Kissy, Waterloo, and other villages. Connaught Hospital at Water Street in Freetown was the main hospital. Patients at these hospitals were only made to pay a token amount of one shilling for treatment.

The prestigious hospital at Hill Station was reserved for the treatment of sick senior British colonial civil servants; officials in commercial organisations, who were mainly British; and a few prominent Sierra Leoneans.

Doctors at these hospitals were dedicated, and none would have asked for "tips". A doctor demanding money before attending to any patient would have been committing serious professional misconduct, and serious disciplinary action would have been taken against any doctor thus lowering himself.

After the professional doctors were off duty for the day, qualified and experienced dispensers and nurses were available to treat patients with minor ailments. But there was a doctor on standby who could be summoned whenever patients were seriously ill or had sustained serious injuries. Normally, the doctor on standby would visit the hospital at night.

After a patient had been examined by a doctor and received prescriptions for any necessary medicines, he or she could collect the medications at the dispensary in each hospital.

Very few commercial pharmacies existed in Freetown. Morgan Pharmacy and City Pharmacy were well stocked with modern medicines, for which moderate prices were charged.

There were also small clinics in a few small villages in the colony area. These were staffed by qualified government dispensers, who would examine patients and give initial treatment for minor ailments and injuries. They would also prescribe medications, which were supplied at the dispensary, also on payment of a token fee of one shilling. Villages around Freetown – Wilberforce, Murray Town, Regent, Wellington, and so on – were served by clinics. Citizens who were seriously sick or injured in any of these villages would be conveyed to the Connaught Hospital in Freetown.

In the protectorate (now provinces), there were hospitals in the large towns. Each of these hospitals was staffed by doctors and qualified nurses. In addition, the hospitals during colonial days were supplied with basic medicines and equipment. Such medicines would not be carted away and sold by dishonest officials.

Doctors at hospitals were properly dressed in white gowns when attending to patients. Doctors would not be seen improperly dressed when on duty.

Medicines in those days were almost entirely liquid, mixed in the dispensary by qualified druggists. There were very few tablets. Each patient had to provide his or her own clean empty bottle to serve as container for the medicine. One medicine for malaria was quinine. This was a very bitter liquid. It was then the only medicine for the effective treatment of malaria. But it should not be taken in large doses. It was reported that, if quinine were taken in too large a quantity, the patient would be deaf.

Idoform was a powder medication for wounds and sores. There were then no antibiotics.

It is most unfortunate that long after independence had been attained and the government is with Sierra Leoneans there has been a lowering of standards and discipline in almost all public services. Both senior and junior staff perform their duties lackadaisically. Gross irregularities are perpetrated with impunity. Presently some doctors on duty attending to patients do not wear their white gowns or coats as used to happen during pre-independence days.

Some doctors would charge patients extra fees before these patients would be attended to by the doctors. Few years ago, some doctors had certain number of beds in wards allocated to them where patients were admitted and treated by these doctors on payment of exorbitant and unofficial fees. It is not known whether the same system prevails at present.

Not too long ago a certain doctor at the Connaught Hospital in Freetown was alleged to have ripped tubes containing drips from patients. The doctor was alleged to have lost control of himself and gone berserk during a political upheaval in Freetown. The doctor was not even penalised for his unprofessional conduct. Such an unprofessional display would never have occurred during colonial days.

As an indication of how deterioration in public services has been allowed to prevail, there are kiosks which are manned by illiterate sales people and selling various drugs of questionable quality near hospitals. After doctors have issued prescriptions for medications to patients, nurses would inform the patients that the medicines could be obtained from the illegal kiosks nearby.

Some other illiterates openly hawk controlled drugs in public places.

The government seems unable or unwilling to stop these grossly illegal and dangerous activities because politicians fear that stopping these activities means they will not be able to get the votes of the public.

How sad for all these grossly illegal and unprofessional activities to be permitted by the government to happen now when the country has attained independence.

Sanitary Inspectors

The colonial government had a strict public health system. To keep the city clean and to reduce the spread of mosquitoes and diseases, sanitary inspectors were employed. These officials, recognised by their khaki uniforms, carried out daily (Monday through Saturday) inspections of compounds of houses in and around Freetown. They would also visit surrounding villages frequently. The owner of any compound that was found filthy or in which empty cups with waste water were discovered was summoned to court, where fines were imposed against the defaulters.

At times, some of these sanitary inspectors would issue written warnings to owners of houses with slightly filthy compounds. But warnings were for minor negligence to keep compounds clean.

In general, the frequent inspections acted as an effective deterrent to people keeping their compounds filthy and untidy.

In addition, health officials sprayed chemicals in gutters and other places where stagnant water was found. By such measures, mosquitoes were deprived of their breeding grounds, and consequently, the number of mosquitoes was substantially reduced in and around Freetown. In fact, mosquitoes had almost been eradicated in Freetown by the early sixties.

Water Supply

The Freetown City Council was responsible for the supply of water in Freetown. One of its departments was Freetown Water Works (FWW). At the time, relatively few citizens had houses with private water supplies. These compounds had only water standpipes from which water was collected for all domestic purposes. Very few houses had water supplies to the interiors to serve toilets and kitchen. In fact, most houses had only dugout toilets located in a suitable place in the compound. Only the privileged few had toilets with flush systems.

To serve the general population in Freetown, standpipes were located in vantage points along many streets in the city. Each of these standpipes had a knob that, on being depressed, opened a valve, thereby releasing water, which gushed out from a tap. On releasing pressure from the knob, the valve would shut off the flow of water, thereby preventing waste.

Citizens would go to these public standpipes to collect water in buckets to be used for all domestic purposes. Usually water was collected and stored in 44 gallons or smaller drums called "dog iron." Why these drums were called "dog iron" is not known by me.

It was the common practice for children in each household to collect water from the public standpipes and fill the large storage drums. They would perform this chore in the morning before going to school and in the evening after school.

Throughout the thirties and into the fifties, Freetown suffered an acute shortage of water during the dry season. During this period, citizens would rush to collect water from any public standpipes that weren't dry. As citizens did not always queue patiently to await their turns, it was not unusual for fracas to erupt. Inconsiderate behaviour was often the spark that would set off fighting. People would take many buckets to the public standpipes and expect to fill them all before anyone else had the opportunity to collect water. On such occasions, attempts to prevent this unreasonable behaviour would sometimes result in scuffles.

It was not until the Guma Valley Water Company project was completed in about 1961 that Freetown no longer experienced acute water shortage during the dry season. However, I have now learnt that the situation has almost reverted to pre-1960s days. Several factors have contributed to the current acute water shortage. First, since 2002, Freetown has experienced an unexpected rush of citizens from the provinces, people who are seeking refuge and hope to escape the atrocious civil war. Most of these refugees refuse to return to their towns and villages in the provinces because almost all of their houses were destroyed during the eleven years of civil war in Sierra Leone, which completely devastated most of the country's infrastructure.

Another factor is incompetence and lack of planning. The widespread indiscipline and dishonesty that now prevail among the public is another cause of the water shortage. Irresponsible and dishonest individuals have illegally diverted water from the main pipe, through which flows water from Guma Valley Water Company's main dam at Sussex Village, to their private residences. It is also alleged that dishonest officials, who should monitor and report this illegal diversion of water, succumb to financial enticements. Lastly, incompetence of the senior staff is partly responsible for the deplorable situation.

COMMUNICATIONS

Telephones

With very few exceptions, up to about the sixties, private houses had no telephones. The country's telephones were almost all in government offices and in the buildings of commercial and religious organisations. A few schools, as well as houses where British administrators resided, also had telephones. No one communicated over the phone with relatives abroad.

But starting from about the late sixties, Sierra Leoneans were able to have telephone communications with relatives abroad. But anyone who intended to phone his or her relative had to go to the cable and wireless office (later named Sierra Leone External Telecommunication) at Water Street (now Wallace Johnson Street). They also had to pay fees in advance. In addition, people had to wait for half an hour or more before the connection would be made. There were no satellites to beam phone signals quickly and clearly from one location to another. Nor were there any cell phones.

Cable

To communicate with someone abroad, one had two options – letter or cable. Letters would be conveyed by ship or, starting about the mid-thirties, by air. But air service was not frequent.

Quickly communicating with someone abroad meant wiring a cable. One had to go to Cable & Wireless Office (now Sierra Leone External Telecoms) down at Water Street (now Wallace Johnson Street) and prepare the text of the message on a special form. The charge for each message depended on the number of words. The cable would then be laboriously transmitted to the town abroad by Morse code (wireless dots and dashes), which would then be transcribed letter by letter into words upon receipt at the other end. The cable company abroad would then dispatch the cable to the recipient either by a special courier or by mail. The same happened the other way round. In those days, there was no fax. Neither were there any Internet or cell phones.

PUBLIC TRANSPORT

Motor traffic in the thirties and forties

Prior to the commencement of the Second World War, Freetown was a rather dull city. Relatively few cars and lorries (trucks) were driven along the streets at irregular intervals. After a vehicle had passed along a street, it would take a couple of minutes before another would be driven along. Some of the vehicles would belch smoke from the exhaust pipes (mufflers), and the cars would create a cloud of dust, as most streets in Freetown were not yet tarred.

The warning sounds from these vehicles were not made by electric horns. Rather, the sounds came from small horns fixed on the outside right front window of the driver. This equipment had a black or brown rubber bulb at its rear, which, when squeezed, would force air through a pipe. The resulting sound would be a croak – *pom, pom* or *awooah, awooah*. It was from about the late thirties to the early forties that cars with electric horns arrived in Sierra Leone.

Also, most vehicles then in Freetown had no electric starters. Vehicles had to be cranked by hand using handles on the front before they would start. It was from the late thirties to the early forties that vehicles with electric start mechanisms were available locally.

The Second World War (1939–1945) soon brought an increase in the number of vehicles in Freetown. The occasional movement of vehicles soon gave way to an avalanche of vehicular flow as British military vehicles engaged in various assignments in the prosecution of the war – transporting troops, building materials, war equipment, ammunition, and on and on.

Bus service

In the thirties and up to the early fifties, only a handful of affluent people could afford to own private cars. And they were primarily doctors, lawyers, and the random Lebanese trader. A few young men owned motorcycles. Many other young men owned modest bicycles.

To move around Freetown, the majority of citizens, including pupils and workers, would walk to schools or to their workplaces.

But there was also a bus service, which ran regularly from Cline Town in the east end of Freetown via the bus station at Oxford Street (now Lightfoot Boston Street) to Congo Cross in the west end of the city. There were also regular bus services to and from Wilberforce (a suburb of Freetown). But the bus services to Wilberforce and Lumley did not run as frequently. They ran only during rush hours in the morning and evening, as well making a few runs during other times of the day and late in the evenings.

Government buses were formerly under the management of the general manager of the Railway Department. I have now forgotten the year when the management of the buses was separated and transferred to the general manager of the Road Transport Department.

The government bus services were well organised. Buses ran regularly and on time. Timetables were posted at bus stations and bus halts along the routes, showing the times buses were available to and from all destinations. Small shelters at many bus halts protected passengers from the sun and rain.

There were also buses to and from some of the seaside villages around the peninsular – York, Kent, and a few others. This bus service would depart from Oxford Street bus station late in the evening every day en route to York via the neighbouring villages along the route. It would depart from Kent very early in the morning, picking up passengers in villages along the route and arriving at the main bus terminal at Oxford Street, Freetown, in time to enable those who worked to get to work on time and pupils in secondary schools to get to school. This bus service, to a great extent, facilitated the journey to and from Freetown of people who resided in the villages, especially workers and secondary school pupils. However, the circumstance was, to a certain extent, quite inconvenient for workers and students. They would have to wake up very early in the morning to make it on the bus and would return home very late in the evening.

The distance between Freetown and York via these small villages is about 30 miles. The major problem that impeded the fast movement of motor vehicles between Freetown and York via these villages was the deplorable condition of the roads. The roads were not tarred. Nor were they maintained regularly. Consequently, large potholes dotted many sections of the roads.

Sometime in the sixties, the Road Transport Corporation was created and made responsible for bus services throughout the country. This new organisation was different from the Road Transport Department.

The Road Transport Department was then made responsible only for the acquisition and supply of cars and lorries (trucks) to various ministries, as well as the repairs and maintenance of these vehicles.

Up to the early fifties there were no *poda-podas*. These shared taxis emerged around the late fifties. Poda-podas were privately owned, and as no laws restricted their movements, they were competing with government buses, even inside Freetown.

There was also a privately owned bus service that, to this day, plies passengers between Freetown and Kissy and Wellington. Kissy Bus Service and Company was owned and operated by a prominent family named Tuboku-Metzger who resided in Kissy.

But during colonial days, a law prohibited private bus service collecting passengers along the streets of Freetown. The Kissy Bus Service was only authorised to collect and convey passengers for Kissy and Wellington from central Freetown and vice versa. Only the government bus service was legally permitted to collect passengers along routes in Freetown.

The private buses were not allowed to compete for passengers with the government buses. Therefore, these private buses stopped only at fixed spots, away from the stops for government buses.

The main terminal of this private bus service was along Water Street (now Wallace Johnson Street) beside the Anglican St George's Cathedral.

Unfortunately, after independence had been achieved and the administration of the country was left to Sierra Leoneans, some politicians and a few other people who owned minibuses exerted pressure on the government for the legislation that restricted the movement of private buses in routes around Freetown to be relaxed. As a result, poda-podas were permitted to use Freetown routes, competing with government buses.

There were no restrictions on these buses. The drivers violated the road traffic regulations with complete impunity. Many poda-poda drivers openly tipped traffic policemen to overlook violations. Consequently, these vehicles would be overloaded. Even when the vehicles were full, boys riding the vehicles, known locally as "apprentices" and dressed in shabby outfits, would push passengers to allow additional passengers to board. In addition, the "apprentices" would participate in unruly behaviour, such as hanging on the doors and stretching their legs outside the vehicles while the vehicles were in motion.

All these indecent acts were a result of politics. During colonial rule, such comportment never existed. But soon after the country had gained independence, many believed they could do whatever they liked. They had a misconception of freedom of expression.

Double-decker buses

In 1951, double-decker buses like those in Britain were introduced in Freetown. Before these buses were imported into Sierra Leone, specially selected drivers from the Road Transport Department were sent to Britain to be trained to drive them. These ran from Cline Town in the east of Freetown to Congo Cross in the west end. On important public holidays, double-decker buses conveyed holidaymakers between Lumley Beach and back. Lumley Beach was located about seven miles from the centre of Freetown.

Double-decker buses were a novelty in the fifties, and Freetown citizens would be delighted in going for bus rides in the evenings.

These buses were in the service of the Road Transport Department until their administration was transported to the Road Transport Corporation upon its formation.

The railway

In the Western Area of Sierra Leone, in addition to buses, the Sierra Leone Railway conveyed passengers within the colony from Freetown to Kissy, Wellington, Hastings, and as far as Waterloo and back daily. The distance between the main railway terminal at Water Street (now Wallace Johnson Street) in the centre of Freetown is about twenty-one miles. Runs were provided during the morning hours, in the afternoon, and during the evening. Residents in Waterloo, Allen Town, Wellington, and part of Kissy depended on the train to travel to and from Freetown. Workers, students attending secondary schools (which were all located in Freetown), traders, and others residing in these villages depended solely upon the train to travel to and from Freetown.

Sierra Leone's hinterland was declared a British protectorate in 1896. To establish the British presence in the interior of the country, as well as to facilitate the exploitation and transportation of the natural minerals and agricultural products from the hinterland to the port of Freetown for export, the British constructed a narrow gauge railway (in other words, the parallel rails were only two feet six inches apart). The engine was steam. The train ran from Freetown through Waterloo and Songo, and through the middle of the country. Its route ended at Pendembu in the far east of the country near the Liberian border, traveling a distance of about 230 miles one way. There was also a branch line from Freetown to Makeni in the Northern Province. The construction of this railway commenced in 1898 and was completed in 1909.

Apart from the transportation of the country's resources from the interior to the port in Freetown, the railway facilitated the transport of soldiers to parts of the interior of the country, where there might be unrest. The railway, which was government-owned, also provided relatively cheap transport for people and their luggage from the interior to Freetown and vice versa. This railway was of great importance to the entire country. To travel from Freetown to the provinces and vice versa, vast numbers of people depended on the Sierra Leone Government Railway.

But the railway ran at a very slow speed, 15 to 20 miles per hour maximum. This was partially because of the narrow gauge design. But the major reason the train was so slow was that the rails were not laid out in a straight line but, rather, in sharp S curves. Even the approaches to some bridges were on S curves. Why the British surveyors who surveyed the path for the railway and the British engineers who laid engineers who laid the rails did so along such an awkward path is not known. The journey from Freetown to Bo, a distance of about 130 miles by the railway, would last from about 8.00 a.m. to about 4.00 or 5.00 p.m.; going all the way to Pendembu would take another three hours. And that was when the trains ran "on time". But whenever the engines developed "problems", which were not infrequent, the journey would take even longer. In addition, the engine drivers and their assistants were known to have been intentionally causing "malfunctions" in the engine in order to get large amounts of overtime.

In addition to the rail service from Freetown to the provinces, up to the early thirties, a railway line ran from Freetown to Hill Station. This line ran from Water Street (now Wallace Johnson Street) station in downtown Freetown up Hill Station via Brookfields (that is why a road at Brookfields is known as Old Railway Line), Tengbeh Town, down Wilberforce, and up to Hill Station. The Hill Station railway terminal was located a short distance from St Augustine, the Anglican church at Hill Station on the main road to Regent Village.

This railway was intended mainly for British colonial senior civil servants; the majority of them resided at Hill Station, an area reserved for British expatriate administrators. This was before the introduction of motor cars in Freetown in the late twenties to the early thirties. When motor cars became available to British colonial civil servants, the railway between Freetown and Hill Station was discontinued.

For historical record, another very short track of the railway branched off from Sanders Street and along Campbell Street into the compound of the Public Works Department (PWD) (now Ministry of

Works) at Pademba Road. This short railway line was used only for the transportation of materials and equipment to and from the PWD. This short track of the railway was discontinued in the early thirties when lorries (trucks) were made available to the PWD.

Unfortunately, the Sierra Leone Railway was phased out sometime in 1972 or 1973. There were various versions of how the Sierra Leone Railway came to be closed down. In one version, a World Bank official carried out a survey of the railway and, finding it financially unviable because of large government subsidies, recommended its phasing out.

Another version has it that the government asked some important Sierra Leoneans to carry out a survey of the railway, as it was being operated at a huge annual loss. This group reportedly recommended the railway be phased out and replaced by lorries (trucks) and buses to convey passengers and goods between the provinces and Freetown.

Others blame Solomon A.J. Pratt, who was serving as either the general manager of the railway or the minister of transport (I have forgotten which) – alleging it was he who recommended the closure of the railway. All I can say is that Solomon A.J. Pratt was not personally responsible for the closure of the Sierra Leone Railway. It is not fair to cast blame on Pratt. He just happened to have been in the wrong place at the wrong time. Many undesirable behind-the-scenes manoeuvres by unscrupulous foreign individuals played a role; agents of vehicle manufacturers abroad were lobbying the government to phase out the railway and to purchase large fleets of trucks and buses. These officials, it was suspected, were supported by certain senior officials in the Sierra Leone government, who apparently, through greed, put their love of money above the general interest of the country.

The final decision for the phasing out of the railway was, to use a Churchillian phase, a riddle wrapped in a mystery inside an enigma. But it is certain that Pratt was not personally responsible. Rather, the APC government – aided by the extreme pressure exerted by certain foreign officials – was collectively responsible for the railway's phasing out. Unfortunately, the government succumbed to those individuals' enticements, thereby acquiescing to their diabolical motives.

The government seemed to have completely ignored certain facts when making its decision. For one, the country lacked a network of good roads, making it difficult if not impossible for lorries and buses to travel between the major towns and provinces. In addition, the government did not take into consideration the country's lack of vehicle repair shops, not to mention competent motor mechanics.

Concurrent to the railway being phased out, large fleets of Mercedes Benz lorries were imported. These vehicles were then made to convey produce and other goods from the provinces to the port of Freetown. The general manager of the railway department was charged with managing the large fleet of trucks. It did not take long before the trucks gradually broke down and, due to the lack of adequate spare parts, could no longer be repaired.

It was true that the railway was being run at a loss and had to be subsidised heavily by the government annually. The huge losses were partially attributed to the staff of the railway, some of whom were allegedly engaged in widespread misappropriation of railway revenue.

In addition, there were systematic thefts of produce loaded into wagons in the provinces and bound for the port in Freetown. This I know because, when I was serving in the CID in the sixties, the traffic manager of the Sierra Leone Railway, Mr Terry, requested our help implementing adequate security measures to stop the rampant theft. Produce loaded into wagons in towns in the provinces would never make it to the port in Freetown. The CID implemented appropriate security measures, and the theft came to an abrupt end.

The Sierra Leone Railway was confronted with another problem. The narrow gauge railway was antiquated. Manufacturers abroad were no longer manufacturing spare parts necessary to repair. Furthermore, steam engines were being replaced by either diesel engines or electric engines all over the world.

But while it's true that the railway was being heavily subsidised by the government, it was rendering invaluable services to the country as a whole. The government could have replaced the narrow gauge railway with a wider gauge railway. Furthermore, the railway lines could have been realigned. Of course, these improvements would have required large amounts of money. But the government might have been able to convince the World Bank or the IMF to loan Sierra Leone the money for these major projects. In addition, the projects would have provided a substantial number of jobs for many years.

Rather than exploring all other avenues, the government phased out the railway. With precipitate speed, the rails were sold to an Afro-Lebanese national, who exported the steel rails to factories abroad to be smelted. How much the individual paid the government for the steel rails is, to this date, a mystery. The government never made the deal public. In addition, a group of private individuals quickly and illegally acquired the land along which the railway line was laid and erected buildings on it. The government did not seem to have taken any action to prevent this illegal encroachment on government lands.

And so, the railway has been phased out, and the entire country is now feeling the adverse effects of absence of a railway.

MAIL

During colonial days, the post office and the telephone system were lumped together under one department. The nomenclature of the head of the department was postmaster general.

Uniformed postmen delivered mail daily and promptly around Freetown. Letters with postage stamps already affixed could be dropped inside red public mailboxes, located in several areas around Freetown. Those post boxes were exactly the same as those in Britain. Postal officials collected the letters in them at certain fixed times each working day.

Pilfering of mail by dishonest postmen was almost unheard of in those days. Severe penalties, such as mandatory terms of imprisonment, were inflicted on any officials who were caught illegally tampering with public mail. Ex-convicts were all but finished and wrecked for life. They could no longer obtain employment in any government department or with most commercial businesses, which were mostly owned by British companies. Such severe punishment served as an effective deterrent to dishonesty in the public service as a whole.

MEDIA

Newspapers

Only a few major daily newspapers were in regular circulation in Freetown. One was the *Daily Mail*, whose proprietor and editor was a Mr Dephon Thompson of Wilberforce. The editorial office and printing press were all in one small building at Howe Street, near where the present *Daily Mail* the offices are located. The other daily was the *Daily Guardian*. Its editorial office and printing press were located on Percival Street, almost at its junction with Oxford Street (now Lightfoot Boston Street). The price for a copy of each of these newspapers was one penny.

The editors of both papers behaved quite responsibly. Their editorials and news reporting were within normal bounds. There were no intentional blackmailing or threat of blackmailing of certain citizens with the aim of extorting money from them. Journalism then was quite a decent profession into which only well-educated people would enter.

Freetown also had a weekly paper, the *West African Standard*. Its editor was radical politician and trade union leader I.T.A. Wallace-Johnson. But during the Second World War, the *West African Standard* was shut down. Wallace-Johnson was accused by the British colonial government of being subversive. He was, therefore, arrested and banished to Bonthe Island to keep him quiet and from allegedly inciting citizens against the British colonial government.

Radio Broadcasts

Wired "radio" (locally called Rediffusion) was first installed in Freetown in 1934. In the thirties, the few wireless radio receivers in Freetown were owned by individual citizens. These receivers were large and had no transistors; instead, they had large valves similar to electric light bulbs but smaller. Only top British administrators and affluent citizens owned them.

When left switched on for a long time, the wireless radios became hot because the valves generated small amounts of heat. Consequently, after being turned on for a while, they would have to be switched off for several minutes so they could cool down.

The common equipment that existed then, and which several citizens in Freetown possessed, was locally called a rediffusion box. This was a small, light brown box (about one foot by one foot and about six inches from front to back). The box contained a small loudspeaker. Rediffusion boxes were installed in private houses, offices, and some schools. These rediffusion boxes were connected to a central radio receiving station located up at Tower Hill, Freetown. This radio receiving station received news and other programmes from the BBC in London, England by short wave. It then retransmitted the BBC programmes (news, music and other programmes) to houses, offices, etc. in Freetown through the rediffuson boxes.

Small fee for each rediffusion box was paid monthly to the government post office department, which was then responsible for the operation and servicing of the radio receiving station and the rediffusion boxes.

The central radio receiving station up at Tower Hill, Freetown also broadcast notices by the government as well as private announcements by members of the public. A small fee was paid for each private announcement. These private announcements were mainly obituaries and notices for public functions.

The entire organisation responsible for the rediffusion service was called the Sierra Leone Broadcasting Service (SLBS). It was government owned. After the end of the Second World War, the SLBS was relocated to New Englandville at a site that the British military had used as a wireless station during the war.

The rediffusion service was costly to maintain. The pairs of wires conveying the signal from the central receiving station to all the rediffusion boxes sometimes became entangled. Also, since the wires were copper, vandals would cut them be sold to scrap metal dealers.

Shortly after the war ended in 1945, in addition to the "broadcast" through the rediffusion network, local broadcasts began to be made by medium wave. By then, many citizens owned individual radio receivers.

When FM broadcast became available, the entire country eventually received broadcast through FM. Thus in the fifties, rediffusion boxes were replaced with portable wireless receivers. Members of the public would then buy wireless radios from the few large commercial shops in the country. These shops were United African Company (UAC), G B Ollivant, CFAO, SCOA and a few others. The popular brands of portable wireless radio receivers then were Grundig, Pye, KB.

Also sometime in the sixties, the government imported thousands of portable wireless radios which were leased to the public on payment of a small fee monthly. This fee was being paid at the general post office. But the SLBS had by that time become a separate entity with its own director.

The director of broadcasting throughout the colonial period was a British expatriate. The first Sierra Leonean director of the Sierra Leone Broadcasting Service was the late John Akar, who was appointed in 1960. He was a most talented individual. He was the one who composed the words of the Sierra Leone National Anthem.

THE WEST AFRICAN YOUTH LEAGUE

When I was about ten years of age, I would hear my grandfather conversing with his friends about a man called Wallace-Johnson. The conversation would turn to the youth organisation Wallace-Johnson had formed, the West African Youth League, which was attracting hundreds of men and women in Freetown. As I grew older, these conversations attracted me more and more. I learned that Wallace-Johnson was unearthing and publishing in his newspaper a lot of secrets of the British colonial government and about how he was fighting for the rights of Sierra Leoneans.

I later came to know that Wallace-Johnson was a young, fearless, charismatic and nationalistic leader who had just returned from studying in Russia. He had organised workers in Freetown into trade unions so they could be united and fight for their rights. His newest organisation, the West Africa Youth League, had spread to other West African countries, mainly the Gold Coast and Nigeria. By the late thirties to the early forties, the name Wallace-Johnson had become a household name in Freetown, and there was even a popular song about him.

Wallace-Johnson the revolutionist was soon to become a thorn in the flesh of the colonial government in Sierra Leone. He would publish news about secret government machinations and about suppression of Sierra Leoneans. He would petition the governor about certain matters, and if he was not satisfied, he would petition as far up as the Secretary of State for the Colonies in London. He petitioned the Secretary of State for the Colonies and parliamentarians in London to issue boots to Sierra Leonean soldiers. He also petitioned for a pardon for Emanuel Cole, the rebellious Sierra Leonean soldier, who, together with some of his colleagues, had been court-martialled for agitating for higher pay and allowances for Sierra Leonean soldiers, as well as boots.

TRADE AND COMMERCE IN FREETOWN

Trade

The wholesale and retail trade in Freetown was formerly dominated by a few European firms. United African Company and G.B. Ollivant were British. The French firms were SCOA, CFAO, A. Genet, and M. Jourdan P.Z. & Co. was Greek. There was also a German firm in Freetown before the Second World War.

The Lebanese, who were then known locally as Syrians, had always dominated the retail trade in Freetown. The Foulahs dominated the petty retail trade. Lebanese shops were primarily along Kissy Street (now Sani Abacca Street), Little East Street (now Malamah Thomas Street), East Street (now Ecowas Street), the bottom of Westmoreland Street (now Siaka Stevens Street), part of Rawdon Street, and the bottom of Oxford Street (now Lightfoot Boston Street).

These Lebanese shops formerly sold rice and other local produce, as well as cotton goods and various imported consumer goods. Customers would go from shop to shop to buy rice, which was sold in various grades. There was a kind of rice the citizens of Freetown "chicken rice". This was rice from which the husk was barely removed. Husk rice was not much in demand. Rice sales by the Lebanese shopkeepers suddenly came to an end during the Second World War, when Sierra Leone faced an acute scarcity of rice and other edible produce.

The Foulahs also played a very important role in the petty trade in Freetown. They sold various provisions and small quantities of other articles in small kiosks in the basements of dwelling houses throughout Freetown. The services they rendered to the citizens of Freetown were most invaluable, and the public could not have afforded to live without their services. One incident demonstrated how invaluable the Foulah's services were. The Foulah petty traders went on strike on a relatively minor matter and closed all their kiosks. During the few days the kiosks were closed, almost the entire population of Freetown was in disarray.

Banks in Freetown

In the thirties and even until the sixties, Freetown had only two commercial banks. There was also one government-owned savings bank, which was a subsidiary of the government post office. The commercial banks were Bank of British West Africa (BBWA) (now known as Standard Chartered Bank) and Barclays Bank DC&O (now known as Rokel Bank).

BBWA was located in a bungalow-style building on Oxford Street, near the current location of Standard Chartered Bank. Barclays Bank DC&O was on the ground floor of a small three-storey house along Westmoreland Street (now Siaka Stevens Street) by Charlotte Street junction. After the Second World War ended, the old buildings in which these two commercial banks were located were demolished, and new buildings were erected to replace them.

Post Office Savings Bank

The savings bank was a subsidiary of the General Post Office (now known as SALPOST). This savings bank was quite small. Money deposited in the Post Office Savings Bank by citizens was quite safe. There was no misappropriation of money in this bank in those days. In colonial days, misappropriation of public funds, either in the banks or in the civil service, was almost unknown.

Probity by clerks in commercial organisations and in the civil service

The very few civil servants or bank clerks who were foolish and irresponsible enough to incur a shortage of even relatively small amounts would be placed on criminal charges. If they were found guilty, they were sent to jail and disgraced. Furthermore, those culprits would be unable to obtain employment after their convictions and imprisonment. This acted as a strong deterrent, and well-respected civil servants and clerks in commercial organisations refrained from engaging in dishonest practices.

SUNDAYS IN FREETOWN IN THE THIRTIES AND FORTIES

Sundays in Freetown during the thirties and up to the late forties were Puritan-like or reminiscent of Jewish Sabbath Day. The custom, particularly among Creoles, was to refrain from any physical work or any activity that would generate a lot of noise. Rice would not be pounded inside mortar to clean it; nor would firewood be split to kindle fire for cooking purposes. All such work should have been carried out on Saturday. Sunday was considered too holy a day to engage in such activities.

Thus, Freetown was a relatively quiet city throughout Sunday. Games were not to be played. Nor did citizens engage in any form of dancing or merriment. Even the singing or playing of light music or dance music was frowned upon. As a matter of routine, in the morning, citizens (generally the Creoles) dressed in their best dresses (called Sunday clothes) and attended church services in the various Christian churches in Freetown and neighbouring villages. After that, children returned for Sunday school from about 1.00 to 2.30 p.m.

Somewhere around 4.00 p.m., there was an evening service.

It was forbidden to stage dances or any form of social activities on Sunday. Neither would there be any parade of masked devils or any similar procession in the streets on Sundays, except religious or school processions. Selling was frowned upon.

This Puritan-like Sunday was shattered during the Second World War. The British had to carry out war activities associated with the prosecution of war around Freetown. Buildings and other installations had to be constructed. These activities necessitated building materials, troops, ammunition, and other war materials being transported in lorries to various locations. All these movements and activities generated noise.

Moreover, British soldiers and sailors would play games on Sundays. These activities soon became contagious in Freetown and in neighbouring villages. In no time, the Puritan kind of Sunday in Freetown and in the surrounding villages disappeared forever.

SOCIAL CUSTOMS AND TRADITIONS IN FREETOWN

Weddings

In Freetown during the good old days (in other words, up to recently), a Creole man who wanted to become engaged to a woman adhered to a strict traditional practice. The engagement ceremony was termed "Put Stop". A few of the man's relatives would assemble in the evening and proceed to the residence of the intended woman. Among the man's delegation would be at least one man who could speak flowery English. There would also be in the man's delegation a young girl, who would carry a calabash wrapped in white cloth and containing a Bible, an engagement ring, a certain amount of money enclosed in an envelope, cola nuts, needle and thread, and a few other items.

The delegation would proceed to the woman's house, where a group of relatives and friends of the woman would have already assembled. Among this group would be several young girls dressed in pretty clothes. These girls, as well as the woman to be engaged, would be kept in a bedroom of the woman's residence. When the man's delegation would arrive at the woman's residence, they would meet the door locked.

An interesting dialogue would then begin. There would be a knock on the door of the woman's residence, and a man from within would enquire who had come to disturb the family, who were relaxing. From the entryway, a gentleman from among the man's delegation would respond in flowery language that it was a delegation from afar who had espied a rose in the garden of the residence. And because the rose was so beautiful and enticing, they had come to pluck it. The response from within would insist that there was no rose in that particular household. The man outside would insist that there was indeed such a rose.

The dialogue would continue, and the representative of the woman would enquire what proof the delegation had that they were not armed bandits. This dialogue would continue. Eventually, the entrance door would be opened, and the man's delegation would enter amid cheering from the woman's delegation inside the woman's residence.

The dialogue would continue between a man in the woman's family and the representative from the man's family. Eventually, one young girl after another from inside the locked bedroom would be presented to the man's delegation. The man's delegation would reject all these young girls as not the particular beautiful and enticing rose they sought. Then for the event's climax, the particular lady, dressed in pretty clothes, would be presented, and there would be a roar of applause from the delegation of the man.

The dialogue would continue. And after it had ended, the main speaker from the man's delegation would present the calabash containing the previously itemised articles that the young girl had carried, as a token from the bridegroom-to-be. The speaker would say that the articles were a token of assurance that the delegation would return later in grand style to acquire the particular "rose".

A few of the men's delegation and a few of the representatives of the woman would then retire to a bedroom, and after they'd emerged, a representative of the woman would disclose the items brought by the man's delegation, including the Bible and the engagement ring. He would also have disclosed the intended date of the wedding whilst inside the bedroom. In some cases, it would be stated that the intended date would be revealed in due course.

Refreshments would then be served all around, after which the man's delegation would take leave of the representatives of the woman's delegation.

When the man's delegation returned to the man's residence, there would be merriment, including a song entitled "Yahwoh Mammy don answer Yes oh". Refreshment, which may include alcoholic drinks, would be served. The ceremony would then come to an end, leaving the man to plan for the big day.

Special distinction for married Creole women

It was formerly the practice among Creole women who had married to hang on one of their shoulders a shawl – a piece of handwoven decorative cloth – to indicate that they were married. This shawl would be nicely folded to about twelve inches in width and from four to six feet in length. The married women typically wore printed cotton dresses with floral designs.

This style of dress was mostly used for social functions. The women would also wear a pair of canvass slippers. The slippers, called "canvass", were manufactured by local cobblers. These canvass slippers were so named because the upper part was handwoven with short coloured pieces of wool on canvass to form various designs.

The designers were rendered by women who had made doing so their specialty. The soles of the canvass slippers were manufactured by local cobblers from dried and cured hides of sheep of cow.

The dead

Up until the sixties, there were no funeral homes in Freetown. There was only one mortuary in the Connaught Hospital along Oxford Street (now Lightfoot Boston Street). When people died, they were buried with minimum delay. This would place some people in financial crisis. Not many people were able to get the large amount of money needed to cover burial expenses.

When there was a death of someone in a household, some of his or her relatives would become hysterical, shouting in grief, "Fire. Fire. Fire. Oh ..." That expression did not mean that the house was actually on fire. Rather, it was an indirect expression of concern about where to get the money right away for all the funeral expenses. This expression was particularly used when the death of the relative was sudden.

Later on close relatives and friends of the deceased's relatives would donate funds towards the funeral expenses.

"Companies" for mutual assistance

In view of the fact that there was then no embalmment, bodies had to be buried either late in the afternoon of the same day if the death occurred early in the morning or, if the death was late in the evening, the burial would have to be early on the following day.

Most people could not immediately spare the money to purchase timber for the manufacture of the coffin. Therefore, in some villages, there existed benevolent societies called "Companies". Their primary purpose was to render financial and other assistance to families of the deceased during the bereavement period.

One company in Gloucester was called Horn Company, and the other was called Christian Company. A very old cow horn was sounded by the "town crier" in the village to alert members of the Horn Company of the company's meetings, as well as the death of any member of that company.

Members of each of these two benevolent societies held meetings monthly, and each member paid a modest fee of about two shillings either monthly or yearly (I have now forgotten the period of payment). A treasurer was appointed from among the members. That treasurer was responsible for the safekeeping of the fees collected. The money would be used to purchase timber, which was stored in the compound of one of the members of the company. Whenever any member of the company died, the carpenters in the village would be requested to manufacture a coffin with the timber kept in reserve. A certain amount would also be paid to the family of the deceased. The money would be used for the entertainment of mourners.

During the death of someone in the village, in the evening, some of the villagers would congregate in the house of the deceased where a vigil (known as *wakin*) would be conducted. During wakin, solemn Christian songs, commonly known as "shouts" would be sung, and some passages would be read from the Bible. Light refreshments and, in some cases, alcoholic drinks would then be served to mourners. The wakin would be conducted by someone who could raise the tune for each of the shouts. Some people were experts at conducting these shouts.

Awoojor

It used to be the tradition among the Creoles to celebrate the third day, as well as the seventh day, and also the fortieth day following the death of a relative. The fortieth day ceremony was marked by a large feast called Awoojoh. During Awoojoh, a variety of cooked food would be prepared and served to relatives and friends.

The climax of this ceremony would be the poring of libation to the deceased in the evening. A small hole about a foot in both diameter and depth would have already been dug in the front entrance of the residence of the deceased. Inside this hole would be placed a small quantity of each of the food items.

The libation consisted of rum (or any other alcoholic drink). A close relative of the deceased would then be called upon to pour the libation to appease the spirit of the deceased. The ceremony included rum (or any other alcoholic drink) and two pairs of cola nuts (one pair white and one pair red). The pairs of cola nuts would be unplugged. Water and the alcoholic drink would be poured into the hole in which the food would have already been placed.

The relative pouring the libation would "talk" to the spirit of the deceased while pouring the mixture into the hole. Such talk included calling on the spirit of the deceased to protect the surviving relatives, some of whom would be named individually.

After the libation had been poured, the pourer in would toss the four pieces of cola nuts on the ground near the hole. If the colas turned one red and one white up and the others turned down, the person performing the ceremony would announce that the deceased had "accepted" and that he or she was pleased.

But if the four cola nut pieces landed in any other combination, the ceremony performer would say that the deceased was "annoyed" and, therefore, had not "accepted" the cola nuts.

The ceremony would be repeated, only now the person performing the ceremony would beg the deceased to accept the cola nuts. The cola nuts would again be tossed on the ground near the hole. In some cases, this tossing of cola nuts would be repeated until the right combination of one red cola nut and one white would face up and the other pair of one white and one red cola nuts were facing down.

A few of the deceased's relatives and friends would also proceed to the grave where the deceased was buried, and the same ceremony would be performed on the grave of the deceased.

I have my own personal opinion of the ceremony.

Also on the Sunday following the fortieth day of the death of the individual, there would be "Berrin Church", during which relatives and friends of the deceased dressed in black or dark dresses and attended service at the church where the deceased had been a member. The preacher would include in his sermon the good qualities of the deceased and offer words of consolation to relatives of the deceased.

The Berrin Church service would be followed by a repeat of the pouring of libation.

Close relatives of the deceased would wear dark clothes for a one-year mourning period.

Mr Lumpkin, aka Pa Alimamy Bungie

Since there were no funeral homes in and around Freetown, there were a few shops known as "undertakers", which specialised in making coffins. In addition, there were no funeral limousines or vans. The vehicles available for the conveyance of the corpse to and from the church to the cemetery were called hearse. The coffin would be placed inside a large black rectangular box, and the box was placed on top of a wagon with four wheels. The hearse accompanying the funeral procession was pushed by boys who were employees of the undertaker.

One famous undertaker in Freetown was Mr Lumpkin, popularly known as Alimamy Bungie. His business was known as Sympathetic Undertaker for the Living and the Dead. His shop was on Kissy Street by Upper East Street. He was quite popular. When he died sometime in the late thirties, many people attended the wake (or vigil) and the funeral service, which was held at the Roman Catholic Sacred Heart Cathedral on Westmoreland Street (now Siaka Stevens Street).

Funeral Homes

Up until the fifties, if I can remember well, there were no funeral homes. It was in the early sixties that someone from Liberia introduced the first funeral home in Freetown. The funeral home was situated along a stretch of grassy field on King Harman Road in Brookfields. I have now forgotten the name of that funeral home.

It was several years later that additional funeral homes were established. Presently, there are several funeral homes in Freetown.

SOME SIGHTS AND SOUNDS IN AND AROUND FREETOWN IN THE THIRTIES AND FORTIES

No narrative about Freetown during the thirties and forties would be complete without mention of some of the sights and sounds around that city, particularly during the Second World War. Throughout the day, someone, at the behest of Muslim leaders would ring a gong at the top of the hour to indicate the time. This was more typical in the eastern part of Freetown than in the other parts of the city.

The pervading sounds heard all over Freetown were those of the fighter airplanes and other aircraft of the Royal Air Force (RAF). And, in some areas near the sea, the sounds of motor boats and launches of the British Royal Navy (RN), as well as launches of the many ships anchored in the harbour were also part of the soundscape.

Some of the vessels ferried sailors from ships to shore or vice versa. Others supplied goods to vessels at anchor in the harbour.

During those years, the main aircraft seen above Freetown were the fast-flying Hurricane fighters and the rather clumsy Albatross planes and Sunderland flying boats. A lone dark bulky Sunderland flying boat (or one of its smaller counterparts, the Catalina flying boat) with floats hanging beneath it, flying clumsily west toward the Atlantic Ocean from its base in an inlet at Jui, east of Freetown, was almost a regular morning sight. These aircraft were engaged in patrol duties, observing German U-boats close to the coast and waiting to attack any vessels in sight.

The high-pitched sounds of the Hurricane fighters were quite distinctive. Even without seeing an aircraft, we boys in those days could identify a Hurricane fighter from the sound generated by its engine.

On a few occasions, a Hurricane fighter would perform aerobatics above the city to demonstrate its agility, as well as to reassure citizens of the might of the British naval and air forces. The Hurricane fighters were based at one of three airfields – Hastings Airfield, Waterloo Airfield, or Lungi Airfield across the river.

TIME CHANGE

It is of interest to note that there used to be change of time in Sierra Leone, just as there is in Britain. During the latter part of April, the time was advanced one hour, and at the end of September or thereabouts, it was brought back one hour. This practice ended, if I remember correctly, during or after the Second World War.

SOUNDING OF THE SIREN TO INDICATE 9.00 P.M.

Another matter relating to time in Freetown was that, at nine o'clock in the evening, a siren would sound. If my memory serves me well, I think the sounding of the 9.00 p.m. siren was stopped sometime during the Second World War, so that the 9 signal would not be confused with the sounding of the siren in case there was an air raid by enemy planes.

RESTRICTION OF THE BEATING OF TOM-TOMS

Up until the sixties, it was illegal to beat tom-toms in and around Freetown from about 9.00 p.m. to about 6.00 a.m. Tom-toms are small drums that are beaten during ceremonies of local indigenous societies, such as Ojeh, Bondo, hunting, and others. The law was strictly enforced, and the police would swoop on the site anywhere there was beating of tom-toms at night, seize the drums, and arrest the players, who would be taken to the nearest police station and charged with beating tom-toms after hours. The law gradually became dormant after the country had achieved independence.

PLAYING MUSICAL INSTRUMENTS TO THE ANNOYANCE OF THE PUBLIC

Another law made it an offence to play musical instruments loudly and to the annoyance of members of the public. Anyone who violated that law would be arrested and charged to court, and the musical instruments would be confiscated.

SOME AMENITIES IN FREETOWN

Meat vans

Young people may like to know that, in the thirties and even up until the sixties, the Freetown City Council provided meat vans, which conveyed meat in bulk early in the mornings from the abattoir at Magazine Court to the various markets around Freetown. The meat vans were painted red.

This contrasts with the present unhygienic practice of placing uncovered meat in bulk in omolankays or poda-podas for conveyance from the abattoir to the various markets in the city.

The Victoria Park

The Victoria Park, a relatively small park along the top of Garrison Street at the top ends of Howe Street and Gloucester Street, served as a relaxation area. Trees provided shade, and metal benches sat underneath the branches of the trees. In addition, nice flowers grew in various areas in the park opposite or near each of the metal benches. The star amenity was a water fountain whose water always flowed. Inside the fountain were fish.

A circular rotunda bandstand with a raised stage stood in the centre of the park. The rotunda was used for public performances and entertainment. Periodically during the dry season, the band of the Sierra Leone Police Force would stage concerts in the evenings. During the concerts, light classical music; martial music; and other music, including local music, would be played. Everyone knew Capt. McWeen, the British bandmaster.

Park goers could avail themselves of four public toilets inside the park.

The park was serviced by a park manager, together with several labour assistants who were responsible for the maintenance of the park and all amenities therein. They would clean and paint the metal benches, paint the flower mounds, tend the flowers, clean the toilets and the fountain, and take care of the fish. The park also provided fresh flowers, with which wreaths were made and sold to the public.

It was a pleasure on Sundays to see groups of citizens, including young couples in tight embrace, walking along the lanes or relaxing on the benches inside the park.

There were strict rules for the park. Anyone with a large bundle on his or her head was prohibited from passing through the park. Petty traders and hawkers were prohibited from selling inside the park. And hooligans were not permitted inside the park.

The park was small in comparison with parks in other countries. Nevertheless, it was a symbol of the pinnacle of the development of Freetown at the time.

When I visited Freetown a few years ago, the Victoria Park had been closed, and grasses were all around the park. It is a shame that city councillors allowed the park to deteriorate.

Public Toilets

There used to be a few public toilets around the city. These toilets were cleaned daily by special labourers, who were hired for this purpose.

All the foregoing public amenities exist no more. The present councillors of the Freetown City Council do not appear to be interested in such amenities. This is an indication of the management of the Freetown City Council by the present city councillors.

ENTERTAINMENT

Wilberforce Memorial Hall

Freetown once boasted a historic building situated at the junction of Water Street (now Wallace-Johnson Street) and Gloucester Street overlooking the seafront. The Wilberforce Memorial Hall was dedicated to the memory of William Wilberforce, one of the Christian philanthropists who persistently advocated for the abolishment of the slave trade in Britain and its former colonies in America until the slave trade was finally declared illegal.

This building was situated in part of the area now occupied by the former Town Hall, which I understand was burnt down by the RUF rebels when they invaded Freetown on 6 January 1999 during the Sierra Leone Civil War (1992–2002).

The Wilberforce Memorial Hall was a two-storey building with red stone walls and a wooden interior. Unfortunately, it was destroyed by fire in 1959.

Wilberforce Memorial Hall was the venue for almost all major public functions – formal dances, concerts, public meetings, electioneering campaign meetings for the Freetown City Council, and many more. During the thirties and part of the forties, this building was also the only centre where movies were shown to the public by a private company, Freetown Cold Storage Company. In those days, movies included performances by the famous British comedian Charlie Chaplin, news of British forces at war, and some American movies.

Odeon Cinema by the junction of Howe Street and Westmoreland Street (now Siaka Stevens Street) opposite the Roman Catholic Sacred Heart Cathedral was built around 1946.

Formal dance bands

Formal dances in Freetown back then were really formal. Gentlemen dressed in formal evening wear – dark jackets or white dinner jackets, black trousers, and well-polished shoes. Ladies wore floor-length dresses. Each lady had to be accompanied by her gentleman partner. No ladies would attend dances unaccompanied by gentlemen.

Music was usually provided, though not electronically amplified as at present. Electronically amplified music was not yet known in Freetown. Rather, music for formal dances was supplied by formal dance bands, with each member playing a different musical instrument.

One famous dance band was Mr Mann and His Orchestra. The leader, who was a half-caste, was called Mr Mann. His orchestra consisted of several players with brass, woodwind, and string instruments, as well as drums. Among the brass wind instruments was a large double bass wind instrument known as a bombardine.

The Cuban Swingers was another lead dance bad. There were also a few other bands in Freetown. The bands would be hired on an hourly basis.

Dance music of the time included formal foxtrot, sidestep, quick step, rhumba, waltz, and lancers (a form of group dancing). Strict protocol and decorum were observed at dances. Before a gentleman would dance with a lady who was not his partner, he would first approach the male partner of the lady to seek permission. After permission was granted, the gentleman would approach the lady and, with a bow, ask permission to dance with her. When the dance piece was over, the gentleman would escort the lady to her seat and thank her for the dance.

Dances that were not formal were called socials. Socials were typically held by youths in a small private hall or a dwelling houses with enough space for dancing. Dresses at such socials were casual. Music was provided by the gramophone. Later on, in the fifties, amplified dance music was being supplied by electronic equipment.

Ebenezer Calendar

No narrative about the music in Freetown from the thirties and even through the seventies would be complete without mention of Ebenezer Calendar, the soloist, and his guitar. Ebenezer Calendar was quite popular. He would sing solos, accompanying himself on his guitar, about social customs and activities in Freetown.

Ebenezer Calendar was actually a carpenter. But he took to playing the guitar and singing in his spare time. He became quite popular, providing songs at wake keeping ceremonies, as well as for entertainment. One of his best known songs was "Fire, Fire, Fire, Fire, Fire dae Cam". Ebenezer Calendar died in 1985.

Gramophones

Gramophones were imported from Europe (mainly from Britain) or, in a few cases, from America. Gramophones were not available in every household. In general, it was mainly the affluent who could afford to purchase this instrument. Its presence in a house was evidence of affluence.

Gramophones were generally operated by adults. But in some cases, grown-up children were permitted to operate them. Gramophones played 78 rpm plastic records, which had to be handled carefully, as they were brittle. One had to also take care not to wind the spring of the gramophone too tightly, or it would snap. Many a child received punishment, such as severe flogging, for accidentally causing a gramophone record to fall to the floor and break.

The Ascico Band

An indigenous band known as Ascico supplied local music. The band was popular and quite cheap to hire. The four to six band members played different crude musical instrument. The "instruments" consisted of a drum that had to be hit with the naked palm, an old carpenter's wood saw on which a flat piece of metal was rubbed rapidly to and fro along the flat side, a flute, sometimes a bombardine, cymbals, and a few other articles used to produce musical sounds. The combination of the rhythmical sounds created by the deft hands of the players would soon entice young women to jump in the centre of the crowd and wriggle their buttocks whilst moving in circles. When the dance was at its climax, some of the women would tighten their dresses around their buttocks so that they became more pronounced. They would then turn their heads as if trying to view the rapidly gyrating movements of their flabby hips. This delighted males in the crowd.

Not everyone was able to dance the "Ascico." This type of dancing was unsuitable for men, as men don't have flabby hips to vibrate.

CHRISTMAS AND BOXING DAY CELEBRATIONS

Christmas and Boxing Day celebrations were joyful occasions for all citizens, particularly in Freetown. Masked "devils" would parade in the streets or perform in enclosed compounds. There were Gongorlis (men with large, ugly, wooden masks); Mamapara (dancers on stilts); hunters with their own masked "devils"; and on and on.

No rowdy, disorderly, or violent behaviour marked these celebrations. Adults and children alike accompanied the masked devils. But they all behaved decently. No hooligans took delight in perpetrating riotous and obscene conduct, drinking intoxicating liquor, littering the streets with broken bottles, and obstructing streets and preventing vehicles from being driven. There was back then no need for truckloads of police to accompany the masked devils and their followers to enforce law and order.

It is most unfortunate that so-called politicians are now using masked devils to perpetrate indecent and disorderly behaviour, on the pretext that these masked devils are "Sierra Leone's cultural heritage". Masked devils *are* the cultural heritage of Sierra Leone. But indecent comportment, violence, and disorderly conduct among the masked devils and their followers are not. The Gongorlis and other masked devils that used to parade Freetown from the thirties to the sixties were well behaved. Their followers did not perpetrate indecent and disorderly behaviour. They did not drink alcoholic beverages or climb and walk on the top of cars, oblivious to the damage they were causing. They did not break bottles or carry all sorts of offensive implements.

At present, even young children innocently accompany these rowdy and disorderly groups, singing all sorts of immoral songs. It was long after Sierra Leone had gained independence that some irresponsible politicians – in order to gain what, in their polluted minds, they perceived as "popularity" – used the masked devils and their followers to perpetrate all sorts of immoral and indecent comportment, as well as violence.

When I was a cabinet member in 1979, I personally heard certain irresponsible politicians justify the immoral comportment and violence among masked devils and their followers as part of "Sierra Leone's cultural heritage". These so-called politicians must change their views in order to bring about high standard of moral comportment among the children who will be the future leaders of the country, or else I foresee doom in Sierra Leone.

On Boxing Day (the day after Christmas), sports would be held at the recreation grounds (the site of the present Brooksfield National Stadium). The sports were organised by the Young Men's Christian Association (YMCA). Large crowds, including men, women, and children, would attend the activities, which included flat races, bicycle races, the climbing of greasy poles, tug of war matches, and more.

The land on which the building containing FSSG (Freetown Secondary School for Girls) and Youyi Building now stands used to be filled with monkey apple trees. Indeed, those were halcyon days, which if the present trend of the abominable behaviour by hooligans is any indication, may never return.

HOTELS

During the thirties and thereafter, the hotels in which Freetown had prided itself became objects of ridicule. There was the City Hotel along Oxford Street (now Lightfoot Boston Street), whose building stood inside a relatively large compound. This "hotel" had a few rooms for guests.

The other hotels were what I might term third-class guests houses. There was the hotel with the prestigious name of Grand Hotel. It was anything but grand. It consisted of just a handful of rooms in a building belonging to Genet & Sons, opposite the Roman Catholic Sacred Heart Cathedral at Westmoreland Street (now Siaka Stevens Street).

The other hotel, established during the Second World War, was on Oxford Street on top of the building where Sweissy shop was located. That hotel was called Sugar Ball Hotel.

The City Hotel was the most popular during the Second World War. It was even mentioned in the novel *The Heart of the Matter* by British author Graham Green.

BULLOM BOATS

Bullom boats, sailing to or from Bullom (Lungi) on the mouth of the River Rokel, where the river joins the Atlantic Ocean, have been unique sights along the seafront of Freetown since the thirties. These sailing boats conveyed foodstuffs and various other commodities for sale in Freetown.

Bullom boats sailed, usually in groups, to and from Freetown every Tuesday, Thursday, and Saturday. These days were called market days. Most of the sailing boats would land at King Jimmy Wharf in downtown Freetown, where they would dislodge their passengers and cargo around 11.00 a.m. A few of the boats would sail to other wharves – Moa Wharf, Kroo Bay, and so on – with their cargoes, mainly mangrove firewood. By somewhere between 3.00 and 5.00 p.m., the boats would set sail on their return journey to Lungi. In those days, boats with outboard engines were non-existent.

These sailing boats with their sails fully deployed against the wind and sailing majestically across the River Rokel in groups was a beautiful sight. Their large white sails, filled with the wind that propelled them, were unforgettable. But these sights gradually faded and disappeared completely when sails lost the battle to outboard motors.

GODERICH STREET

The Second World War years (1939–1945) brought some improvements to Freetown. Goderich Street did not then extend to Kissy Road. It ended in a filthy and unhygienic creek a short distance after crossing Ambrose Street. A few shacks and ramshackle buildings stood along the creek.

Freetown was not designed for vehicles (if ever it was designed). Prior to the war, the main routes from central Freetown to and from the east end were along narrow Kissy Street and the equally narrow Mountain Cut. To provide easier movements for the many large military vehicles in transit all over the city, the British government confiscated all properties along the creek, bulldozed the ramshackle shacks, and extended Goderich Street to Kissy Road.

REGENT/GRAFTON ROAD

As has already been mentioned, the only major roads to and from the provinces from central Freetown were Kissy Street (now Sanni

Abacha Street) and Mountain Cut and then either through Kissy Road or Fourah Bay Road through to Waterloo. All these streets were narrow. The road round the peninsular was too long and not developed. To facilitate the movements of military vehicles from Freetown to and from the provinces during the Second World War, the British Army constructed the road from Regent to Grafton between 1942 and 1943. That road, which wound its way through the hills and dense forest between Regent and Grafton, was constructed mainly by Nigerian troops under the supervision of British officers. It provided easy passage for the British military vehicles travelling from Freetown through Wilberforce, Hill Station, to Regent; on to Hastings Airfield and Waterloo Airfield, from which war planes operated; and on to the provinces.

The British military constructed all three airfields during the war. These were important airfields for the British Royal Air Force (RAF).

MASSIVE LANDSLIDE AT CHARLOTTE VILLAGE

A little less than two years after the construction of the Regent/ Grafton road, a massive landslide devastated part of the road. This incident occurred during the rainy season on a Friday sometime in 1944. A heavy and continuous downpour all day caused a massive landslide from the hill overlooking Charlotte Village down towards the village. Thousands of tons of earth, trees, and rocks were dislodged from top of the hill and cascaded down into the village. Countless residents – men, women, and children who then resided in the valley close to the stream in Charlotte – were permanently buried underneath tons of rubble.

VACANT HOUSES OR ROOMS FOR RENT

In the earlier forties, it was common practice for notices to be placed on the front of houses available for lease. These notices contained the words, "To let, apply within" (or otherwise indicated where would-be tenants should apply). Nowadays, no signboard advertising a vacant house or vacant room would be seen anywhere around Freetown. In fact, there are no longer any vacant houses or rooms to rent.

NATIVE PASTORATE FUND

From the thirties and up until the sixties, the Anglican churches in Freetown had what was called a "Native Pastorate Fund." Members of the Church Missionary Society (CMS) established this scheme in 1861. Every Sunday, special collections were taken up in each Anglican church, and the donations were given to the Native Pastorate Fund. The funds were used to build schools in the protectorate for the education of children there. It also built a few churches in the protectorate, to convert the people there to Christianity.

Since the Christian churches in Freetown consisted mainly of Creoles in those days, most of them gladly made donations to this Native Pastorate Fund.

DORCAS ASSOCIATION

The Dorcas Association was another establishment of the Anglican churches. This association was for female parishioners of Anglican churches. Members would donate money and clothes, to be sent to the people in the protectorate to assist with the education of children, as well as the general welfare of adults.

"MONTH BOYS"

The following is in no way intended to demean anyone or any group. It is only my sincere effort to portray part of the history of Sierra Leone.

The affluent in Freetown and its environs sometimes had "month boys" (in other words, monthly paid domestic servants). These were mainly boys from the protectorate who were hired to assist with domestic chores, such as cleaning the house, doing laundry, cooking, and so on. Month boys were paid monthly. In addition, they were served meals daily.

Some of us in the villages had month boys as well. In the villages, month boys assisted in the tending of gardens and farms and carried out a few domestic chores.

In some cases month boys were made to attend churches and converted to Christianity. In other cases, the children of the month boys were sent to primary and even secondary schools by their employers. In general, month boys lived a relatively good life. Periodically some of those who were recruited directly from the provinces were given leave of about a month, during which they would visit their families in the provinces. In due course, some of the month boys acquired the habits of their Creole employers and were assimilated into Creole society.

In the villages, as many of the educated Creole youth sought white-collar jobs in Freetown, they abandoned gardening and farming with their parents. Some of the month boys leased the gardens and farms. By the late fifties to sixties, an appreciable number of the farms and gardens in the Mountain Villages (Leicester, Gloucester, Regent, Bathurst, and Charlotte) were owned by former people from the provinces.

In due course, the children of the month boys who had acquired an education obtained employment in Freetown as clerks, motor drivers, mechanics, and so on.

THE GREAT FIRE IN FREETOWN ON CHRISTMAS EVE 1940

On Christmas Eve 1940, Freetown experienced the greatest fire in its history. The fire completely devastated the area now known as Fire Burn along Fourah Bay Road in Freetown's east end.

The fire engulfed the entire area along Fourah Bay Road starting near Eastern Police Station up to Magazine Cut and around the then railway line behind that section of Fourah Bay Road. All the houses were razed to the ground. I understand that the rampaging fire even spread across the other side of Fourah Bay Road behind Holy Trinity

Church. But the flames were extinguished before they could engulf the church. Consequently, the church was spared from destruction.

The area that was devastated by the fire has thereafter been called Fire Burn.

chapter 11

SIERRA LEONE AND THE SECOND WORLD WAR

———————— ▬▬▬▬▬▬▬ ————————

IMPORTANCE OF SIERRA LEONE TO THE BRITISH DURING THE SECOND WORLD WAR

In September 1939 when the Second World War commenced, Sierra Leone was still a colony of Britain. Freetown has a large natural harbour able to accommodate a large number of vessels The harbour was ideally located on the coast of the Atlantic Ocean. And its narrow channel at the entrance to the open ocean could be easily sealed with nets, preventing German U-boats (submarines) from sneaking in and attacking ships docked in the harbour.

Consequently, Freetown's harbour served as an assembly area for convoys of vessels, which were provided with armed British naval escorts for their journeys across the Atlantic Ocean.

Freetown, therefore, became a strategic naval base of the Royal Navy. The headquarters of the British South Atlantic Naval Command were located at the Prince of Wales School in Kingtom, Freetown. Consequently, Freetown was transformed into a very active port city during the war years.

As a result, on any given day, especially during the peak of the war in 1943, large numbers of vessels of all kinds and sizes and from various nationalities, but mainly British, could be seen at anchor in the harbour. At one point, fifty or more ships would be in the harbour at any time. These included small merchant ships, large passenger vessels such as the *Queen Mary*, oil tankers, large battleships, destroyers, minesweepers, and submarines.

On some occasions, ships would be seen trailing thick black smoke, listing and crawling into the harbour. These were the lucky ships that had been crippled after they'd been attacked in the Atlantic Ocean by German U-boats. The less fortunate vessels would have already gone to their watery graves under the Atlantic Ocean, victims of the determined and well-deployed packs of submarines prowling along the Atlantic Coast of parts of West Africa.

Along with the presence of so many ships in Freetown came men as well as few women of various nationalities, and one would see them roaming around downtown Freetown and on the outskirts of town.

On some occasions, pitiable groups of foreign nationals, some of whom were injured, would also be seen roaming around as if they were in a daze. These were survivors who had been passengers and sailors of merchant vessels that had been torpedoed and sunk in the Atlantic Ocean off the West African coast. These survivors wore a variety of clothes, and some of them looked sullen and dejected.

Military bases were constructed around Freetown, as well as in the outskirts of the city and in other parts of the country. Lungi across the mouth of the River Rokel in Freetown, as well as both Hastings and Waterloo about 15 miles and 21 miles respectively from Freetown, became very important to the British Royal Air Force (RAF). Airfields, from which war planes operated, were constructed in these towns. Daru in the far eastern part of the country became a major training area for Sierra Leonean troops.

Other areas in Freetown and its outskirts that were taken over for the construction of installations in the prosecution of war were parts of Kissy up Jui, a small cove near Hastings. Those areas were converted from virtual wastelands to servicing areas, as well as shelters for various kinds of small vessels and seaplanes. The seaplanes, mostly Sunderland flying boats and Catalina flying boats, were sheltered in an inlet at Jui near Hastings. It was from there that they took off daily to patrol parts of the Atlantic Ocean off Freetown and hunt for German U-boats.

The feverish construction of these airfields and ancillary buildings at Lungi, Hastings, and Waterloo made the towns, as well as nearby villages, prosper during the war. But as soon as the war in Europe ended in May 1945, the British gradually withdrew all their forces and equipment. And so Lungi, Hastings, and Waterloo's prosperity declined. But Lungi was resuscitated, as it was chosen to house the international airport for Freetown a few years later.

JOE-KHAKI AND JIG-JIG

Large numbers of British sailors in their white uniform and troops in their khaki uniforms would also be seen roaming around Freetown when they were off duty.

In addition, the war brought a few new words to Freetown. British troops and sailors usually called each other Joe. "Hi, Joe," they would say when they encountered each other in the streets. Because of the khaki uniforms (in those days, there were no camouflaged uniforms) and these frequent friendly greetings, the British troops and sailors soon became known in Freetown and its environs as "Joe Khaki."

In the forties, several private "welfare centres" popped up around Freetown. But the main, most popular welfare centre was located in a building at 9 Walpole Street, by Oxford Street (now Lightfoot Boston Street) and the back of Wesley Church. The immoral activities around that area caused the sailors and soldiers to coin a euphemistic expression, *jig-jig*. So when drunken Joe Khakis would go around asking street boys, "Where is jig-jig?" they would be directed to these private welfare centres. The street boys would hang around the welfare centres and beg these soldiers and sailors for few pence

Decent well-bred young boys needed to be very careful not to associate with the street boys. They also needed to avoid carelessly mentioning such words as *jig-jig* in the hearing of their parents or other elders. One's indiscretion in uttering such comments would result in hi buttocks and back soon being hot and, perhaps, blistered by severe lashes. Decent and well-bred kids were taught not to mention jig-jig or roam around areas where Joe Khakis and sailors often congregated.

ENEMY ACTIVITIES IN THE AIR OVER FREETOWN

Although it was known that Freetown was an important British naval base in West Africa during the Second World War, there were no air raids in Freetown throughout the war. Nor did any German battleships shell Freetown from the sea. Only on occasion would hostile aircraft on reconnaissance operations fly over Freetown harbour. It was suspected that these aircraft were from Dakar, which was then occupied by Vichy France and sympathetic to the Germans. Any hostile aircraft that flew over Freetown would draw a lot of anti-aircraft gunfire, both from the many British naval vessels at anchor in Freetown harbour and also from numerous ack-ack (anti-aircraft) batteries installed at vantage points in and around Freetown – Tower Hill Barracks, Wilberforce Barracks, Murray Town Barracks, Juba Barracks, Cockerill gun emplacement, Kissy naval installations, Hastings, and Waterloo.

On one occasion, a few pupils including me were on our way from schools in Freetown to Gloucester and Leicester villages when, at about 4.00 p.m., the sound of a hostile aircraft was heard flying over the harbour. Almost immediately, it was met by barrages of gunfire from anti-aircraft batteries. Also as it flew towards the east end of Freetown, an RAF Hurricane[7] was seen pursuing it. We learnt late in the evening from workers returning from Waterloo that the hostile aircraft had been shot down by the Hurricane fighter around Waterloo and had crashed in flames. The crew of two, who were suspected to be Frenchmen, had perished.

[7] Spitfires and Hurricane were the two most powerful British airplane fighters during the Second World War. These crafts were deployed successfully against the seemingly formidable might of the Luftwaffe (the German Air Force) and greatly contributed to the victory of the RAF over the Luftwaffe in the skies over Britain.

On another occasion, an enemy aircraft was damaged by anti-aircraft gunfire, and it was reported to have crashed in the sea off Isles de Los near Guinea. It is believed that other hostile aircraft on reconnaissance missions were shot at and damaged and later crashed somewhere in Sierra Leone.

AIR RAID PRECAUTIONS IN FREETOWN

During the Second World War, Freetown was subjected to strict blackout at night. Street lights that, prior to the war were regularly lit late in the evening and turned off early the next morning were permanently turned off during the war. All buildings were prohibited from allowing interior lights to be seen from outside. Consequently, glass windowpanes were darkened with black paint or had very thick dark curtain draped across them so that light was visible from outside. The purpose of this was to make it difficult for the city to be seen at night by any hostile aircraft or hostile war vessels.

To enforce these precautions, several local officials, called air raid precaution wardens, were deployed at night to patrol streets and warn residents who were violating the law by allowing streaks of light to be visible through windows. These officials had uniforms with armbands as a sign of authority.

As further precaution in case Freetown was attacked by hostile aircraft, to try and extinguish the initial fires that might have been started by incendiary bombs, large metal tanks filled with water were erected in several areas in Freetown. Stirrup pumps were issued to government offices, various organisations, and individuals, as well as to many schools in and around the city. These stirrup pumps were to be used to dowse the initial fires. Workers, pupils, and others were taught how to operate them.

I now look upon such precaution as a big joke. First, incendiary bombs were dropped in hundreds, and they burn initially with such intensity that it would have been very difficult to extinguish the resulting flames. Also, highly explosive bombs might have been dropped together with the incendiary bombs, and these would have devastated everything around. Furthermore, no plans were made to extinguish fires that might have been started by incendiary bombs that fell on the roofs of tall buildings in Freetown. Since most of the buildings in Freetown were constructed of timber, there might have been a great conflagration around the city.

But there was never any cause to use the large water tanks, as no hostile aircraft ever bombed Freetown. These water tanks remained as permanent fixtures around Freetown after the war had ended and eventually became breeding grounds for mosquitoes. They were subsequently dismantled gradually.

APPEALS BY THE COLONIAL GOVERNMENT FOR DONATIONS TOWARDS THE WAR EFFORT

By 1941, Britain was in the midst of a bitter struggle against the almost invincible Germans, supported by the Italians under Il Duce, Mussolini, who was head of the Italian government.

Therefore, Britain appealed to all its colonies for support of the war effort. In Sierra Leone, notices were put out in public places appealing to citizens contribute financially towards the purchase of a bomber. Many citizens, even schoolchildren (myself included), made small donations. Later on, pictures showed a Lancaster bomber with its round, blue white and red emblem in an airfield somewhere in Britain and marked "Sierra Leone." On seeing the pictures, we were all glad that Sierra Leone had purchased a bomber that would be deployed in bombing Germany. It was later when, I had become older, that I realised that the pictures were probably faked and were only designed for propaganda purposes, to arouse interest among people in the county to support the war effort.

Although I was then a youth, as far I knew, apart from the serial number and the RAF emblem, there were no other marks on the aircraft.

GERMAN PRISONERS OF WAR

Before the Second World War started in September 1939, there were a few German firms in Sierra Leone, including a branch of the German shipping company Wormann West Africa Line. The supervisors in these firms were German nationals. Immediately after Britain declared war on Germany on 3 September 1939, the German nationals in all the German firms were rounded up, arrested, and detained in the Model School compound, which had been converted into a prisoner of war detention centre. They remained in this detention centre for several weeks, after which they disappeared. It was believed that they were transferred to detention centres in Britain until the end of the war, when they were repatriated to Germany.

ITALIAN PRISONERS OF WAR

During the serious fighting in North Africa between the Germans and the Italians on the one part and the British and Americans on the other part, the American forces and the British forces defeated the combined German and Italian armies and took many thousand prisoners of war in 1943. The majority of them were Italians.

Sometime in 1943 to 1944, several Italian prisoners of war were brought to Freetown. They were made to work in the railway department, the Public Works Department, and other workshops. These prisoners of war were not locked up but were free to roam about. Many of them were accommodated in war buildings at Grafton/ Hastings, where they had access to scrap metals from abandoned aircraft.

Some of these prisoners of war cleverly used salvaged metals from broken and abandoned aircraft to turn out cigarette lighters, ashtrays, aluminium pots and cups, and several other handy items. They even taught some Sierra Leoneans living in Hastings and surrounding villages how to smelt aluminium to make pots and other household items.

The Italian prisoners of war were in Sierra Leone until the end of the war in Europe, when they gradually disappeared. It was assumed that the British repatriated them to Italy.

SCARCITY OF FOODSTUFFS AND OTHER ESSENTIALS DURING THE SECOND WORLD WAR

By1943, Sierra Leone was seriously feeling the adverse effects of the war. Toys that used to be in abundance before the war all but disappeared from shops. Imported foodstuffs like flour, sardines and other canned fish, corned beef, and shoes, to name a few, disappeared from shops. Staple foodstuffs like rice and fufu and became scarce.

This scarcity of local foodstuffs was partly due to the fact that there were, by then, large numbers of soldiers from Nigeria and the Gold Coast (now Ghana), in addition to Sierra Leonean soldiers. These soldiers depended mainly on rice and by-products of cassava for their staple food.

In view of the fact that there were shortages of flour, which had to be imported, there were also shortages of bread. It was a common sight to see large crowds struggling to obtain one or two loaves of bread from the few bakeries, which had limited quantities of flour. Sierra Leoneans weren't used to queuing for any service. Whenever crowds gathered to wait for a service, scuffles would break out in the early morning, sometimes with resulting injuries.

Rice, which had hitherto been in abundance, was rationed by the colonial government. Consequently, there were struggles among people trying to buy rice from the few shops that would occasionally sell small quantities.

WORK AND ECONOMY DURING THE SECOND WORLD WAR

In pursuit of the war and in defence of Sierra Leone, especially Freetown, the city that was so vital to the Royal Navy, the British constructed various buildings and installations as quickly as possible. Machines had to be manned. Workers had to be hired to construct these buildings and installations. There was a great demand for workers of all types in Freetown and all around the suburbs. Almost every male who wanted to work was able to find employment.

At the same time, quite a lot of quacks emerged. It was not unusual to see someone who was not a known mason or a known carpenter now passing around buildings with trowel or a hammer or some other tools in his hand.

Wages of those engaged in war projects were relatively high. Plus, workers on war projects weren't paid at the end of each month, as was the practice in the civil service and in the few commercial firms, but fortnightly on every other Friday. The local word that emerged for war-related work was *tangains*. Payday was termed *terma*.

Quite a lot of dishonest practices were carried out by some of the Sierra Leoneans who were in charge of hiring and paying workers and even with the connivance of some of the British military officers. The common practice was to put extra names of non-existent workers on the payroll. On payday, the extra pay was surreptitiously collected by other workers, and later, the money for the fictitious workers was handed over to the paymaster, who would then give "commission" to the workers who were in connivance with him.

Sierra Leonean foremen did this, and so also did some British officers who were responsible for dishing out the money to the Sierra Leonean foremen. The term related to this dishonest practice was *dieman*, or in other words, "ghost workers."

The large demand for various categories of workers resulted in there being a large amount of money in circulation. Many workers, especially foremen, found themselves "rich" overnight. Some workers, especially the reckless ones, squandered their new-found "riches". Some pasted British West African currency notes of ten shillings and one pound denominations on the walls of their bedrooms.

Other workers would perform certain ceremonies and say they were "christening" newly born kittens or puppies. Such ceremonies were usually accompanied by lavish serving of alcoholic beverages. Other workers took delight in courting other women as wives, even though they were already married. I knew one worker who delighted in seeing naked women. Substantial amounts were wasted by such frivolous men.

On the other hand, some workers were quite responsible and did not waste such unexpected "wealth." They cleverly saved this money and were soon able to build or purchase their own dwelling houses. A few others established commercial enterprises. Unfortunately, most of the commercial projects failed, owing to poor management, as well as to dishonesty of those who were put in charge. Some were relatives of the businesses' owners.

The war years provided an additional source of employment for certain other people. These were those who were chartered by the British Royal Navy, as well as the merchant navy, to supply the crew of vessels in Freetown Harbour various kinds of foodstuffs, including fruits and vegetables. They were known as ship chandlers. There were not many ship chandlers, as compared to other workers. Nevertheless, they rendered valuable services to the crews of the warships of the Royal Navy, as well as to the crews of merchant ships anchored in the harbour.

Those of us who resided in the mountain villages about 3 to 5 miles from Freetown and who planted vegetables also benefited. The war years brought us some wealth. Almost all the town's vegetables and substantial quantities of fruits were being grown in the five mountain villages. The produce was purchased wholesale by the ship chandlers for supplying the large number of vessels anchored in the harbour.

The Second World War in the European theatre came to an end in May 1945. The British military quickly evacuated its personnel from Sierra Leone. Military construction projects were gradually halted. Fewer vessels were in the harbour. Mass employment of workers in construction and other projects also came to an end, as did tangains.

THE SIERRA LEONE MILITARY

Sierra Leone soldiers, under the leadership of British officers, played an important role during the Second World War, assisting the British forces in the Asian Theatre. In 1943, the British were engaged in a bitter life-and-death struggle, not only against the Germans and Italians in North Africa, but also against the Japanese in the Far East.

Following the surprise attack by the Japanese against the American navy in Pearl Harbor on 7 December 1941, the aggressive and powerful Japanese launched attacks against British, French, and Dutch territories in the Far East. The Japanese forces were formidable, and by 1943, most of the British colonies, as well as the Dutch and French colonies in the Far East, had been captured by the seemingly invincible Japanese. Burma, Malaya, Singapore, and more had all fallen.

The British forces were too widely stretched in 1943. The British resorted to recruiting soldiers from their remaining colonies in Asia and in Africa to supply additional troops to fight against the Japanese forces in Burma. Soldiers were, therefore, recruited in Nigeria, the Gold Coast (now Ghana), Sierra Leone, and the Gambia, as well as from other British colonies.

Prior to the commencement of the Second World War, Sierra Leone had only a small number of troops. A large number of boys in the then protectorate were recruited into the army by 1943. These additional Sierra Leonean troops were based at Wilberforce, Murray Town, and Tower Hill, which were old military installations used during the First World War. New barracks were also built at Juba near Lumley, at Regent, and at Grafton.

Sierra Leonean soldiers were also based at Daru near Pendembu in the extreme eastern part of Sierra Leone. Daru served as a major training area for Sierra Leonean soldiers.

An appreciable number of Sierra Leonean solders were completely illiterate or semi-literate. But there were a few literates amongst them. Among the literate soldiers were a few Creole boys.

Creole boys in the colony of Freetown in general were rather reluctant to join the military. One of the reasons Creole boys in particular did not enlist in the army was that educated men were, in a subtle way, discouraged by the British from joining the army in those days. Also, Sierra Leonean soldiers were not accorded any form of respect by their British officers, who looked upon African soldiers as inferior people. In addition, the pay to Sierra Leonean soldiers was a pittance of what was being paid to the average Sierra Leonean workers in other spheres. Plus, however educated a Sierra Leonean may be in those days, he would not be promoted to the rank of a senior officer. The highest ranks Sierra Leoneans could attain were sergeant major or sergeant. On top of all that, Sierra Leonean soldiers were denied wearing boots by the British. All soldiers paraded barefoot.

Actually, sometime in 1939 or 1940, a few Creoles joined the military as soldiers. But in view of the unfair circumstances, these Creoles, headed by one Emmanuel Cole, protested vehemently against the subjugation they were undergoing under British officers. The British officers resented the protest. As a deterrent, all the Creole soldiers were arrested, charged with mutiny, and court-martialled. All of them were found guilty and sentenced to various terms of imprisonment. Emmanuel Cole, who was the ringleader, was sentenced to fifteen years in prison, and the others received sentences ranging down to eighty-four days.

Despite the adverse circumstances that confronted Sierra Leonean soldiers, they were, nevertheless, quite loyal and highly disciplined.

The Sierra Leone battalion that was shipped to confront the Japanese forces in Burma acquitted itself excellently by the exceptional bravery of many of its soldiers.

Battle of Arakan Valley in Burma

The climax was at the Battle at the Arakan Valley in Burma (now Myanmar) in 1944, when these brave Sierra Leonean soldiers fought heroically with determination and tenacity. They scored a big victory against the Japanese in this battle and routed sizeable numbers of Japanese forces. There were several reported acts of extreme bravery under enemy fire.

One of the Sierra Leonean soldiers who distinguished himself by his extreme bravery was Sgt Asana Beya. Beya's leadership qualities and outstanding courage earned him a Distinguished Conduct Medal

(DCM). The memorable encounter was reported in detail in volume I of *The Regimental History of Sierra Leone*. Here's a short description of his heroism as recorded in the citation by Sgt Beya's battalion commanding officer, Lt Col H.M. Boxer:

> Sergeant Beya, a platoon commander, led an action against a Japanese force in the Kaladan region of Western Burma, routing the enemy and capturing documents which provided the Allied Forces with very valuable information.
>
> On December 22, 1944, 2 companies occupied Point 887 Thandada last light, and had consolidated during darkness. At approximately 05.30 hours 23 December 1944, a Japanese force penetrated the Sierra Leone army positions from the rear in the vicinity of Battalion Headquarters which was protected by 2 sections of the Defence Platoon commanded by Sgt. Asana Beya. There had not been time to dig defensive positions, but Sgt. Asana Beya took immediate action and organised his platoon to meet the attack. In the early stages, oblivious of the fire, he continually visited his men and encouraged them. When it became apparent that the enemy were on the point of overrunning his position, he took a machine gun and advanced towards the enemy, entirely regardless of the heavy fire directed against him. He showed a complete disregard for his own safety, and firing from the hip as he advanced, personally killed 6 of the enemy, before the remainder turned and fled. His leadership was an inspiration to all around him, and it was largely due to his courage, initiative and resolution, that the attack was finally beaten off and the action brought to a successful conclusion. Through his action, many valuable documents giving enemy strength and dispositions were captured. Among the

enemy killed was one Japanese officer. Sgt. Beya was awarded an immediate DCM.

When Asana Beya died in 1987, His Excellency the president of Sierra Leone, Major General Dr J. S. Momoh directed that he should be accorded full military honours. On the occasion of the ceremonies relating to the fortieth day of his death, a three- mile long access road leading to his village was constructed, and this made possible the presence of a military detachment, as well as representatives of the Sierra Leone Ex-Servicemen's Association. National and state recognition of Beya's unforgettable military exploits was demonstrated by the gracing presence of President Momoh himself.

Up to the fifties, the Sierra Leone Armed Forces had only British senior officers. It included some British NCOs as well.

The British colonial government started promoting Sierra Leoneans into the senior ranks (starting from lieutenant) in about the mid-fifties. The first Sierra Leonean who was promoted to a senior rank in the army and later promoted to the rank of brigadier was Brigadier David Lansana. Subsequently, he replaced the British Brigadier Blackie, who was the commander of the First Battalion, Sierra Leone Military Forces in the sixties.

SIERRA LEONEANS' INVOLVEMENT IN THE ROYAL AIR FORCE (RAF) DURING THE WAR

In 1941, many important towns in Britain were being devastated almost daily. These towns were suffering merciless bombing by the huge fleet of the German Luftwaffe (the German air force). The British recruited young men from her overseas colonies in Africa, the West Indies, and other areas to serve in the RAF.

In Freetown, public notices invited applications from young men to join the RAF. The criteria required were quite high. All applicants must have passed the Cambridge Senior School Certificate Examination and had to be physically and mentally fit. Many young men in Freetown applied.

Following a series of interviews and tests, only a few men were eventually selected. These were:

1. Ade Hyde
2. Ben Davies
3. Christo Davies
4. Horatio Bundu-Williams
5. Johnny Smythe
6. Mitchell Johnson

These young men were sent to Britain, where, after further rigorous physical and other tests, they were enlisted in the RAF and trained in different flying duties. They were allocated to different RAF units in Britain as airmen. All of them saw combat in operations over Germany and the then occupied Europe. They acquitted themselves exceptionally well and fought with gallantry.

The bomber in which Johnny Smythe was flying as a crew member was reportedly hit by German anti-aircraft fire whilst on a bombing mission in Germany sometime in 1943, and the aircraft started to burn. Johnny Smythe and the other crew members parachuted to safety before the plane crashed in flames. They were captured and taken as prisoners of war and spent the rest of the war in captivity in Germany. They were eventually rescued by the Soviet Forces in 1945.

Whilst on leave in Freetown during the latter part of 1945, Smythe gave a series of lectures to secondary school pupils. He narrated this episode in one of his lectures. I was in form five at St Edward's Secondary, and I was present at one of these lectures.

Whilst on an operation over France in 1944, the aircraft in which Ade Hyde was a crew member was hit by German anti-aircraft fire and badly damaged. Ade Hyde was very seriously wounded. According to the pilot of the aircraft, despite his serious injuries, Hyde remained at his post in the aircraft and continued to operate. The pilot managed to land the aircraft safely in Britain, and Hyde was rushed to a hospital. He was awarded the Distinguished Flying Cross (DFC) medal for gallantry.

A few other Sierra Leoneans also travelled to Britain through their own initiative and later succeeded in being enlisted in the RAF. Among these was Leslie William Leigh. He was trained as a bomber pilot and later posted to RAF Coastal Command, where he served bravely till the end of the war. As far as was known then, he was the only Sierra Leonean trained as a pilot in the RAF. The other Sierra Leoneans were trained as wireless operators, gunners, navigation officers, or aground crew.

SIERRA LEONEANS' INVOLVEMENT IN THE BRITISH ROYAL NAVY (RN) DURING THE WAR

As far as I can remember, no Sierra Leoneans actually enlisted in the Royal Navy for active duty on board British warships during the Second World War. White naval crewmen still harboured racial prejudice against blacks and did not want black crewmen to mix with them on board their warships.

However, on shore in Freetown, the Royal Navy enlisted a few Sierra Leoneans, mainly for land-based duties. They served as clerks and mechanics and in other capacities. Some worked on board mine layers and mine sweepers inside Sierra Leone's territorial waters. These Sierra Leoneans wore the white RN uniform. But none of them attained senior ranks in the Royal Navy.

Many Sierra Leoneans served as ordinary seamen on board merchant vessels during the Second World War. Some of these vessels were torpedoed or shelled by German U-boats or warships, and some Sierra Leonean crewmen were among the many casualties.

COMPENSATION FOR SIERRA LEONEAN
AIRMEN AFTER THE WAR

After the end of the war in 1945, the British government compensated the brave young Sierra Leoneans who had joined the RAF. Johnny Smythe was awarded a scholarship to study law. After successfully completing his law studies, he was posted to the then Colonial Service and sent to Sierra Leone as pupil crown counsel.

William Leigh was enlisted in the colonial police force and sent to Sierra Leone as assistant superintendent of police (ASP). He later became the first Sierra Leonean commissioner of police in Sierra Leone in 1963.

All the other Sierra Leoneans who served as airmen in the RAF were posted to various senior posts in the Colonial Service in Sierra Leone. These brave young men were the vanguard of Sierra Leoneans who were later to be elevated to senior posts in the civil service in Sierra Leone to replace the British expatriates.

PART 3

POLITICAL UPHEAVALS
IN SIERRA LEONE

chapter 12

PRE-INDEPENDENCE UPRISINGS

Apart from a revolt started by Bai Bureh in 1898, in protest against the colonial administration's imposition of a tax on each hut in the then protectorate, there were no other significant political upheavals in Sierra Leone until the fifties. That war, known as the Hut Tax War, was quelled within eight to nine months following the capture of Bai Bureh by the British in November 1898. He was then banished to the Gold Coast (now Ghana), which also a British colony. Bureh remained in banishment in the Gold Coast for several years, after which the British returned him to Sierra Leone in 1905 and reinstated him as chief in Kasse Chiefdom.

In February 1955, very serious riots and looting occurred in Freetown – the worst in Freetown in living memory up till then. Sierra Leone was then in transition to independence. The top minister at that time was Chief Minister Dr Milton A.S. Margai, who was leader of the Sierra Leone People's Party (SLPP). The minister of mines and labour was Siaka Stevens. But the country was still effectively under British colonial rule. The police force and the army were still under the control of British colonial officers.

The riots and looting occurred between Friday, 11 February and Saturday, 12 February 1955. The riots and looting started following a pay increase request by Marcus Grant, the secretary general of the Sierra Leone Labour Congress, a coalition of several trade unions.

Member unions included United Mine Workers Union, Railways Workers Union, and Mercantile and General Workers Union. Grant was asking for an increase of six pence in the daily wages of workers in the various trade unions. But the government's minister of labour seemed to be stalling, insisting that negotiations with the Sierra Leone Labour Congress should continue. In exasperation, the secretary general of the Labour Congress called for a general strike, apparently in the hope of exerting pressure on the government so that it might relent and grant the wage increase.

The strike was quickly hijacked by unemployed youths and hooligans, who then spread mayhem throughout Freetown. Substantial parts of the city were seriously vandalised. Railway lines, as well as public water pipes, were uprooted. Telephone and radio rediffusion wires were cut. Widespread looting of Lebanese as well as Foullah shops followed.

But by late Saturday, 12 February 1955, the police and the military had the situation under control. Several people, all of whom were suspected looters and other hooligans, were killed and several were wounded.

During the riots, Assistant Superintendent of Police Everett, a young British colonial police officer, was in charge of a riot unit in the eastern part of Freetown. The desperate and frenzied riotous mob rounded up and overwhelmed the forty-man unit in Everett's charge. He himself was captured and then lynched. Several police personnel were seriously wounded. Ironically, Everett had just been transferred from Malaya (now Malaysia) during the violent and bloody insurgency in that former British colony. Sierra Leone, which had hitherto been considered peaceful, was the place where this young British colonial police officer was to meet untimely and gruesome death at the hands of the violent mobs.

The riot was finally brought under control by late Saturday with the intervention of the army.

During the peak of the riots and looting on Friday, Deputy Commissioner of Police Anthony S. Keeling, a British police officer, together with a handful of policemen, fought their way along Kissy Street, where many Lebanese were being looted.

After considerable difficulties battling their way through violent mobs along Kissy Street, they finally arrived at Eastern Police Station, where a few policemen were based. By then, the vicious mobs had almost surrounded Eastern Police Station and had set part of the building on fire. The large and violent mob was desperately trying to break into the building. Keeling and the handful of policemen inside the station had no way to escape.

Just then, a contingent of soldiers under a British officer arrived and dispersed the large violent mob. Keeling and the other policemen who were inside the station were rescued from what may well have turned into lynching by the mob. The deputy commissioner was, therefore, saved from meeting the same fate as the young British officer Everett, who had earlier in the afternoon been captured and lynched not too far away at Upper Kissy Road.

I did not personally witness these incidents. But the details were in the report of the commission of inquiry, which was set up by the government after these disturbances in Freetown. Particulars about the incident involving Keeling were also in one of the files at Special Branch headquarters.

However, a customs officer at the time, I did personally witness some of the rioting and looting that spread through Freetown on those two fateful days.

The Freetown riots were followed a few months later by very serious revolts in the protectorate. From 1955 to 1956, people, mainly in the northern province, were rising up against the chiefs. The revolts were centred mainly on Lokomasama Chiefdom.

Several casualties among police officers resulted from these riots as well. Those killed included three CID personnel who had smuggled themselves into a meeting organised by the rebels in Lokomasama Chiefdom. These policemen, who were young recruits fresh from the training school, wore plain clothes; but people in the crowd identified them. They were captured and brutally murdered, after which their bodies were dumped into a nearby river.

By early 1956, the disturbances in the protectorate were brought under control by the police force.

I can recall no other serious significant political upheavals in the country until after Sierra Leone had gained full independence in April 1961.

chapter 13

POST-INDEPENDENCE: TWO
~~STRUGGLING PARTIES~~

TRANSITION TO INDEPENDENCE IN 1961

The transition of Sierra Leone from a colony and protectorate of Britain to an independent nation on 27 April 1961 went smoothly. There was no insurgent movement preceding independence as in some former British colonies in Africa and in Asia. All government machinery, including the military and the police force, was headed by British expatriates. All of them continued to function as effectively as they had when the British colonial administration was in charge.

FIRST PRIME MINISTER

The first prime minister of independent Sierra Leone was Sir Milton Margai from Bonthe District. He was formerly a surgeon who became leader of one of the political parties, the Sierra Leone People's Party (SLPP) and, eventually, leader of the country. From the transition government consisting of Sierra Leoneans (1954 to 1961) through April 1961 when the country gained full independence, apart from minor problems, peace and tranquillity reigned in the country under Sir Milton Margai's leadership. Security and the economy were reasonably stable. There was not any haste to replace senior British administrators in the civil service, the police force, the judiciary branch, or the military with Sierra Leoneans (or to implement "Africanisation", as was the common term). Consequently, there were no subtle actions designed to discourage these British administrators and force them to retire. Many top British colonial civil servants remained after independence and served happily under Sierra Leonean ministers. Milton Margai's policies may best be described as "make haste slowly", and his cabinet might best be described as balanced. He appointed ministers based on his assessment of their abilities for the posts and, at the same time, focused on creating "national balance."

But by 1962, slight political tremors began to be felt, as a new political party emerged. The All Peoples Congress (APC) was led by Siaka Stevens, a charismatic and crafty politician who was also an ex-trade union leader. Siaka Stevens was formerly a minister under Dr Milton A.S. Margai's SLPP government before the country gained its independence. He was minister of mines and labour during the serious riots in Freetown in February 1955. But he soon lost his seat in Moyamba as result of an election petition against him. Consequently, Sir Milton removed him from the post of minister of mines and labour.

THE ALL PEOPLE'S CONGRESS (APC)

Either because Siaka Stevens was angry at being left out of the government or with a hidden motive, he then formed his own political party. From its inception, the APC was militant and prone to resorting to violence to achieve its aims. APC members mimicked Communist Party members in the Soviet Union, greeting one another as "comrade." The colour of the party was red, and its emblem was a red rising sun. But the similarity between APC members and practitioners of fundamental Communism ended with the greeting and colour choice. APC members did not seem to be motivated by any revolutionary zeal similar to that which brought the Communists in the Soviet Union to power after the 1917 Russian Revolution or the one that brought the Chinese Communists to power in 1949.

Those were days when the Cold War between the East, led by the Soviet Union, and the West, led by the United States of America, was very intense. Each side was struggling to gain spheres of influence with newly independent countries. Consequently, the Soviet Union encouraged several members of the APC to go and study in the Soviet Union. Also many young men and women who were not even members of the APC were awarded scholarships to study there. All these students were looked upon by the West as having been tainted by Communism. This actually was not the case. The Soviet Union was also very strongly suspected of giving clandestine financial support to the APC.

Siaka Stevens and his APC began to revolt against the policies of Dr Milton Margai. When Sierra Leone was about to be granted independence, Stevens vehemently opposed Margai, alleging that Sir Milton was selling the country to the British. He pointed to an addendum in the agreement granting the British access to her Royal naval vessels and the use of Freetown Harbour after independence. The opposition to the policies of Milton Margai that Stevens and his newly organised APC created was very strong.

As the granting of independence to Sierra Leone drew near, reliable information had it that APC members wanted to disrupt the process. Siaka Stevens and a few of the other leaders of the APC were detained at Pademba Road Prison just before the independence was granted on 27 April 1961. It should also be noted that, despite the fact that Sir Milton Margai had been in charge of what may be termed a transitional government before the granting of full independence to Sierra Leone, the British still had certain influence in the government. Governor Sir Maurice Dorman was British.

AGITATION FOR CHANGE: SECOND PRIME MINISTER

During Dr Margai's initial leadership as prime minister, some in both the government and the country as a whole were eager for rapid and fundamental changes and for Africanisation to be accelerated, as was being done in neighbouring Ghana under the revolutionary and charismatic leader Kwame Nkrumah. Among such impatient and overambitious persons were the younger elements in the SLPP. Gradually, growing agitations commenced among these younger elements for a more dynamic leader to replace Prime Minister Margai. In their myopic view, Dr Milton was not dynamic enough.

Overambition also encouraged the eagerness to replace Dr Margai. Foremost among the contenders within the SLPP was Albert Margai, a southerner who was the first lawyer from the protectorate and Dr Margai's younger brother. Another was Dr John Karefa-Smart, a young medical doctor who'd had some experience abroad in the World Health Organization. But whereas Dr Margai might have seemed to be leaning toward Dr Karefa-Smart as his shadow, it should nevertheless be noted that Dr Karefa-Smart's original roots were from the Northern Province. Albert Margai, on the other hand, was Mende and from the Southern Province. Most of the influential members in the SLPP were Mendes.

As the agitation for change continued within the SLPP, nature stepped in, and Dr Margai died suddenly in April 1964. His unexpected death was immediately accompanied by brief tremors within the governing SLPP, caused by the quiet but tense contest to fill the sudden vacancy in party leadership.

The contest was short, and Albert Margai eventually emerged victorious. After being selected as leader of the SLPP, Albert Margai became the second prime minister of the new nation, in accordance with the provisions of the then existing constitution of Sierra Leone. There were doubts in some circles as to whether or not his appointment as prime minister was constitutional. But these doubts soon gradually faded. Albert Margai seemed to command the support of many of the young elements within the SLPP. He quickly established his dominance in the party and as leader of the country.

Not too long after Albert Margai became prime minister, the country started to feel the effects of violent political tremors, which continued during the limited period of his leadership. These violent political tremors culminated in Sierra Leone's first military coup. This was to presage the political turmoil and instability that would engulf the country for more than thirty-five years and climax in the atrocious RUF rebel war from March 1991 to 2002.

In the mid-sixties Dr Kwame Nkrumah of Ghana was in the zenith of his revolutionary activities in Africa. His country was leading other African countries in revolutionary zeal. He had pioneered a republican and one-party democratic system of government in Ghana. He had also replaced almost all the former British administrators in the civil service and officers in the military and the police by Ghanaians. Other emerging leaders in Africa were desirous of following Nkrumah's examples. Albert Margai was one of them.

NEPOTISM, FAVOURITISM, AND CORRUPTION

One of the problems created by Albert Margai was his seeming haste to install his own tribesmen in top positions in the civil service, as well as in quasi-government organisations. Within a relatively short time after he became prime minister, he promoted several of his tribesmen in both these arenas, over officials of other tribes. Appointments included the establishment secretary, the secretary training and recruitment, the chief accountant of the Marketing Board, and several other official positions. It also happened that the head of the military, Brigadier David Lansana, was his own tribesman as well.

As for the police force, it was rumoured that secret plans were afoot for the first Sierra Leonean police commissioner, William Leigh – who had been appointed by Sir Milton Margai in 1963 following the departure of the last British expatriate commissioner, Anthony S. Keeling – was to be replaced by another tribesman of Albert Margai. But the ensuing political developments prevented him from completing his agenda.

Growing opposition to the SLPP

The policies of Albert Margai started to meet with serious opposition from several sectors in the country. Alleged widespread corruption, as well as nepotism and favouritism, gradually emerged in Albert Margai's government. Apart from the Creoles, who were seriously opposed to the policies of Albert Margai and his SLPP, the APC was also in the forefront of the opposition to Margai's policies. APC founder Siaka Stevens exploited to the fullest the growing discontent in the nation, as well as the Creoles' apprehension and strong opposition to the SLPP.

Effective propaganda of the APC

The propaganda machinery of the APC was, without a doubt, most effective. The party's newspaper *We Yone* carried almost daily news about alleged corrupt activities of the SLPP government under Albert Margai.

Another lawyer/politician was vehemently opposed to Albert Margai and his SLPP government. That person was a wily lawyer turned politician whose name was Cyril Rogers-Wright. Rogers-Wright had a newspaper called *Shekpendeh*, which was also involved in the publication of news exposing the corruption of Margai and the SLPP government. Together, he and Siaka Stevens tormented Sir Albert Margai, and consequently, Margai found his position in the government of the country most untenable.

Some of the allegations against Margai and the government were even supported by immutable and irrefutable documentary evidence. The APC, together Cyrus Rogers-Wright, thus became a thorn in the flesh of Albert Margai.

The APC used every method available to increase and fan the flames of widespread public discontent and opposition. The resentment felt towards the SLPP by a wide section of the public created for the APC a wide network of informants, who were happy to disclose information about all alleged dishonest and irregular activities by the leaders of the SLPP. Such informants included civil servants, employees in parastatals (quasi-government organisations), personnel in both the military and the police force, and also some civilians. Hardly any secret moves by the SLPP government would not eventually be leaked to the APC.

THE "INSURANCE POLICIES" OF SENIOR CIVIL SERVANTS

As a result of the precarious position in which the SLPP government found itself, several top civil servants took out what may be described as "insurance policies." They secretly registered in the APC. Somehow or the other, the membership list of the APC got to the Special Branch. Surprisingly, several senior civil servants, army and police officers, and other important persons were paying members of the APC.

This list was considered so delicate and sensitive that its existence was not revealed to Prime Minister Margai. It was feared that, if he were aware of the scale of disloyalty within the core of the civil service, he might be tempted to take drastic retaliatory measures, a situation that could well lead to a catastrophic outcome.

chapter 14

A Proposed New System of Government

POLITICAL UNEASINESS AND THE GATHERING STORM

The strong opposition against the SLPP and Albert Margai increased inexorably and rapidly in most parts of the country. Albert Margai's popularity continued to plummet. Uneasiness prevailed everywhere. Even the discipline and strong cohesion within the military the British had left behind started to crumble.

In April 1967, after only six years of independence from Britain, and following a series of serious political dissensions, this fledging and relatively peaceful country suddenly erupted into serious political upheavals, which culminated to the first military coup in the country. A counter-coup followed two days later. And in the following years, a series of coups would be followed by a vicious civil war that would last from March 1991 until 2002. As of this writing, Sierra Leone is still wracked with occasional political tremors.

Military coups had, up to 1967, been undreamt of in Sierra Leone. They were viewed as something that happened in South American countries. Little consideration was given to the possibility of a coup in Sierra Leone. But the sudden emergence of coups in Africa, first in Nigeria and then in Ghana, jolted many in Sierra Leone. The possibility of a military coup in Sierra Leone became a reality.

Meanwhile, the Special Branch received persistent intelligence about surreptitious and suspicious activities among certain officers in the military. Uneasiness followed. In the midst of this uneasiness, several officers in the military were arrested and detained for alleged subversive activities. Among those arrested and detained was a very senior and popular lieutenant colonel called John Bangura. He was not a Mende but a Temne from the Northern Province of the country. The uneasiness in the military, which at first had been imperceptible, now gradually became palpable. The uneasiness in the army was felt everywhere.

THE PROPOSED REPUBLICAN AND ONE-PARTY FORM OF GOVERNMENT

Oblivious to the gathering storm around his regime, Albert Margai, either in emulation of Ghanaian President Kwame Nkrumah or to fulfil his own wild ambitions – and also as a means of neutralising the gathering opposition to the SLPP – determined to force on the mostly reluctant citizens a republican and one-party system of government.

This unpopular proposal met with very serious opposition from many sections of the country headed by the Creoles. The APC, under the dynamic and charismatic leadership of Siaka Stevens, seriously exploited this determined and widespread opposition. The intention was to prevent it from being implemented and to expedite the downfall of Sir Albert Margai and the SLPP.

Margai still had a core of loyal supporters. In this group were his cronies, as well as some senior civil servants, most of whom were his own kith and kin and who he had promoted to senior positions over senior officials of other tribes. The exception to this group was one Tejan Kabba, a young civil servant and a Madingo by tribe, who rapidly gained favour with Albert Margai and emerged as the permanent secretary in the Ministry of Trade and Industry. He was a close confidant of Margai's, and thereby, he wielded considerable influence in the civil service. Several top civil servants were alleged to have been paying obeisance to Tejan Kabba on account of his special relationship with Margai.

There was widespread opposition to the proposed one-party republican government. Margai's unpopularity increased amongst the public. Despite these, Margai forced through parliament the initial stages of his proposals. But the constitution of Sierra Leone then required that, before such fundamental change could be made, Parliament had to be dissolved and a fresh general election held in order to obtain a new mandate from the citizens.

The widespread condemnation of Margai and other's alleged corrupt activities continued with unabated fury. And so did the tussle over the proposed republican, one-party constitution – with ever increasing acrimony.[8]

THE INEVITABILITY OF A FRESH GENERAL ELECTION

Prime Minister Albert Margai could not circumvent the very important safeguard in the constitution. He had no other option but to dissolve Parliament and call for a fresh general election. Presumably, his hope was that the SLPP would win, allowing him to reduce the powerful influence of Siaka Stevens. The election was eventually held in March 1967. The opposition parties headed by the more popular APC campaigned vigorously to get the public to reject the proposed system of government.

The APC capitalized on the widespread and serious opposition, especially by the Creoles in the Western Area. The Creoles saw the proposed one-party, republican constitution as a serious threat to the

---

[8] It is of interest to note that the republican, one-party system of government that APC leader Siaka Stevens so vehemently opposed was the very system he would later, as prime minister, manage to get the people to swallow in the form of a referendum, alleged to have been highly rigged. And he would do so by employing crafty and, more or less, violent methods.

When he was asked about this turnaround of fundamental policy, he was reported to have craftily explained that, in 1967, the people were not yet ready for a republican, one-party rule. During his regime, the people had become enlightened and, as they had acclaimed the system, they were ready for it!

dominant and powerful position they hitherto had held in the country. In addition, the alleged widespread corruption among ministers and senior civil servants was met with widespread disgust.

Indeed, never before had there been such intensive and tense political campaigning in Freetown and all over most of the country. It was like a fight between two bulls.

THE GENERAL ELECTION OF 1967

In Freetown and environs, the general election was conducted in a free and fair atmosphere. As far as I can remember, no serious attempt was made to prevent anyone from voting. Nor were any surreptitious attempts made to rig the elections in the Western Area of the country. During the election, Albert Margai himself went around some polling stations in Freetown to provide moral support to his supporters.

In Freetown, this 1967 election was unique. In the past, citizens of Freetown, particularly the Creoles, had manifested lukewarm interest in voting. Elections had hitherto been with considerable indifference. But this one was different. The fears over the intended imposition of a republican, one-party system of government, as well as the disgust with the alleged widespread corruption and nepotism, galvanised the majority of Creoles to put up very stiff opposition to the SLPP.

The voter turnout in Freetown during the election was unprecedented. So unpopular had the SLPP become and so serious were the apprehensions among Creoles of an SLPP victory that Creoles went out in unprecedented numbers to vote. In some polling stations around Freetown, old people were seen patiently awaiting their turn to cast their ballots.

Whatever were the accusations being made against Albert Margai, it was obvious that, as a lawyer, he respected the constitution. As far as was known, neither he nor his agents made any serious attempts to rig the election. Furthermore, the electorates were not openly prevented from voting, as would become the trademark of the civilian government that emerged later, when voters were subjected to various forms of intimidation. Armed thugs, who seemed like ferocious animals, manned polling stations, ready to attack anyone attempting to vote who was considered an opponent to the particular political party the thugs represented.

ELECTION RESULTS

As mentioned, the main opposition to the proposed republican, one-party system came from the Western Area, especially in Freetown. Substantial opposition was also brewing in the Northern Province. On the other hand, most people in the Southern and Eastern Provinces, though not unanimously, were diehard supporters of the SLPP and its policies.

The contests in the ensuing general election were very stiff and tense. The initial results released by the elections secretariat indicated a very close race between the SLPP and the APC. Eventually, the APC gained a thin edge over the ruling SLPP.

UNEASY DEVELOPMENTS

Reliable information from impeccable sources told of ominous and dangerous developments within a clique in the SLPP. This, to some of us in the Special Branch, did not seem to augur well for the peace and tranquillity in the entire country. Our anxieties increased daily. But all we could do was observe and keep our fingers crossed, hoping for the best. Unfortunately, as the situation was to evolve, what unfolded wasn't what was best for the country.

VICTORY SNATCHED FROM SIAKA STEVENS AND THE APC

The results of the general election of ordinary Members of Parliament, excluding the results of the general election of paramount chiefs, now showed that the APC had won by a slight edge over the SLPP. In accordance with the provisions of the constitution then, Governor General Sir Henry Lightfoot-Boston decided to swear-in as prime minister the leader of the political party that seemed to have carried the majority in Parliament. It was the view in certain quarters that the chiefs would traditionally support whatever party was in power.

Siaka Stevens, the leader of the APC, was, therefore, invited to the State House to be sworn in as the new prime minister. The news spread rapidly around Freetown. Large crowds of APC supporters, many dressed in red, swarmed the areas surrounding State House and the Cotton Tree, singing songs, dancing, and proclaiming victory. In an unprecedented display of ecstasy, some young men and women, many clad in red dresses, were seen rolling on the ground along Pademba Road in celebration of what was seen as victory for the APC. This was not hearsay; I personally saw these exuberant manifestations of ecstasy.

The over-joyous waiting crowds saw Siaka Stevens being driven into the State House compound accompanied by a few other APC leaders. The crowds erupted into loud bursts of applause, some singing religious songs and Negro spirituals, such as, "Oh, Oh Freedom". A substantial number of people in the exuberant crowd were Creoles. Everyone waited in high expectation for the eventual emergence of Siaka Stevens from the State House as the new prime minister. The Creoles who had given strong support to Siaka Stevens and the APC were not aware that the Negro spirituals they were joyously singing were the death knell of the Creoles under the rule of Siaka Stevens.

Meanwhile, the SLPP contended that swearing in anyone at that stage was unconstitutional. In their opinion, the results of the election were not yet complete. Election results of paramount chiefs were still being received at the election secretariat at Tower Hill, Freetown. This created a constitution toggle. One view was that the results of paramount chiefs' election had nothing to do with the results of the general election of ordinary members of Parliament. The other view held that the election would not be complete until all election results were published.

In the midst of the serious contention, Governor General, Sir Henry Lightfoot Boston, a Creole and a lawyer, apparently on the advice of some legal experts, decided it was within his constitutional powers to swear in Siaka Stevens as prime minister.

The swearing-in ceremony reportedly went ahead inside the State House. But there seemed an unusual delay in the emergence of the newly dubbed Prime Minister Siaka Stevens.

THE CEREMONY'S DRAMATIC HALT

It was reported that a company of soldiers under the leadership of a young lieutenant, Hinga Norman, of the Sierra Leone Military Forces, on orders of the army commander, Brigadier David Lansana, stormed into the room in the State House where the March 1967 swearing-in ceremony was being held. Lt Norman was reported to have commanded a halt to the ceremony.

The governor general, together with Siaka Stevens and all others present, were then placed under house arrest. But the huge crowds outside were, for the time being, oblivious to all these dramatic developments inside. Soldiers had blocked all the exits leading out of State House.

As the expected triumphant emergence of Prime Minister Stevens continued not to be forthcoming, uneasiness started growing among the crowds. They suspected that something was amiss. Some expressed serious concern for the safety of Siaka Stevens and his supporters inside.

chapter 15

FIRST MILITARY COUP

MILITARY INTERVENTION: FIRST MILITARY COUP IN SIERRA LEONE

Amid this suspense and quite surprisingly, the head of the military, Brigadier David Lansana, made a dramatic announcement over the national radio system. He contended that the results of the general election were not yet complete, as the final results for the election of paramount chiefs had not been announced. He argued that it was unconstitutional for the governor general to swear anyone in as prime minister until such results were in. Brig. Lansana declared the immediate imposition of martial law and the suspension of certain parts of the constitution until all the results of the general election were in. He ordered the dispersal of everyone from the streets.

Simultaneously following this announcement, detachments of soldiers started to disperse the large crowds of ecstatic citizens, who had, not long earlier, been in a celebratory mood. Gunshots rang out all around. But apparently, the soldiers were shooting into the air. Pandemonium broke loose, as the large and restive crowds scattered in panic in all directions. Many were dumbfounded and confused and refused to believe that, indeed, a military coup had been staged in Sierra Leone.

Certain aspects of this military intervention ought to be mentioned, although some may tend to disagree with them. It is doubtful whether it was Brig. Lansana who gave the direct order to halt the ceremony. He was a professional soldier who had, throughout his career, been well trained in the traditions of the British military. He had very high respect for British military tradition.

In addition, before the intervention, rumours had spread that some of the top SLPP leaders were determined to have the military step in if the opposition, APC, seemed to be winning the election. Additional rumours had it that, when eventually it seemed as if the SLPP had lost the election, though by a small margin, panic overcame certain militant female SLPP leaders and others. Some of the SLPP leaders had congregated in Flagstaff House[9], the official residence of the head of the Sierra Leone Military Forces, when the results of the election were being announced.

Some of the important SLPP leaders were alleged to have exerted great pressure on Brig. Lansana to have the army to intervene. According to these rumours, Lansana was reluctant to get the military involved in this unconstitutional activity. But he allegedly later succumbed to the extreme pressure. He was suspected to have consumed large quantities of alcohol and was allegedly under the influence of Bacchus when he announced the imposition of martial law, shortly after having sent Lt. Norman and a detachment of soldiers to the State House.

It is unfortunate that, after Siaka Stevens was eventually installed as prime minister, following the coup organised by junior ranks in the army in April 1968, he had Brig. Lansana extradited from Liberia. Lansana was arrested and charged with treason, found guilty, and sentenced to be executed. He was hanged at Pademba Road Prison.

---

[9] Flagstaff House at Hill Station was a large house that had been the official residence of the brigadier in charge of the army since colonial days. It was mysteriously destroyed by fire during the NRC government's regime.

COUNTER-COUP

An uneasy night prevailed, with frequent sporadic gunshots being heard around Freetown. This continued through the next day and the day after. No other announcements were made over the national radio, further increasing anxiety among citizens. All normal programs over the national radio were suspended. On the third day, martial music was heard over the national radio.

Sometime in the afternoon, the tense and uneasy atmosphere that had gripped the citizens was suddenly broken by an announcement over the national radio by Major Charles Blake. He announced that they the young military officers were not in favour of the action taken by Army Commander Brig. Lansana. Blake added that Lansana, together with Prime Minister Albert Margai and a few others had already been arrested and detained. He added that certain sections of the constitution had been suspended and that a curfew had been imposed throughout the country.

THE NATIONAL REFORMATION COUNCIL (NRC)

Blake stated further that an interim council called the National Reformation Council (NRC), comprised of a few senior military officers, as well as a few senior police officers, had been formed to govern the country as an interim measure. This seemed to ease the tension among citizens to a certain degree. Major Blake also announced that Lt. Colonel Ambrose Genda would be the chairman of the NRC in absentia and that Commissioner of Police L.W. Leigh would be the deputy chairman of the NRC.

After several days, Lt Colonel Genda, who was then abroad, did not arrive in Sierra Leone to head the NRC. The officers then invited Major Andrew Juxon-Smith, who was on a training course in Britain, return and head the NRC.

The NRC was composed mainly of senior military officers and included Major Andrew Juxon-Smith, Major Charles Blake, Major

Jumu, and several others. In addition to Commissioner, Leigh, the third in command of the police force was invited to join. The deputy commissioner of police at that time was a British expatriate officer named R.A.I. Nicholson. But for obvious reasons, he opted not to get involved in the emerging political situation. So the third in command, Alpha Kamara, who was then the most senior among the assistant commissioners of police was invited to join.

MAJOR ANDREW JUXON-SMITH

Major Andrew Juxon-Smith heeded the call of the other officers in the military. He returned to Sierra Leone from Britain after a few days and assumed chairmanship of the National Reformation Council.

Following the arrival of Major Juxon-Smith, the business of governing the country by the military started in earnest. Juxon-Smith demonstrated martinet discipline, as well as strong leadership. He tolerated no nonsense and no indiscipline. His initial rule brought signs of hope to a country that seemed to have been going astray under the previous civilian administration.

Within a relatively short time, he had jolted the majority of civil servants from their former complacency. He had made them more responsible agents of the people. He caused senior civil servants to adopt a more responsible attitude in their work, ensuring that they went to work on time and were appropriately dressed when on duty. He ensured offices were clean and tidy. He personally visited offices without prior warning, and the head of that department or the permanent secretary would be held personally responsible for any lateness of staff or dirty and filthy offices. Many government employees were, thus, jolted from their complacency.

COMMISSIONS OF INQUIRY

Within a relatively short time, Juxon-Smith and his NRC got the situation in the country under control. The NRC ruled by decrees.

Commissions of inquiry looked into various irregularities and dishonest practices that had allegedly been perpetrated during the leadership of Albert Margai by his ministers and others in position of authority. These commissions unearthed many gross irregularities and dishonest activities.

One of the commissions investigated alleged irregularities in the Sierra Leone Rice Corporation. The inquiry unearthed gross irregularities, both financial and otherwise, in the corporation's store at Kissy Dockyard. The storekeeper was found to be short several hundreds bags of rice. He could not give any satisfactory account how these bags of rice had gone missing from the warehouse. When he was pressured by the chairman for an explanation, the storekeeper gave the ludicrous explanation that the hundreds of bags of rice had been eaten by rats! The rats were so voracious that had eaten not only the rice but also the bags the rice was stored in. This response incited laughter among the audience.

Several other irregularities and dishonest activities were unearthed via Justice Beoku-Betts' commission of inquiry. As a result, he recommended the confiscation of the state properties of several leaders of the SLPP and other senior officials, as well as of the newly built SLPP headquarters building along Water Street (now Wallace Johnson Street).

Based on these recommendations of Justice Beoku-Betts, the chairman of one of the commissions of inquiry, the NRC government under Brig. Andrew Juxon-Smith ordered the confiscation to the state of the assets already mentioned. The fickle public in general acclaimed these disclosures as well as the confiscation of properties to the state.

Furthermore, as a compromise and in an effort to bring about tranquillity in the still restive military, the NRC released Col. John Bangura from detention and sent him away as Ambassador to the USA. Siaka Stevens was also released from prison but held under house arrest. Other actions were taken in an effort to neutralise simmering opposition and placate some of those who were adversely impacted by these developments until some practical compromise could be arrived at.

By any standard, and compared with the rule by the ousted Sierra Leone People's Party, the National Reformation Council ruled the country relatively well. The NRC brought sanity and discipline to the country and financial discipline to the government. They were able to suppress all open political activities for a time but not for long.

Juxon-Smith's genuine efforts to reform the country unfortunately earned him hatred by those who were adversely impacted by those efforts.

Furthermore, politicians who were eager to gain power that seemed to have been snatched from them resented his efforts. These politicians began to stir up opposition to his rule. Eventually, they succeeded in their diabolical plans. The country soon began to groan under the rule of the emerging government.

Brig. Andrew Juxon-Smith's time at the helm of the military government and the NRC lasted from March 1967 to April 1968. Some say he was arrogant, conceited, and power-hungry. I strongly disagree with the accusations against Juxon-Smith.

He was not present when the young officers led by Major Charles Blake overthrew Brig. David Lansana, who had just staged the first military coup in Sierra Leone with the suspected hidden intention of somehow or the enabling the SLPP to prolong its stay in power, despite the party having lost the general election to the APC. Furthermore, Juxon-Smith was not these officers' first choice after they had overthrown Lansana. Their first choice was Lt Colonel Ambrose Genda, who was then in Britain. But when several days had elapsed and Genda did not show up, the young officers then selected Major Juxon-Smith, who was also in Britain undergoing a course of study in the military. He heeded the call of the young officers, who were his professional colleagues, and returned to Sierra Leone to lead the NRC.

As for his supposedly being arrogant and conceited, well, it all depends on one's perception of the personality of another. Juxon-Smith was no more than a very strong disciplinarian who ruled with an iron fist. He was apparently overenthusiastic in seeing that discipline returned to Sierra Leoneans.

Some may also say that he was somewhat eccentric. Juxon-Smith was in no way an eccentric military officer. If that were the case, the British senior officers under whose tutelage he advanced would have detected the eccentricity in his character, and he would not have been promoted to a senior officer. Juxon-Smith, when he assumed command of the NRC and, with it, the government of the country, was genuinely enthusiastic about improving the country. He might have been considered overenthusiastic, and he may have used unorthodox methods in his enthusiasm to restore a country that seemed to have lost its sense of direction. But he was never eccentric; nor was he power-hungry.

All the positive reforms he implemented in the public service were, unfortunately. resented by those who were adversely impacted. They therefore branded him arrogant and conceited.

The actions of Juxon-Smith have now been vindicated by the desperate struggles by successive governments to restore the gradually crumbling rule of the country; the widespread indiscipline among students in colleges, as well as pupils in secondary and primary schools, and that in the civil service and in Sierra Leone society in general.

After his regime was overthrown, has Sierra Leone seen any substantial improvement in government of the country? What does Sierra Leone have to show as its achievements during over fifty years of independence from colonial rule?

It should also be noted that, when Juxon-Smith was chairman of the NRC, he did not cause any citizens to be executed on questionable criminal charges, as would be the hallmark of the emerging civilian and military governments.

Very soon, political activities began to rear their ugly heads. Clandestine and subversive activities suddenly became widespread.

The APC, which had been denied victory, allegedly began to engage in subversion clandestinely and to incite the junior ranks of the military to revolt. Concomitant to that, Special Branch personnel in the Northern Province received reliable information that several Sierra Leoneans, mainly from the Northern Province, were going to Guinea, where it was speculated they would join the APC members who had already escaped to that country. Information also had it that then Guinean President Shekou Toure was allegedly assisting APC leaders, allowing them to set up a base, where Sierra Leonean were being trained. Their purported goal was to attack the NRC and eventually take over the government by force, if the NRC was unwilling to hand it over peacefully to the APC.

Siaka Stevens, who was under house arrest in Freetown, reportedly pleaded with members of the NRC to be allowed to travel abroad on the pretext of obtaining urgent medical treatment. The NRC gave approval as a gesture of humanitarianism. Unfortunately, the members of the NRC were apparently naive and were deceived by the very crafty Siaka Stevens. The request was a subterfuge, allowing Stevens to flee the country and join the other members of the APC in Guinea, where they had sought refuge. The next thing anyone heard of Stevens, he was already in Guinea.

DEVELOPING OPPOSITION TO THE NRC

Despite all efforts by the NRC to placate the public, nefarious plans were being made by certain disgruntled political groups aimed at subverting the NRC. Civil servants who had been jolted by the stern action of Juxon-Smith resented his martinet discipline. Some saw his genuine efforts to rectify a country already adrift as a serious threat to their hitherto privileged positions. The flames of political embers were soon being blown to high intensity. Quite effective, scurrilous, and hostile propaganda against the NRC started emerging. There were agitations for the NRC to step down immediately and for power to be handed over to Siaka Stevens, the leader of the APC, who was viewed to have won the general elections and had already been sworn in as prime minister in March 1967. These destabilising activities rapidly increased. Serious but unfounded allegations of corrupt activities were secretly circulated against the leaders of the NRC.

The APC's insidious and forceful propaganda was effective. The public soon became disenchanted with the NRC. As public hostility against the NRC increased, so did public outcry for the handover of power to Stevens, the perceived winner of the general election.

SUBVERSIVE ACTIVITIES AGAINST THE NRC

Simultaneous to all this agitation against the NCR, intelligence flowing into the Special Branch pointed to the secret and heinous plans of certain politicians to ignite an insurrection in the army against the NRC. Subversive activities increased within both the military and the police force. Far more ominous were credible reports that some of the APC leaders who had sought refuge in neighbouring Guinea were planning revolutionary activities against the NRC. These included the alleged training of young men (and a few women) from Sierra Leone to attack Sierra Leone and oust the NRC by force if they did not quickly hand over power to the APC. Such reports from credible sources increased in the coming weeks.

Soon, news was received that Col. John Bangura had disappeared from his diplomatic post in the USA and was in Guinea, where he had joined the APC leaders already there.

As the one-year mark of NRC rule drew nearer, intelligence from impeccable sources disclosed subversive plots in the Sierra Leone Military. The loyalty of some personnel within both the military and the police force became seriously eroded.

Anonymous phone calls tipped police off about arms and ammunition being hidden in certain houses. The calls were deceptive, their intention to confuse the police force, compel officers to carry out searches of the houses of innocent citizens, and increase antagonism against the NRC.

At the same time, anonymous persons – suspected to be politicians – were circulating insidious and false propaganda about the extreme corruption NRC members. The propaganda falsely accused NRC members of amassing wealth and building several large houses.[10]

---

[10] The ridiculous propaganda claimed that Her Majesty the Queen of Britain had given £750.00 to each officer in both the army and the police force. But the alleged money, according to the propaganda, was not shared among the other ranks. At that time, even though Sierra Leone was an independent country, it was not yet a republic. The queen of Britain was still regarded as queen of Sierra Leone.

The queen could not have afforded to give such "gifts" to senior army and police officers in Sierra Leone. How this amount was arrived at, God only knows. Where had it ever been heard that the king or queen of Britain gave money to officers? They did not even give money to officers in the British military. Unfortunately, gullible soldiers and policemen believed such trash.

The insidious propaganda eventually turned against the emerging politicians who assumed power after the NRC had been ousted from power. In due course, it became evident that they were corrupt and lacked any sense of patriotism. This revelation would result in the public outcry that eventually climaxed in the student revolution against the APC in 1977. As of this writing, the country still suffers from the evil effects of the government policies that emerged immediately after the overthrow of the NRC.

Chapter 16

COUNTER-COUP

_____

MUTINY AND MASS ARRESTS OF SENIOR OFFICERS

April 1968 arrived. For some of us in the Special Branch, the intelligence being received almost daily was unnerving. Various reliable reports indicated that the plans for the final overthrow of the NRC were being finalised. This prospect was no pleasure to some of us. Our thoughts were directed toward self-survival – in other words, toward what actions we could take to escape the approaching doom. Eerie reports told of a two-fold plan of action by the APC dissidents in Guinea under the leadership of Siaka Stevens and others. First, the military would be incited to revolt against the NRC. The second and more ominous plan involved with would have if the NRC resisted and the planned mutiny failed. Then bands of young men (and even a few women) already trained in Guinea as guerrillas would enter Sierra Leone to overthrow the NRC by force and to kill members of the NRC as well as their supporters.

Fortunately for some of us and for Sierra Leone as a whole, when the military revolted on the night of 17 April 1968, the NRC put up no resistance. Within a very short time that night, the junior ranks of both the military and the police force had seized control and arrested many of their senior officers. Those arrested included the Chairman

Andrew Juxon-Smith, Deputy Chairman Police Commissioner William Leigh, Col. Charles Blake, and many other senior military and police officers. I was among the senior police officers who were arrested. In the following days, many more officers, both in the army and in the police force, were arrested and detained at the maximum security prison at Pademba Road.

THE ANTI-CORRUPTION REVOLUTIONARY COUNCIL

I understand that, immediately after the senior officers in both the army and the police force had been arrested and detained, the junior ranks set up what they called the Anti-Corruption Revolutionary Council (ACRC). A Sergeant Kengeyeh of the army was appointed the chairman of this council. The council accused the senior officers they had detained of corruption. The hidden hand of the APC was behind all this. The junior officers who were then in control were being effectively manipulated by some of the APC leaders.

SIAKA STEVENS INSTALLED AS PRIME MINISTER

A few days after this mutiny had commenced, Siaka Stevens, who was then in the neighbouring republic of Guinea, was invited by the ACRC members to return to Sierra Leone. On his return, he was reinstalled as prime minister and the ACRC members quickly stepped aside.

The new government then appointed Malcolm Parker as the interim commissioner of police and Tinga Sesay as the interim deputy commissioner.

After Parker had been commissioner for about a year, he went on retirement and was replaced by Jenkins Smith, who had previously been deputy commissioner before he was arrested and detained together with other senior police officers in April 1968.

After four months in detention, most of the army and police officers were released.

After retiring from the police force, Malcolm Parker was ordained as a priest in the Anglican Church. He served as priest in the St George's Cathedral, Freetown, for many years until his death.

FATE OF THE MEMBERS OF THE FORMER NRC

The members of the former National Reformation Council were kept in detention and subsequently charged with high treason. They were convicted in the High Court and sentenced to death. But following appeals in the Supreme Court, they were set free. After being set free, Brig. Andrew Juxon-Smith travelled to the United States of America, where he reportedly joined a religious group. He died there after few years. Leslie William Leigh, ex-commissioner of police travelled to Liberia, where he was reported to have been appointed an adviser to the Liberian Police Force. He died during the coup by Samuel Doe in 1980, in unknown circumstances. Charles Blake was employed as chief security officer at the Sierra Leone Produce Marketing Board. He died several years later.

When the mutiny commenced on the night of 17 April 1968, Major Jumu, also an NRC member eluded capture and escaped. He later sought refuge in Ghana, where he remained for long. I do not know what was his eventual fate.

The fate of the other NRC members has now become blurry in my memory.

chapter 17

SIMMERING DISCONTENT

─────────────────████████████████████─────────────────

CHALLENGE TO THE APC GOVERNMENT

During the early years of the APC, Karefa-Smart, a former SLLP member, formed his own party. Smart had vied against Albert Margai for leadership of the SLPP following the sudden death of Prime Minister M.A.S. Margai. He called this new party the United Democratic Party (UDP). The UDP attracted many members, mainly from Sierra Leone's Northern Province.

The UDP put up very serious opposition to the APC. Under the leadership of John Karefa-Smart, the UDP made the APC very uncomfortable. After a few years, the crafty Siaka Stevens was able to neutralise the very strong opposition of the UDP.

TREMORS WITHIN THE APC

In April 1971, there was an abortive coup against Siaka Stevens, during which a determined attempt was made to assassinate him. He eluded his attackers with the help of loyal members of the Internal Security Unit (ISU). Stevens escaped to neighbouring Guinea.

A few days later, he returned to Sierra Leone on board a Guinean military helicopter under the escort of a strong contingent of Guinean soldiers, who were accompanied by tanks and armoured cars and protected by Guinean jet fighters. Siaka Stevens was reinstated as prime minister. Brig. John Bangura, who it was alleged was the primary leader of the abortive coup, was arrested, together with other military officers. They were charged with high treason, found guilty, and sentenced to death by hanging. Brig. John Bangura was subsequently executed by hanging. The other conspirators were given sentences of many years imprisonment.

After this very serious attempt on the life of Prime Minister Siaka Stevens and his return to Sierra Leone, he seemed rather distrustful of Sierra Leone's army. Thus, he retained a sizeable number of heavily armed Guinean security personnel. They served as his security guards for about a year. During this period, no Sierra Leonean soldiers were seen as part of Stevens's security entourage. Only selected personnel of the ISU were permitted to be around him and only under the very watchful eyes of the Guinean security personnel.

IBRAHIM TAQI AND OTHERS ARRESTED
AND CHARGED WITH HIGH TREASON

Another individual who had been among the foremost leaders in the APC during its early days and who had been instrumental in bringing Siaka Stevens to power later fell out with him. After having helped bring the APC to power, Ibrahim Taqi was appointed minister of information and broadcasting. But he reportedly started to encounter fundamental differences with Siaka Stevens.

Eventually Taqi, as well as Dr Mohamed Fornah, the finance minister, and others were alleged to have been plotting against the APC. Taqi, Fornah, and a few others were arrested and charged with high treason. They were tried in the High Court, where they were found guilty and sentenced to death by hanging. They were consequently executed by hanging at Pademba Road Prison.

"NO COLLEGE, NO SCHOOL": THE
STUDENT REVOLUTION OF 1977

Hitherto, discontentment had been simmering among the public, including students of Fourah Bay College (FBC). The APC government was allegedly propagating corruption, mismanagement, and suppression. Clamours for reforms gradually arose among both the public and the students. At the forefront of the movement were militant members of the Fourah Bay College Students Union. All these goings-on were being reported by Special Branch to government through the president. But no positive action was taken to address the alleged grievances. Rather, the president and other top leaders of the government seemed to depend on the unreliable information of private informants, who in general did not report the actual facts but, instead, reported what would be sweet to the ears of the president and his able lieutenants.

For several weeks, intelligence from impeccable sources warned that the executive members of the Fourah Bay College Students Union under the chairmanship of Hindolo Trye were secretly planning a demonstration, to be staged when President Siaka Stevens arrived at the college for its annual convocation. The week before the convocation, union members were reliably reported to be printing placards that would be displayed during the demonstration. This was reported to the president in the daily intelligence reports.

Rather than taking action to neutralise the planned demonstration, the president questioned the accuracy of the Special Branch reports and ordered that the alleged intended action be further investigated.

DEMONSTRATION BY FBC STUDENTS

The president, who was the dean of the college, his entourage, and the usual invitees (diplomats and other important persons) converged at Fourah Bay College in the afternoon of Saturday 29 January 1977 to witness this important annual event of the oldest university in Sierra Leone.

During the president's address, the convocation ceremony was disrupted. Students shouted out against him and displayed placards with inflammatory slogans. Soon, they were hurling rocks and other missiles at the president and other VIPs at the ceremony.

Special Branch personnel at the campus reported that the president, the vice president, and other dignitaries were having difficulty escaping the belligerent students and ensuing chaos that had erupted.

Later on that afternoon, Commissioner of Police Kaetu-Smith, who had earlier accompanied President Stevens to the convocation, summoned me and a few other officers to his office at police headquarters and narrated what had happened. He added that the president was very annoyed, and it appeared as if heads might roll. I calmly reminded the commissioner of the series of reports that had indicated the restiveness and simmering discontent among students, as well as the latest reports that had positively revealed the intention of FBC students to demonstrate during the convocation. I added that, if the government did not take any action beforehand to forestall the intended demonstration, then there was nothing else that could have been done at our own level to stop it. Commissioner Kaetu-Smith advised us to be on alert for any further developments.

RUMOURS OF COUNTER-DEMONSTRATION AGAINST FBC STUDENTS

On Sunday morning, 30 January 1977, the commissioner summoned all heads of police formations in Freetown to an urgent meeting at police headquarters.

The commissioner disclosed that he had received information on the alleged intention of members of the youth section of the APC to stage a counter-demonstration against FBC students on the next day, Monday, 31 January.

We discussed the potential threats of violence if the alleged proposed counter-demonstration went ahead. It was decided that all of us senior police officers present at the meeting should go to the president to advise him. Deputy Commissioner Gbassay Kamara (alias Kornie Karta) cleverly and tactfully excluded himself from the group of officers that was to see the president, on the pretext that he would remain at police headquarters to make decisions on reports of any disturbances that might likely erupt that Sunday while we were at the president's residence.

DELEGATION OF SENIOR POLICE OFFICERS TO PRESIDENT STEVENS

The delegation of senior police officers went to visit with President Siaka Stevens at his residence at 1 King Harman Road, Brookfields. The commissioner of police, on behalf of all of us, in as diplomatic a manner as possible, apologised for the embarrassment the president had encountered at the hands of the students the previous day. The commissioner pledged the loyalty of the police force and all senior officers. He reassured the president of our determination to deal firmly with any further disturbances by the students. He tried to discourage the president from permitting the alleged counter-demonstration to take place. He also reassured the president of the capability of the police force to deal with any further disturbances by Fourah Bay College students.

PRESIDENT ADAMANT ON COUNTER-DEMONSTRATION

President Stevens would hear none of the commissioner's pleas. Nor would he listen to the assurance that he could leave matters in the hands of the police. President Stevens responded in his usual crafty way that the APC youths were not going in any aggressive manner. Nor did they intend to fight against the FBC students. Rather, they were simply going to the campus to indicate to the students that they, the APC youths, were disgusted with the demonstration by the students. Stevens reiterated that the APC youths were not going to fight with FBC students.

To add to the already delicate situation, that Sunday morning, the Rev. Dr Leslie E.T. Shyllon had delivered a fiery sermon against corruption in one of the churches in Freetown.

President Stevens was visibly enraged as he referenced the sermon. Turning to me in particular, he said, his tone menacing, "Coker, go tell your Creole people that any incitement of the populace to revolt against the government will backfire and that, in due course, when the provincials dominate the political scene, they are not going to look on the so-called 'superior education' that the Creoles profess to have." He went on to say that they (the provincials) would place their own provincial brothers in senior positions "irrespective of the perceived superior education and enlightenment of the Creoles."

President Stevens was prophetic in this respect. The other Creole officer present at the meeting with myself was Chris Thomas, the chief police officer in the Western Area Division. On hearing the pronouncements of the President, Chris Thomas, who was standing near me, quietly nudged me.

It was quite obvious that President Stevens was in no mood for compromise. We took our leave and returned to police headquarters with heavy hearts. We knew that very serious problems would confront us the next morning. We therefore made plans to maintain law and order for whatever would be the consequences of the APC youths' intended action the next day.

chapter 18

WIDESPREAD RIOTS AND LOOTING
AND THE END OF A REVOLT

COUNTER-DEMONSTRATORS ASSEMBLE

Early Monday morning, 31 January 1977, all senior police officers went to their respective formations to ensure that personnel were deployed to take appropriate action on whatever might be the consequences of the APC youths' trip to Fourah Bay College.

By 7.00 a.m., I was in my office at Special Branch headquarters when I learnt from some of the personnel deployed around Freetown and up at the college that truckloads of APC vigilantes were already on their way to Fourah Bay College campus.

SKIRMISHES BETWEEN FBC STUDENTS
AND COUNTER-DEMONSTRATORS

We received reports that some FBC students were already deployed in tactical positions around the campus up at Mount Aureol. They were reportedly throwing rocks and other missiles at the truckloads of rowdy and belligerent APC youths who were approaching the college campus.

Several minutes later, reports of running battles between some of the students and the APC vigilantes who had by then overrun the college campus came in.

DEMONSTRATIONS SPREAD AMONG OTHER STUDENTS IN FREETOWN, FOLLOWED BY RIOTING AND LOOTING

Demonstrations broke out at Brotherhood Secondary School, not too far from Albert Academy. Students were shouting, "No college, no school." Almost simultaneously, we received reports that students of other schools around Freetown were shouting the same slogan. From Tuesday, Freetown was the scene of riots and looting.

During the evening I went to the president's residence at Kingharman Road to brief him on the current situation. I met the president in a pensive mood. Commissioner of Police Kaetu-Smith and several women were also met with the president.

President Stevens seemed to be seriously pondering the next steps to resolve the situation. While I was in the president's compound at Brookfields, about a mile from downtown Freetown, I saw flares being fired in the sky over downtown Freetown. The women and several others who had congregated inside the compound also saw the flares.

Some of the women started wailing, saying that rebels had invaded the city. They became hysterical, urging the president to do something. A few minutes later, some youths in the residence emerged. They were agitated and armed with light machine guns and saying that they were going to confront the alleged rebels.

PRESIDENT REGAINS CONTROL AND ACTS RESOLUTELY

Throughout all this President Stevens had remained pensive. He appeared to be considering what should be done to get the delicate situation under control.

Seeing the youths and hearing what they had to say seemed to galvanise him to action. As if jolted, President Stevens sprung from his hitherto ponderous mood and, uttering expletives, he firmly ordered the youths to put down their weapons and stay at home. The president then turned to the hysterical women and addressed them with similar expletives, saying that they should shut up and keep calm. Turning to Kaetu-Smith, President Stevens ordered him as commander of the police to go down to his headquarters and take control of the situation. This moment, though spontaneous, was one that showed President Siaka Stevens at his best.

What started as a local event at Fourah Bay College on 29 January 1977 had transformed to a critical national event in less than a week. The short and volatile situation nearly resulted in the overthrow of Stevens and the current APC government.

DEMANDS BY FOURAH BAY COLLEGE STUDENTS

The executive officials of the Fourah Bay College Students Union had made several demands to the government, including changing the name of the Internal Security Unit (ISU), the withdrawal of the weapons from the ISU, and that a fresh general election be held throughout the entire country.

To give the students a semblance of appearing to agree to some of their demands, President Stevens reluctantly but cleverly consented to one of the least controversial demands of the students—that the name ISU be renamed. This was a tactical move, hoped to placate the students.

As for the demand that ISU personnel no longer carry weapons, neither the president nor the senior police officers agreed to this. It was felt that the students had gone too far with their demands.

A few days later, calm returned to the country. Thus ended one of the most desperate students revolts in Sierra Leone – a revolt that was, at points, on the brink of overthrowing the APC and Stevens.

Though the student revolution of 1977 failed in many respects, it laid the foundation for revolutionary activities that culminated in a far worse revolt fifteen years later. The rebellious war of the RUF, termed the Sierra Leone Civil War, started in March 1991.

During the next seven years, the country remained relatively peaceful. In 1984, President Stevens got the army commander, Major General Joseph Saidu Momoh, elected as chairman for the All Peoples Congress.

A few months later, general elections were held. Major General J.S. Momoh was elected as president of Sierra Leone. President Stevens resigned and went on retirement after being in power for sixteen years.

chapter 19

THE "REVOLUTIONARIES" OF THE CIVIL WAR

ABORTIVE COUP AGAINST PRESIDENT MAJOR GENERAL J.S. MOMOH

In March 1987, a coup plot against President Momoh was unearthed. Some of the conspirators included a senior police officer named G.M.T. Kaikai and Vice President Francis Minah. Together with other conspirators, both were arrested and charged in the High Court. Kaikai and Minah were found guilty and sentenced to death by hanging. They were hanged at Pademba Road Prison.

The country continued to be rocked by political instability. Despite the evidence of this instability, President Momoh and members of his Limba tribal group, "The Akutay", spent their time enjoying themselves at the president's chateau. The chateau was located in his home town, Binkoloh, in the Northern Province, and many cronies joined him there regularly.

THE REBELS OF THE REVOLUTIONARY UNITED FRONT (RUF) AND THE SIERRA LEONE CIVIL WAR

President Momoh did not seem to take the threats to his country and power seriously. Meanwhile an ex-army corporal named Foday

Sankoh collected a few unemployed Sierra Leonean youths who were in Liberia and formed a group that he named the Revolutionary United Front (RUF). In March 1991, the RUF launched an attack on a small town called Bomaru in the extreme eastern part of Sierra Leone.

This attack seemed like a minor affair. There were casualties among a few of the Sierra Leone soldiers. But this was concealed from the public in Sierra Leone. The government announced that the incident was a minor dispute between Sierra Leonean soldiers based in Bomaru and some Liberian soldiers.

This incident was to become the commencement of the worst political upheaval in Sierra Leone. Hideous brutalities would be perpetrated on hapless citizens and the country's infrastructure would be destroyed.

Foday Sankoh claimed that he was only fighting to free the country from the allegedly corrupt APC government under President Joseph Momoh leadership.

This civil war also saw a very large displacement of the country's population – primarily from rural areas of Sierra Leone to Freetown.

The war, which raged for eleven years from 1991 to 2002, seriously affected the nation's psyche. It is necessary to know something about RUF head Foday Sankoh to understand how and why this destructive war started and continued for so long, as well as its calamitous effects on the nation.

Sankoh was formerly a corporal in the army. But he was implicated in an abortive coup against President Siaka Stevens in 1971. Sankoh was arrested, together with the other alleged conspirators. They were tried, and some who were found guilty were sentenced to death by hanging. Sankoh managed to escape the gallows because the evidence against him was not substantial to justify a death sentence. Nevertheless, he was found guilty and sentenced to imprisonment for many years.

On his release from prison, he engaged in photography in Kenema and Bo. It is not known whether the military intelligence or the Special Branch kept an eye on him after his release from prison.

But somehow or another, he reportedly went to Libya, where he was alleged to have received training in guerrilla warfare. After his training, he went to Liberia. His activities there were not known. But he was suspected to have been in touch with revolutionary leader Charles Taylor, a charismatic person who had started a revolutionary war against the Liberian government.

I do not know the extent of Sankoh's liaison with Taylor. But it appeared to have been a close liaison, and it also seemed that Taylor wanted to use Sankoh to gain access to Sierra Leonean diamonds in Kono. Whether or not Sankoh was ordered or cajoled by Charles Taylor to commence a civil war in Sierra Leone remain unclear.

What is clear, however, is that after Sankoh returned to Liberia after his training in Libya, he collected a few jobless Sierra Leone boys in Liberia and formed a ragtag army that would become the RUF. He then launched his initial attack on Sierra Leone on March 1991 in a small town called Bomaru in Kailahun District in the eastern part of the country on Liberian border.

Taylor was alleged to have given Sankoh a lot of support, even providing some of his own boys to fight alongside Sankoh's ragtag army. The presence of these extra fighters was discerned when residents in the overrun areas reported that some of the rebels spoke English with a Liberian accent. Some of the RUF rebels were even suspected to be from Burkina Faso.

The Sierra Leone Army at first underestimated the potential strength of the demonic force that confronted them. And the APC government, then under former Major General Joseph Saidu Momoh, treated the emerging affair with levity.

Momoh had been the commander of the Sierra Leone Army before he was handpicked by President Stevens and "transplanted" as president. Whether or not President Siaka Stevens "transplanted" Momoh in the country as President in place of him was not known.

President Momoh turned out to be an inept leader. His government was riddled with corruption. He was surrounded by cronies from his own tribe. Instead of concentrating on this enormous attack on the country, he and other members of his tribal cabal, the Akutay, preferred weekly merrymaking at a chateau in his home town, Binkolo, in the northern part of the country.

The pretext that Sankoh gave as the cause for having launched the Sierra Leone Civil War was that he wanted to rid the country of the suppressive, incompetent, and corrupt APC government. But as it turned out, rather than venting his anger on the APC government and its supporters, Sankoh instead turned his revenge against the hapless citizens of Sierra Leone, including innocent children.

The APC government, under President Momoh, neglected to take prompt and resolute action to nip the problem in the bud. Neither Momoh nor his cabinet made comprehensive plans to confront the RUF rebels under Sankoh's leadership.

President Momoh and his cabinet intentionally refused to inform Sierra Leoneans that the incident was a serious affair. Nor did they share that the rebels were, for the most part, Sierra Leoneans, who were far better armed – bearing AK-47 rifles and other sophisticated modern weapons – than were the Sierra Leonean soldiers based in Kailahun.

The Sierra Leonean soldiers were armed only with obsolete and inferior weapons of Second World War vintage. Furthermore, they were not being supplied with adequate food. These Sierra Leonean soldiers were reported to have been compelled to forage for food in surrounding villages. In addition, the soldiers were not being paid regularly.

The circumstances resulted in a very low morale among the Sierra Leonean government soldiers. They suffered heavy casualties during the determined and vicious attacks of the RUF rebels. Consequently, the RUF rebels met only minor resistance. They were thus able to advance rapidly throughout Sierra Leone.

The rebels first concentrated their major attacks on Kono, the main diamond area. After they had captured Kono, they began digging for diamonds, which were then reportedly sold to Charles Taylor, who in turn supplied the rebels with modern weapons.

The RUF rebels were also joined by some jobless youths in Sierra Leone. These young people joined the bandwagon of the RUF and, with them, vented their anger on innocent civilians.

In revolutionary warfare, it is the intention of the revolutionaries to overthrow the government in power because of some real or perceived fault by that government. So the revolutionaries concentrate their forces on defeating the government forces by attacking the main installations and supporters of the government. Consequently, it is the government soldiers, as well government supporters, who are the main targets of the revolutionary forces.

There has never been a "clean" war. Innocent civilians inevitably become casualties in all wars. Collateral damages to the infrastructure of a country at war are inevitable. But in the case of the Sierra Leone Civil War, perpetrated by the RUF, the rebel forces specifically targeted hapless civilians and committed countless atrocities and horrendous and hideous brutalities on men and women and even children and babies.

In some cases, the RUF rebels were reported to have locked people in their houses and set the houses on fire, leaving the victims to die a horrible death. The other trademark of the RUF rebels was the amputation of the limbs of civilians. The rebel forces perpetrated other forms of hideous atrocities.

chapter 20

THE LONG, BLOODY ROAD TO PEACE

ARMY OFFICERS' COUP AGAINST PRESIDENT JOSEPH MOMOH

The terrible conditions under which the Sierra Leonean soldiers live compelled some of the officers to leave their posts and come to Freetown, ostensibly to explain to their commander-in-chief (the president) the very serious conditions on the front lines. But President Momoh turned out to be only a paper tiger and fled. He sought refuge in neighbouring Guinea, rather than face the music.

In consequence, the young officers had no option but to assume power in place of their former commander-in-chief. This eventually resulted to a military coup against President Momoh and his APC government. The young military officers hastily formed the National Provisional Ruling Council (NPRC) and selected Captain Valentine Strasser to be their leader and to head the government.

With the emergence of the NPRC government, the hitherto rapid advance of the seemingly invincible RUF rebels was blunted. Modern weapons were supplied the troops and fresh life given to them. In addition, the NPRC government contracted with a South African commercial mercenary military organisation, the Executive Outcomes, to pursue the war against the RUF rebels. This mercenary organisation brought into the country modern and sophisticated weapons, which they deployed against the rebels.

The Executive Outcomes halted the rebels' rapid advance throughout the country. But after a short period, the Executive Outcomes disappeared from the scene. Several rumours floated around about why they left. But I had no reliable knowledge of the circumstance that resulted in their pulling out of the country.

The NPRC turned to another mercenary group. This group consisted mainly of the famed Gurkhas but was under the leadership of American mercenary officers. The formidable RUF was reported to have mounted a successful ambush against a unit of these Gurkhas in Mile 91 or thereabouts and killed a substantial number of these troops, as well as one of their American officers. A Sierra Leonean officer who was acting as liaison officer between the Gurkhas and the NPRC, along with a few Sierra Leonean soldiers, was also killed in this military debacle. After this catastrophe for the Gurkhas, they also quietly disappeared from the scene.

Meanwhile, whilst the rebel war waged on with unabated fury, some overambitious politicians were agitating for a general election to be held to reinstate a civilian government.

Sankoh and his rebels, full of confidence and emboldened by their recent success against mercenary troops, continued the fighting with undiminished vigour and moved forward their determined advance against government forces.

Eventually, a palace coup in the NPRC resulted in Valentine Strasser being overthrown. His deputy, Maada Bio, who was responsible for the coup, said as a pretext for his actions that Strasser had not wanted to hold the general election for the reinstatement of a civilian government. Bio installed himself as head of government.

Negotiations with Sankoh were underway. But the arrogant and overconfident leader of the rebel forces had, by then, become very powerful. And he also became intransigent. He stalled, and the war continued.

GENERAL ELECTION

In view of Sankoh's intransigence, detachments of ECOMOG forces[11] were brought into the country in an effort to stop the civil war. But still the war continued. Desperate efforts were made to hold a general election. But this brought about a tussle between two groups. One group held that, as substantial parts of the country were under RUF control, the general election should be postponed until peace had been restored throughout the entire country. This group's slogan was "Peace before Election."

The opposing group held a vague suspicion that the NPRC military government wanted to prolong the war in order to hold on to power. Therefore, this group agitated for the general election to be held immediately in the areas not under RUF control. "Election before Peace" was their slogan.

In all such differences in human opinion, one group will win. But that does not mean that the group that wins will, in the end, prove to be right. In the ensuing tense tussle between the two groups – one of which was headed by James Jonah, a former Sierra Leonean senior UN official, who suddenly emerged like a comet on the political scene in Sierra Leone – the Election before Peace campaign won. Consequently, a general election was held under a scheme known as proportional representation, which Jonah strongly advocated.

Dr Karefa-Smart had been struggling to become prime minister/president since the sixties under the SLPP. He would later form his own party, United Democratic Party (UDP). He now formed a new political party, United National Democratic Party (UNDP).

Several political parties participated in this general election, including the UNDP and the RUF, which had by then metamorphosed into a peaceful political party. Each of the political parties put forward candidates for the post of president. The primary contestants were the SLPP's Tejan Kabbah and Karefa-Smart of the UNDP. In an effort to

---

[11] ECOMOG, Economic Community of West African States Monitoring Group, was a multilateral armed force of West Africa that arranged for separate armies to work together.

bring peace to the country and as a show of chivalry, Tejan Kabbah and Karefa-Smart were seen together driving around Freetown in an open car.

THE ELECTION OF PRESIDENT AHMAD TEJAN KABBAH

Ahmad Tejan Kabbah and the SLPP won the general election, and he was installed as president of Sierra Leone. Tejan Kabbah continued negotiating with the intransigent Foday Sankoh. Peace for the entire country became elusive.

Tejan Kabbah made several major blunders. When he assumed office, he was reported to have surrounded himself with only Nigerian soldiers and security personnel. Sierra Leonean soldiers resented this apparent snub by their own president.

This and some other grievances resulted in yet another alleged military plot. This one was discovered before the conspirators could carry out their diabolical plans. Several army personnel were arrested in connection with the alleged plot. Among them was Major Johnny Paul Koroma. They were detained at Pademba Road Prison, pending investigation into the alleged plot to overthrow the government of President Tejan Kabbah.

As a further snub to Sierra Leonean military officers and police officers, rather than using local investigators, Tejan Kabbah employed Nigerian senior military officers to go to Freetown to investigate the alleged coup plot. On arrival, these Nigerian military officers allegedly became rather arrogant. Their comportment was resented by Sierra Leonean army officers.

Later on, when asked why he had sent for Nigerian military officers to investigate the alleged coup plot in his own military, Tejan-Kabba replied that the initiative had not come from him. Rather, it was the Nigerian president himself who, in sympathy, had offered the help.

Nigerian soldiers had played a very important role in the fighting to protect Sierra Leone from the RUF rebels. Nigerian soldiers fought bravely against the rebel forces. Some Nigerian soldiers were brutally killed during the fighting. Indeed, Nigerian soldiers had played a very important role in the defence of Sierra Leone when the country was facing a grave crisis never witnessed before.

Nevertheless, as far as President Tejan Kabbah was concerned, it seemed he was under the spell and domination of the Nigerian president, to whom Tejan Kabbah would run in order to seek advice. He therefore appeared to have become a sycophant to the Nigerian president.

Shortly after he had become president, Tejan Kabbah set up a small commission of inquiry under the chairmanship of Dr Sama Banya to investigate the cause of the drop in the efficiency and effectiveness of the Sierra Leone Police Force. Many of us who had retired were glad at this move by the newly elected president. Some members of the Sierra Leone Ex-Senior Police Officers Association, including myself, gave evidence at this one-man commission of inquiry.

After all the relevant facts had been collected, Dr Banya compiled a comprehensive report containing his recommendations and submitted the report to the president. When several weeks had elapsed and nothing was heard from the president, discreet enquiry revealed that Tejan Kabbah had sent the report to the Nigerian president for his views. Nothing further was heard about this report, and absolutely no action was taken in terms of implementing Dr Banya's recommendations.

In addition, Tejan Kabbah changed the name of Kissy Street in Freetown to Sanni Abacha Street.

The president was also alleged to have been treating lightly intelligence affecting the security of the country. It was reported that, rather than taking immediate necessary action to forestall such security threats, upon receiving the intelligence, he would express grave doubts about the reliability of the reports.

Furthermore, during the RUF rebel war, President Tejan Kabbah was reported to have disbanded an appreciable number of the Sierra Leone Army and caused many army officers to be court-martialled for their alleged role in committing treason. Rather than getting senior Sierra Leonean officers to sit in the court martial, President Tejan Kabbah was reported to have sent for Nigerian senior army officers to preside. The subsequent court martial convicted some twenty-four Sierra Leonean officers, including a female colonel, who the Nigerian officers had found guilty. These Sierra Leonean army officers were then reported to have been executed by a firing squad, which consisted mainly of Nigerian soldiers.

The other soldiers of the Sierra Leone Army who had been disbanded regrouped and formed a new organisation, the Westside Boys.

The relentless advance by the RUF rebels all over the country could not be halted. The RUF rebels recruited children as soldiers, indoctrinating them and giving them drugs. When high on drugs, these child soldiers were sent to perpetrate heinous atrocities on even their own parents.

Owing to the relentless and determined advance of the RUF rebels against Sierra Leonean government forces, a special group known as Karmajors was called upon to help in the fight against the rebel forces. The Karmajors were originally peaceful traditional hunters. But owing to the crisis Sierra Leone faced, these traditional hunters were called upon to assist government soldiers in the effort to defeat the RUF rebels.

Feverish efforts were made to bring the civil war to an end. But Sankoh continued to refuse to agree.

On 25 May 1997, soldiers of the Sierra Leone Army staged a coup against President Tejan Kabbah, who escaped to neighbouring Conakry, Guinea. The Sierra Leonean soldiers broke into Pademba Road Prison and released Major Johnny Paul Koroma who was being held for his alleged involvement in an earlier plot to overthrow the president. Other soldiers, as well as ordinary prisoners, were also released.

Koroma was appointed head of the new military government, which was named the Armed Forces Revolutionary Council (AFRC). The AFRC government invited the RUF rebels to join them in Freetown. Speculation was that AFRC members naively believed that the invitation would appease Sankoh and entice him to agree to peace negotiations.

But Sankoh refused to make peace. While President Tejan Kabbah was in refuge in Conakry, he made several insensitive broadcasts urging the Nigerian government to bomb Freetown. In one such broadcast, Tejan Kabbah urged Nigerian military forces to bomb Freetown. He said that the bombing of Freetown to force the mutinous soldiers and the RUF rebels out of the city was the price Sierra Leoneans had to pay for democracy. But whereas he was safely in Conakry, it was the citizens in Freetown who would suffer.

Nigerian army jets did bomb areas in Freetown where RUF rebels and dissident Sierra Leonean soldiers were believed to have taken shelter. In addition, two Nigerian frigates arrived in Freetown and started bombing the military headquarters at Cockerill along Wilkinson Road, as well as Wilberforce Barracks.

Panic overcame the citizens in Freetown. Some scrambled to board a rusty coastal vessel that carried frightened Freetown citizens to the capital of Gambia at exorbitant fares. Others travelled by sailing boats, hoping the boats would convey them to Conakry. But several of these boats were reported to have capsized, their passengers drowned. The main cause of these disasters was the irresponsible conduct of boat owners, who would overload the small boats with passengers, bags of rice, large cans of palm oil, and other edible goods.

THE INVASION OF FREETOWN BY THE RUF AND THE WESTSIDE BOYS IN JANUARY 1999

On 6 January 1999, the RUF rebels, together with their new compatriots, the Westside Boys, in a rather surprising move, rapidly advanced on Freetown. Upon arrival, they spread mayhem throughout the city, focusing mainly on the eastern and central parts and killing and wounding many civilians. The combined forces also burnt some houses in Freetown.

They did not meet any resistance whatsoever in their initial invasion of the city – not even from the Nigerian troops who were supposed to provide effective defence of Freetown.

According to reports, the rapid advance was halted at the bridge between Brookfields and Congo Town. It took the combined force of the United Nations, Nigerian soldiers, the Sierra Leonean soldiers with their Kamarjoh allies, and the British Special Forces to finally overcome the RUF rebels.

Tejan Kabbah had surpassed the previous presidents of Sierra Leone for the total number of army officers he had executed. Reportedly, part of the army was disbanded. When no one (including the Nigerian troops intended to defend Freetown) stopped the terrible invasion that January day, it was reportedly some of the soldiers Tejan Kabbah had disbanded who somehow or another got hold of weapons and bravely put up stiff resistance against the rampaging and triumphant rebels. When the rapid advance was finally halted at the bridge, the western part of Freetown was saved from devastation.

ECOMOG detachments, thousands of UN forces, and the Sierra Leonean military forces supported by the Kamajors were deployed in the country in an effort to bring the civil war to an end. Yet these combined forces were unable to defeat the RUF and bring about peace. It was after the British had intervened, sending detachments of the elite Special Forces to join the other international forces, that sufficient pressure was exerted on the rebels, and the RUF compromised and agreed to negotiate peace.

In an effort to cajole Sankoh to agree to make peace, he was appointed minister in charge of all the mineral resources, including diamonds, in the entire country. This position was almost equivalent to that of vice president of the country.

Having been ensconced in this lofty position, Sankoh exploited his powerful position. He quickly made suspicious deals with certain unscrupulous foreign businessmen for the mining of diamonds, as well as gold. Protected by loyal and vicious security guards at his office and residence at Spur Road in the western part of Freetown, he was confident. But his luck would soon run out.

A few months later, a peaceful civilian demonstration agitated against Sankoh for some thing or the other. During the demonstration, his security guards were reported to have opened fire on the peaceful demonstrators, killing many. Sankoh allegedly tried to escape, during which time he became separated from his security guards. After a few days in hiding, he was eventually apprehended by a determined and angry mob of youths. He was handed over to the government and put on trial for war crimes. He died whilst in detention awaiting trial.

But his death did not bring about an immediate peace. Some of his senior officers in the RUF continued the fighting. It was after heavy pressure and protracted negotiations that the other RUF leaders at last conceded to make peace and to allow their troops to be disarmed by the United Nations forces. Peace at last returned to Sierra Leone in 2002, after the country had been ravaged and its citizens submitted to traumatic events during eleven years of civil war. Thus ended the most serious political upheaval this hitherto tranquil and peaceful country had ever faced.

chapter 21

REIGNS OF TERROR

━━━━━━━━━━

REVENGE BY SLPP SUPPORTERS FOLLOWING THE RETURN AND REINSTATEMENT OF TEJAN KABBAH

History is the impartial judge of events. Three major political upheavals in Sierra Leone resulted in the heads of state and government seeking temporary refuge in neighbouring Guinea. The first was Siaka Stevens, who, a few minutes after having been sworn in as prime minister by the governor general in April 1967, was placed under house arrest in what was the first military coup in Sierra Leone. A counter-coup brought in the military's National Reformation Council (NRC). Siaka Stevens continued to be held under house arrest. As crafty as he was, he managed to fool the NRC alleging he intended to seek medical treatment abroad. Stevens later emerged in Guinea, where he sought refuge together with some of the APC leaders who had previously escaped to that country. After another counter-coup by soldiers, Siaka Stevens was reinstated as prime minister in April 1968.

The second was President Joseph S. Momoh, who was overthrown by another coup, which brought in the National Provisional Ruling Council (NPRC) led by Capt. Valentine Strasser. President Momoh also escaped to Guinea. But as developments were to unfold later, he was never reinstated.

Then there was Tejan Kabbah, who, a few years after he was elected, was ousted from power in May 1997 by a military coup. President Tejan Kabbah escaped and sought temporary refuge in Guinea, where he set up a temporary government-in-exile.

It may now be necessary to take a look backward and compare the activities of each of the two political leaders who were reinstated to power (Stevens and Tejan Kabbah) while in exile in Guinea, their subsequent returns to Sierra Leone, and their reinstatements.

While Stevens was in temporary exile in Guinea with some of the leaders of the APC, he did not arrange with the Guinean government or with any other government to bomb his own citizens. It was reliably reported that Stevens and members of the APC were reportedly planning to invade Sierra Leone and oust the NRC by violent means. But subsequent events made their planned invasion unnecessary. Junior ranks of the army and the police staged a mutiny, wherein they arrested and detained all their senior officers. This group formed a temporary military government called the Anti-Corruption Revolutionary Council (ACRC). Stevens returned from exile in Guinea in April 1968. He might have been protected by Guinean soldiers on his return to Sierra Leone. He was reportedly welcomed by jubilant crowds. APC supporters were not revengeful against opponents. They did not perpetrate any brutalities and atrocities against anyone who might have made any uncomplimentary remarks against Stevens or the APC. Stevens was reinstated as prime minister peacefully.

On the other hand, when Tejan Kabbah was in temporary exile in Guinea with some SLPP leaders, he arranged with the Nigerian government for Nigerian forces to bomb his own citizens in Sierra Leone. He was heard to have broadcast the message that the bombing was the price Sierra Leoneans had to pay for the restoration of democracy. I heard this broadcast. I was then in Freetown.

On the subsequent routing of the AFRC/RUF forces from Freetown – with the help of UN Forces; British Special Forces;

ECOMOG, which consisted of an appreciable number of Nigerian troops; and the Sierra Leonean soldiers supported by the Kamajors in February 1998 – Tejan Kabbah was able to return to Freetown. His return was like a parade of Satan and his cohorts spewing fire, brimstone, destruction, and death. Tejan Kabbah reportedly unleashed a reign of terror equal to the terror the RUF had been perpetrating against innocent citizens of Sierra Leone, on the pretext of restoring democracy. This reign of terror reportedly lasted for several weeks. Violence, brutalities, and atrocities too horrible to mention here were committed. Hordes of SLPP supporters, like rabid wild animals, were reported to have sought out all those who had expressed even slightly uncomplimentary remarks against President Tejan Kabbah and his SLPP supporters and to have beaten them mercilessly. Some of those who were arrested, beaten, and brutalised were not even known to have expressed any dissent against Tejan Kabbah and his SLPP government. They were simply arrested and beaten up to settle old scores. Many of these hapless victims were not just beaten up. Some were burnt alive, their blackened, rotten, and fly-ridden corpses left along the streets for several days.

This reign of terror reportedly lasted for several weeks after President Tejan Kabbah had returned to Freetown and had been reinstated as president. That was the price citizens of Sierra Leone had to pay for "democracy" according to President Tejan Kabba! Democracy was trampled upon, brazenly, shamelessly, and mercilessly.

PART 4

THE CREOLES (KRIOS) OF SIERRA LEONE

chapter 22

THE MAROONS

The history of Sierra Leone would not be complete without mentioning the dominant roles the Creoles (Krios) played in the development of the country and, rather unfortunately, their ultimate decline as a group. I will, therefore, endeavour to explain who the Krios of Sierra Leone are, their ascendancy, and how they ended up being virtual ethnic dinosaurs.

WHO ARE THE CREOLES (KRIOS) OF SIERRA LEONE?

To know about the Creoles (Krios) of Sierra Leone, one has to understand the complexities of the slave trade – how lucrative it was to the Europeans, as well as to plantation owners in the Americas and the West Indies. In these territories, dominated mainly by Britain, France, Portugal and Spain, plantation owners wanted cheap labour for their vast plantations, on which they grew cotton, tobacco, sugar cane, and coffee. The Europeans, led originally by Portugal, found cheap labour in Africans, whom they would catch with the alleged connivance of the tribal chiefs and transport to the Americas to be sold as cattle to the plantation owners. Other European nations soon embarked on the lucrative but inhuman slave trade, foremost among them Britain. The gentry in England also wanted cheap labour to perform household chores.

The slave trade lasted from the fifteenth century to the late nineteenth century. It is estimated that, during this period, millions of Africans, men, women, and children, were kidnapped from Africa and shipped across the Atlantic Ocean to the Americas, where these hapless victims were sold into slavery as cattle. The conditions they endured in the sailing vessels conveying them across the Atlantic Ocean were reported by historians to be abhorrent and horrendous.

Throughout this period, neither the slave traders nor the plantation owners nor the Roman Catholic Church, which then had great influence on many governments in Europe, considered the affair inhuman and abhorrent in the sight of God. In fact, slave traders justified their actions by saying that the Africans were subhumans and were also not Christians. There also did not seem to have been any awareness among the public of the horrendous conditions of the slaves. It was not until the eighteenth century that certain Protestant Christian leaders in Britain – evangelicals like William Wilberforce, Thomas Clarkson, Granville Sharpe, and other philanthropists – began to preach against the evils and inhumanity of the slave trade, drawing public attention to this horror and abomination.

The emergence of the Creoles of Sierra Leone was partly entangled with the American War of Independence from Britain. Confronted with defeat, the British colonial government in America lured black slaves on American plantations to escape and join the British forces fighting against the rebellious Americans. For this, the British colonial government promised the escapees freedom and to allocate to them large plots of lands.

The response to the lure of the British was overwhelming. Within a relatively short period, thousands of slaves had escaped from their slave masters in America and joined the British forces in British America in the north (Canada). Some of these fugitive slaves (the Black Loyalists) were in Nova Scotia, Canada, as well as other towns in Canada. They were called Maroons.

After losing the war, the British appeared to have stalled in their promise to grant the fugitives freedom and large plots of land. There emerged a Black Loyalist sergeant named Thomas Peters, who had escaped from slavery in America and had joined the British forces in the fight against the Americans. (Some of the fugitive slaves had somehow found their way to England, where they had joined the already emancipated slaves who were left destitute and roaming the streets. These were ridiculed as the "Black Poor."

Peters travelled to London, where he made contacts with several Christian philanthropists who had been preaching against slavery and had pressed the English government to abolish the abominable slave trade. Through his contacts with a few of the abolitionists, Peters was able to present to the English government a petition urging the government not to go back on their promise to allocate large plots of land to the Black Loyalists who had fought on the side of Britain during the war.

The "Black Poor" had become a serious social problem for the British. Coupled with Peters' petition, this destitute group of emancipated slaves presented a complex problem the British were forced to solve. It was eventually decided that these former slaves and their descendants were to be resettled in the land of their origin. Concurrently, the Sierra Leone Company was in need of settlers.

chapter 23

RESETTLEMENT

Negotiations were reportedly held with the chiefs in the area for a large piece of land to accommodate the resettlement of the emancipated slaves and their descendants. A large piece of land was allocated along Sierra Leone's Atlantic coast. The original indigenous inhabitants of this piece of land were the Temnes. The British named the portion of land Freetown (in other words, the land of the free).

Following these negotiations, the British sent groups of freed slaves from Nova Scotia, Canada, as well as some of the Black Poor in England for resettlement. The first batch of former slaves, about 1,190 emigrants, left Britain in a flotilla of sailing ships under a philanthropist and abolitionist named John Clarkson, who was later to be appointed governor of Sierra Leone. The former slaves were mainly of two groups. One of these groups was made up of emancipated slaves who had been roaming the streets of Britain. And the other group were the Maroons – the slaves who had escaped slavery in America and joined the British ranks in the American War of Independence. The British also included among these groups some English harlots and a few others.

The emancipated slaves and their descendants were originally from different tribal and ethnic groups throughout West Africa, including even Sierra Leone, which, at the time, had not yet been established as a British possession. These heterogeneous people lacked a common language and culture. On their arrival, they were settled in Freetown, as well as in other small enclaves around Freetown, together with the indigenous tribes, who were predominantly Temnes.

The new arrivals did not meet a land that had been prepared for their reception. Moreover, they were completely destitute. They therefore had to struggle to make the land inhabitable. They had to brush the thick forests, lay out streets, and construct shelters. For food, they had to depend at first on rations provided by the organisers of the convoy. It must have been tough for these first groups of arrivals in Freetown.

RECAPTIVES (OR LIBERATED AFRICANS)

The abolition of the slave trade in Britain did not end the slave trade immediately. In view of the lucrative nature of the evil arrangement for both slave traders and plantation owners, the slave trade continued to flourish. African children and adults alike, men as well as women, were still being captured by Europeans, with the alleged connivance of some African chiefs, and transported under horrible and inhumane conditions in slave ships across the Atlantic Ocean to the Americas to be sold into slavery.

To try and put a permanent end to the detestable slave trade, the British government sent naval gunboats to patrol the Atlantic Ocean between West Africa and the Americas and intercept slave ships. Many thousand of Africans were, thus, rescued from the slave ships and taken to Freetown to join the emancipated slaves already there. Those liberated from the slave ships were also from various tribes and ethnic groups in West Africa. They were known as Recaptives or Liberated Africans.

EMERGENCE OF CREOLES

The aftermath of the abolition of the slave trade was the catalyst in the emergence of the Krios (Creoles) of Sierra Leone. There had hitherto been no group in Sierra Leone or in any other part of West

Africa known as the Krios. There were only tribal and ethnic groups scattered around the continent, each with its own culture. The Krios emerged after the abolition of the slave trade brought together groups of disparate people with different histories, cultures, and languages in Freetown.

The Krios of Sierra Leone originally consisted of three groups of emancipated slaves – the freed slaves from England known as the Black Poor, the Maroons who had escaped from slavery in the American plantations to join the British forces, and those Africans (Recaptives) who were rescued from slave ships whilst on their way to the Americas to be sold as slaves. The Recaptives who were resettled in Freetown had come from a number of tribes, including Angola, Ashanti, Yoruba, and several other tribes from other areas in West Africa.

The freed slaves, heterogeneous people from different ethnic and tribal groups, had earlier, whilst in captivity, acquired some rudimentary education, as well as being converted to the Christian religion of their slave masters. They had also adapted a language of their own, which basically was corrupted or broken English mixed with some of their original African tribal dialects. The language was called Krio (or Creole), and the people, Krios (or Creoles).

This new language was also assimilated by the recaptives, who were also a heterogeneous group of people. Both the freed slaves, as well as the recaptives who were resettled in Freetown and in the surrounding villages, were collectively known as Creoles (Krios). The Creoles were, thus, an amalgam of heterogeneous tribes and ethnic groups from various areas in West Africa, including even that part of the continent known as Sierra Leone.

Furthermore, it should be noted that these settlers were given hostile reception and attacked frequently by the indigenous inhabitants. Security must have also been provided for the settlers. In fact, in order to protect themselves from the frequent attacks by the indigenous inhabitants, some of the enclaves where these emancipated slaves had settled were walled with rocks.

While the slaves were working for their slave masters in America, some of them had adopted the names of the slave masters. Other freed slaves, as well as recaptives, were given English names by Christians in Britain who had adopted the emancipated or freed slaves. That is why many Creoles have English names.

Some Creoles combined their English names with local names. Consequently names like Bankole-Bright, Beoku-Betts,, Bundu-Williams, Karamba-Coker, Ojukutu-Macauley and other compound names emerged.

LOCAL NAMES (OSE NAMES)

The mixture of the various tribes who now make up the Krios is reflected in what are usually called, in Krio, Ose names or local names. These names are not English. Nor do they reflect any of the names of indigenous tribes in Sierra Leone. Rather, they reflect the roots of names in other regions in West Africa. A few examples are Abiordu, Adebayor, Arbionor, Ayor, Bisodu, Ekundayoh, Ina, Oju, Oloronfeh, Onikeh, Oseh, and Yamede.

In addition, some villages have sections whose names reflect the tribes of recaptives from other West African countries who were originally resettled there. For instance, in Gloucester Village (my village), there is a section known as Oku Tong (Oku Town).

THE BRITISH COLONIALISTS AND THEIR EAGERNESS TO EXPLOIT THE COUNTRY RATHER THAN SPREAD EDUCATION

Of all the former British colonies in West Africa – the Gambia, Sierra Leone, the Gold Coast (now Ghana), and Nigeria – Sierra Leone is unique in that the British divided the country into colony and protectorate. The colony, a relatively small area around a peninsula in the western part of the country, was occupied by the descendants of the detritus of the slave trade (the Krios). And they were more enlightened than the citizens in the interior of the country. These Krios were classified as "British" by the British colonial government, while the protectorate, which is far larger geographically and which contained the indigenous citizens, was termed a protectorate. The citizens there were classified as "British Protected Persons." In my view, this was a very clever or subtle method of the divide-and-rule strategy.

One of the reasons for the original tardiness in the spread of education in the provinces (formerly the protectorate) was that the British colonial administrators were originally more interested in the exploitation of the resources of the country – and in seeing that the populace was subdued so as to facilitate this exploitation. The primary reason for the construction of a railway from the port of Freetown across the middle of the country to the far east and also from Bauya to the north was to facilitate the transport of those resources to the port in Freetown for exportation.

Even in Freetown, all the primary schools and secondary schools were Anglican, Methodist, Roman Catholic, or American UBC. It was later that the colonial government constructed two government schools – first the Model Primary School and later, in 1927, the Prince of Wales School, a secondary institution. The only secondary school constructed by the British colonial administration was the Bo Government Secondary School, constructed in 1906 in Bo, the capital of the Southern Province. That institution was reportedly constructed for the sons of chiefs.

It was around the late twenties that the colonial government took over the supervision and partial administration of schools in the country. This included supplying school materials, as well as text and exercise books to primary schools. But the schools were owned by the various Christian religions and, one or two of them, by the Muslim religion. All the secondary schools were under the direct administration of the Christian churches but under the supervision of the Department of Education.

As a subtle means to exercise firm rule in the country, the colonial administrators seemed at first to prefer to keep the citizens of the hinterland uneducated and, therefore, unenlightened. This would prevent them from agitating for less control over their affairs by the

British colonialists. Also, unlike the French who considered their overseas colonies as parts of France and developed these countries, the British seemed to have had quite a different philosophy. They carried out modest developments in their overseas colonial territories, simply to enable them to trade and exploit the resources of each territory.

The Christians in Britain followed closely on the heels of the British administrators and were eager to spread Christianity among the emancipated slaves and their descendants in Freetown. Consequently, Christian churches and schools were established throughout Freetown and the enclaves (villages) in the colony. There is hardly a village in the colony area where at least a church and school were not established. Christianity was somewhat slow in spreading through the protectorate (now provinces). This was because the Christians lacked adequate resources to spread through the far larger protectorate.

On account of superstitious and somewhat retrogressive tribal beliefs and traditions, in which they had hitherto been shackled, the indigenous citizens in the interior were at first slow to accept education. Some were even opposed to becoming educated or to letting their children be educated. But apart from the foregoing, the British colonial government seemed at first to be more focused on exploiting the resources of the country than on educating the citizens in the hinterland.

In Freetown, Christian missionaries from Britain established higher educational institutions, including the first college in 1827, which later became known as Fourah Bay College. This college was originally established for the training of teachers and catechists. In addition, a secondary school (high school) known as the CMS[12] Grammar School was established in 1845. These two advanced educational institutions were established by CMS members, and these institutions were also the first advanced educational institutions in British West Africa. Students from other British West African

---

[12] The Church Missionary Society was an Anglican organisation.

territories came to Freetown to attend Fourah Bay College. These included several who later became the early political leaders in Nigeria, the Gold Coast (now Ghana), and the Gambia. Freetown therefore earned the accolade "Athens of West Africa".

So it can be seen why the Creoles were at first the better-educated and more enlightened group in the country. Consequently, in due course, the Creoles in Freetown and its environs became the most influential and dominant group in education, trade, and politics. The Creoles turned out doctors, lawyers, teachers, religious leaders, traders, and so on.

Their influence continued to spread to the other British colonies in West African territories. They were also employed as clerks in the public services and in the commercial field. Some of the Creoles were even sent to work in the other British West African colonies, and as far as to the Congo. They, therefore, became the fountain of education and Christianity to the other indigenous tribes in Sierra Leone, as well as to other British West African colonies.

THE GREAT INFLUENCE OF CHRISTIANITY
IN THE SPREAD OF EDUCATION

The unfortunate course of history that resulted in the emergence of the Creoles was also to result to their being better educated at first and consequently far more advanced than the citizens in the provinces.

As the Anglican churches in Sierra Leone lacked adequate resources, they resorted to making appeals in churches in and around Freetown for donations towards the spread of Christianity and the establishment of schools in the protectorate. They established the Native Pastorate Fund and accepted donations of money and clothes, which were sent to the provinces, all toward the aim of establishing churches and schools there.

Another organisation, the Dorcas Association, was primarily for female members of the Anglican churches in Freetown and the surrounding villages. Appeals were made at meetings of this

Association for monies and clothes to be sent to the provinces to aid in the development of the citizens in these areas.

ASCENDANCY OF THE CREOLES (KRIOS)

Given the colonial administration's lukewarm interest in the spread of education, the Christian churches that followed closely in its footsteps not only spread Christianity among the Creole citizens in the colony but also were foremost in educating them. Consequently, all the primary and secondary schools in the then colony were either Anglican or Methodist or Roman Catholic or American UBC. It was in the late twenties or thereabouts that the colonial government took over the supervision of elementary schools in the country, including the supply of school materials as well as text and exercise books. All the secondary schools were under the administration of the Christian churches but under the supervision of the Department of Education.

Having been imbued with Christianity and benevolence, the Creoles were, in turn, benevolent to the indigenous tribes. They sought the welfare of some citizens in the provinces. They adopted provincial children, whom they raised as their own, educating them and converting them to Christianity.

The British colonialists established in Freetown the same system of local government as had been established in Britain. The city was incorporated as a municipality in 1893 and, therefore, had its own city council and mayor.

Political leaders emerged among the Creole to bring political enlightenment to the country. Creole leaders even successfully challenged, on constitutional and legal grounds, some inimical laws the British colonial government wanted to introduce. There was a time in the thirties when the British wanted to establish some form of apartheid system in Sierra Leone, with separate sections for the white British administrators and the indigenous citizens. The Creoles vigorously opposed this intended form of apartheid, and the British colonial government eventually relented. They were only able to establish Hill Station, a suburb of Freetown, as a reservation for whites.

In 1944, the colonial government wanted to remove Fourah Bay College from Freetown and establish in its place a polytechnic. The Creoles most vigorously opposed the intended retrogressive and detestable plan, and they even appealed as far as to the Secretary of State for the Colonies in London. The colonial government eventually had no option but to put the plan away. That is how Fourah Bay College remained in Sierra Leone to become the premier college in the country.

In the civil service, the police force, and the army, the colonial government precluded Sierra Leoneans from senior positions. It took a long struggle by the Creoles before the colonial government gradually opened senior ranks to Sierra Leoneans, starting in the early fifties. And even then, the government made a distinction. British senior civil servants were termed expatriate senior civil servants, whilst the African senior civil servants were termed African senior civil servants. The salaries and amenities enjoyed by the former were greater than those enjoyed by the latter.

chapter 24

THE COLONY AND THE PROTECTORATE

CREOLES WHO WERE IN THE FOREFRONT OF UNITY

Certain Creoles fought relentlessly to harmonise the relationship between the Creoles in the Western Area of Sierra Leone (the colony) and the provincial citizens. Foremost among those was the Rev. Etheldred Nathaniel Jones, who was the son of prominent Creoles. He received his secondary education at the CMS Grammar School, after which he attended Fourah Bay College. There, he graduated with a bachelor of arts in the early part of the twentieth century. He was subsequently sent to England and studied theology and philosophy at Wycliff College in Oxford. On his return to Freetown in 1924, he was ordained priest of the Anglican Church and appointed curate at Holy Trinity Church on Kissy Road.

But Jones was very radical in his ideas, and so the relationship between him and the Anglican Church authorities became frosty. He subsequently resigned from the priesthood of the Anglican Church. He had a burning desire to integrate the citizens of the protectorate and the citizens in the colony. He was a fearless leader in attempting to bring about harmony in the relationship between these two groups. He was so determined to achieve this goal that he changed his name from Etheldred Nathaniel Jones to Lamina Sankoh. *(Not to be confused with Foday Sankoh the leader of the RUF).*

In 1948 or thereabout, Lamina Sankoh formed the People's Party, one of whose aims was to bring about harmonisation in the relationship between the citizens of the protectorate and those of the colony. Later on, he joined with the Sierra Leone Organisation Society, which was under the leadership of Dr Milton A.S. Margai. Together, they agreed to merge the two parties. Thereby was born the Sierra Leone People's Party (SLPP). Some of the SLPP's prominent other founding members included Albert Margai (a lawyer), Siaka Stevens (a trade unionist), H.E.B. John (Educationist), Doyle Sumner, Paramount Chief R.B.S. Koker, Paramount Chief Bai Farima Tass II, Dr. John Karefa-Smart, Rev. Paul Dunbar, I.B. Taylor-Kamara (another lawyer), Pa Randall from Bonthe and several other prominent citizens from both the colony and the protectorate.

At that time Sierra Leone had only two political parties. The SLPP consisted of prominent people in the protectorate as well as many Creoles. The other party, the National Council of Sierra Leone consisted of die-hard Creoles. The former was under the leadership of Dr Margai, and the latter was led by Dr. H.C. Bankole-Bright.

Lamina Sankoh was so motivated by radical fervour to bring about unity between the two groups that he even sold some of his properties at Wilberforce Street in Freetown in order to financially support the SLPP. He transferred ownership of his newspaper, The African Vanguard, to the SLPP so that it became an official SLPP newspaper. On account of his radical views, he was ostracised by some Creoles, who considered themselves to be upper-class and who considered him a renegade.

But not all upper-class Creoles felt that the efforts to harmonise the relationship between the citizens of the protectorate and those of the colony were wrong. Many supported Sankoh's effort. One such prominent Creole was H.E.B. John, who was the son of one of the Anglican Church leaders in Freetown. He was also vice principal of the CMS Grammar School. He allied himself with Sankoh's views, and when the SLPP was created, H.E.B. John was appointed the first secretary-general of the new party. Margai also appointed him as the first minister of education when Sierra Leone had achieved its independence from British colonial rule.

Another ally of Sankoh was Mrs Constance Cummings-John, who was also an upper-class Creole. She received her education initially in Freetown and later in England and the United States of America. She founded the Roosevelt Secondary School for Girls in the early fifties and became the first female mayor of Freetown in the early sixties. Several other Creole intellectuals were also allies of Sankoh's fight to unite the citizens of the two parts of Sierra Leone. One of those was Newman-Smart, who later became a professor of English at FBC. The father of Brig. Andrew Juxon-Smith (the chairman of the NRC) and many others were allies as well. So it can be seen that not all Creoles were antagonistic to the provincial citizens. But unfortunately, the perception among some provincial citizens seemed to be that all Creoles held prejudices against them.

I have personally knowledge of all these goings-on, as all the incidents happened when I was young and idealistic. In fact, I was also a member of the SLPP in the fifties.

The Creoles were foremost in the development of education, the legal profession, the medical profession, the teaching profession, and several other fields in Sierra Leone because they were educated. In fact, Creoles had been teachers and Christian preachers in the protectorate. During the Hut Tax War, several Creole teachers, ministers, and traders were massacred by the rebels. But no Creoles were known to have harboured animosity against any tribe. The British colonial government appointed some Creoles to positions in education, medical fields, and civil service not because the colonial administrators disliked citizens in the provinces but because the Creoles were the ones who were then educated.

Some Creoles employed "month boys", boys from the provinces who were hired on a monthly basis to do domestic chores. Month boys enjoyed almost the same privileges as the children of the Creoles. They ate the same food and played together. Some of them were assimilated into the Creole society, and some were even placed in jobs by the Creole caretakers. Indeed, several citizens from the provinces owed to Creoles their progress in life.

During the Second World War, Emmanuel Cole and a few other Creole boys joined the Sierra Leone army, which then consisted of mostly semi-literate and illiterate men from the provinces. Seeing that these soldiers were not issued or permitted to wear boots and that they were being paid paltry salaries, Cole and the other Creoles protested against the discrimination. The British officers were annoyed and resented these protests. In retaliation, the British had Cole and the others arrested and court-martialled. As was to be expected, they were all found guilty and given terms of imprisonment, ranging from fifteen years for Cole, who was the ringleader, to a few days to the others.

I have thus far enumerated some of the positive contributions Creoles made to Sierra Leone. But unfortunately, the Creoles are now perceived as being hostile to the advancement of the other citizens in the country.

It may be conceded that there were a few Creoles who felt they were upper class and, consequently, were not in favour of a harmonious relationship between the citizens of the protectorate and the Creoles in the colony. These small groups prided themselves on being "British". Foremost among these, as has already been mentioned, was Dr Bankole Bright, president of the National Council of Sierra Leone. Among these few die-hard Creoles was Columbus Thompson, the secretary general of the National Council. As an example of Dr Bright's extreme beliefs, he was reported to have quipped humorously at one of the meetings of the National Council that the difference between the Creoles and the citizens of the protectorate was that, whereas Creoles ate salad, citizens of the protectorate ate cassava leaves.

Despite the fact that a few Creoles supported his hostility and negativity, the vast majority of Creoles were not in favour of this attitude. It may be conceded that, in a situation like that, there will always be some people who hold eccentric views and oppose the positive and progressive intentions of those in favour of creating harmony between two groups of people. Eventually, the National Council of Sierra Leone, under the leadership of Dr Bright, gradually faded into oblivion in Sierra Leone.

But when viewed in another light, Dr Bright did not hate the people in the protectorate. It seemed as if he was only trying to protect the Creoles and preserve their heritage.

The only criticism, if at all it should be criticism, that may be made against the Creoles was that the Creoles in general tended to imitate and emulate some of the customs and habits of the British. But is it a fault to emulate the sterling qualities of someone or a group of people who are more advanced than us? As has already been pointed out, Creoles in general, emulating the British, had contributed quite significantly to the development of Sierra Leone in every aspect.

chapter 25

Rectitude

CREOLES WERE NEVER PUGNACIOUS

The Creoles were never known to be pugnacious or violent. During colonial days there was no parliament; neither was anyone allowed to vote. The government then consisted of what was known as the Executive Council (or the cabinet) and the Legislative Council, which was composed of mainly the heads of departments. With the exception of a very few prominent Sierra Leoneans specially selected (nominated) by the governor, department heads were all British. The few Sierra Leoneans holding these positions included prominent Creoles in Freetown and a few prominent paramount chiefs from the protectorate. The Legislative Council enacted laws for the whole country. Since Freetown had its own city council as well as its own mayor, the British colonial administration permitted citizens in Freetown to vote for the election of councillors and the mayor. But universal adult suffrage did not exist. One of the requirements for both voters and candidates was that they should be owners of houses in Freetown valued at a certain minimum amount.

Electioneering campaigns for councillors and the mayor were conducted in a decent and peaceful atmosphere. Candidates and supporters never resorted to violence against opposing candidates and their supporters. Rather, each candidate tried to emphasise his educational background, achievements, proficiency, and pedigree and to demonstrate his eloquence. In addition (as was typical of most politicians), in order to woo electors, candidates would make dreamlike promises to create a utopian city. It was a pleasure to attend electioneering campaign meetings. The candidates entertained their audience with eloquence and witticisms. Absolutely no violence was unleashed against opposing candidates or their supporters. Neither were any illegal methods used to prevent electors from voting for the candidates of their choice, meaning voters were not subjected to intimidation.

It was after Sierra Leone had become an independent nation that candidates used violence against their opposition. One prominent leader of a political party was alleged to have mentioned that he had 101 "tricks" to win elections. The "tricks", which were later unveiled, relied on violence, as well as brazenly illegal methods. Hooligans were allegedly given drugs, after which they unleashed exceptional violence against those who were suspected of going to vote for the opposition candidates. All these grossly illegal and violent activities during elections were anathema to the Creoles. Unfortunately, violence and illegal activities have now been inculcated in the growing population, as is reflected in the misbehaviour of students and young adults. Given the slightest problem, the youth tend to riot and display all sorts of disorderly or immoral conduct or engage blatantly in dishonest or illegal activities. The present government has been struggling to control these negative attitudes. Unfortunately, the efforts have, so far, been ineffectual.

Who do the growing citizens look up to for rectitude and as the role models who are so essential in the development of any country? Rectitude has almost disappeared from among the rising generation. I leave it to the reader to answer the question of why the government is struggling to impose discipline and rectitude among the citizens.

Up to about the late fifties, trade in Sierra Leone was dominated by about six large European firms. Among these were two British firms, United Africa Company (UAC) and G.B. Ollivant, as well as two French companies, Société Commerciale Occidentale Africain (SCOA) and Commercial Français Occidentale Africain. There was also a Greek Company called Paterson, Zochonis & Co. All these large firms had branches in the larger protectorate towns, which were placed under the management of Creoles, known as "Factors." The branches contained merchandise worth thousands of pounds (British West African pound, equivalent to the British pound sterling). In addition, Factors purchased produce, which they would send by rail to their respective headquarters in Freetown for export.

Consequently thousands of pounds (now the equivalent of billions of leones) worth of merchandise and produce were entrusted to the Factors. All of them displayed great integrity and lived up to the grave responsibilities entrusted to them. That was why there was no need to establish any form of bureaucratic organisation such as the Anti Corruption Commission. There was rectitude as well as discipline in all strata of the society.

If the same situation were set up today, the Factors would have caused the disappearance of billions of leones of goods.

chapter 26

PROMINENT FIGURES

SOME PROMINENT CREOLES (KRIOS) IN SIERRA LEONE'S HISTORY

This chapter tells the brief history of some of the prominent Creoles (Krios) who have made valuable contributions to the development of Sierra Leone, especially Freetown.

ISAAC THEOPHILUS AKUNA WALLACE-JOHNSON, POPULARLY KNOWN AS ITA WALLACE-JOHNSON

ITA Wallace-Johnson was a popular trade unionist and nationalist leader who was born in Wilberforce in the early part of the twentieth century. He attended mission schools in the village. At the age of eighteen, he entered the government service as a customs officer. But he was soon dismissed for helping to organise the first trade union in Sierra Leone. This was during British colonial days, when the colonial government frowned on trade unions.

He later joined the merchant navy as a common sailor and found his way to London, where he began to print a small newspaper dedicated to promoting the welfare of seamen.

In 1931, Wallace-Johnson founded the first trade union in Nigeria, and in1936, he was jailed in the Gold Coast (now Ghana) for publishing a scathing attack on colonialism. The Gold Coast was then a British colony and under colonial rule.

After his release from prison, he returned to Sierra Leone. Within a short time, he had organised eight trade unions in the country. He also began to publish a newspaper called *The African Standard* and organised a radical and mass political movement named the West African Youth League. That movement was dedicated to urging the colonial government to permit more participation of the citizens in the government of their country, as well as to pressure the government to increase the wages and general welfare of workers. He also urged national unity among all Sierra Leoneans. The West African Youth League was a radical, national movement that was very popular among all Sierra Leoneans. Many Sierra Leoneans, including several lawyers and civil servants who joined clandestinely, became members.

Wallace-Johnson ignited the flame of nationalism among Sierra Leoneans, as well as in citizens of the other British West African colonies, whose emerging political leaders emulated him in nationalism.

In the thirties, Wallace-Johnson was so popular that his name was being sung everywhere in Freetown. He became a very popular national leader in the country and was even able to unearth secret documents exposing methods of suppression of citizens by the British colonial government.

He therefore became a thorn in the side of the colonial government, and the colonial governor tried to have him arrested for alleged subversion. This effort failed, as the government could not get sufficient evidence.

But when the Second World War commenced in September 1939, the colonial government enacted the Emergency Act. The government was thereby able to declare him a threat to national security and had him arrested and banished to Bonthe Island to keep him "quiet".

After the end of the Second World War in 1945, Wallace-Johnson was released from banishment and returned to Freetown, where he resumed his radical political and trade union activities. After Sierra Leone became independent in1961, Wallace-Johnson was elected as Member of Parliament for Wilberforce rural area.

He continued his political and trade union activities and joined several international trade union organisations. In 1965, he was on his way to attend a conference of an international trade union when the vehicle in which he was travelling through Ghana was involved in a serious accident, and Wallace-Johnson suffered fatal injuries. So ended the life of a most illustrious Creole (Krio) and citizen of Sierra Leone.

REV. ETHELDRED NATHANIEL JONES
(ALIAS LAMINA SANKOH)

The Rev. Etheldred Nathaniel Jones was a fighter for unity between the people of the colony and the people of the protectorate. He was born to a prominent Krio family in Gloucester Village on 28 June 1884. In the twenties, he changed his name from Etheldred Nathaniel Jones to Lamnah Sankoh to signify his dedication to nationalism and unity among all Sierra Leonean citizens.

Rev. Jones was educated at Gloucester Elementary School, CMS Grammar School, and Fourah Bay College, where he graduated with a bachelor of arts. He then studied theology and philosophy at Wycliffe in Oxford. He suffered his first racial discrimination in Britain when, after the competition of his studies in theology, a bishop in the Anglican Church in Britain refused to ordain him as a priest in the Anglican Church. This greatly embittered him.

He returned to Sierra Leone in 1924 and was ordained a priest and appointed a curate in Holy Trinity Church on Kissy Road in Freetown. He also lectured in logic for a short time at Fourah Bay College. But he was very radical in his views and soon fell out with the authorities in the Anglican Church in Sierra Leone. The Anglican Bishop then was a British Bishop during colonial days.

Lamina Sankoh resigned his priesthood on account of fundamental differences with the Anglican authorities and returned to London, where he became involved in several radical organisations fighting for freedom from colonial rule. One of these was the West African Students Union (WASU), a pressure group of West African students agitating for independence of the British colonies from Britain. He was a regular contributor of the WASU journal, and he eventually became editor of this magazine.

Later, he travelled to the United States of America, where he lectured students at the Tuskegee College in Alabama, Lincoln University in Pennsylvania, and a few other colleges in the States, at a time when there was strong race prejudice against blacks in America.

He returned to Sierra Leone in the early forties and immediately embarked on radical political activities. He became a councillor of Freetown City Council, which he helped reorganise. He also became president of the Freetown Adult Education Society, and he lectured at Fourah Bay College's Extra Mural. He also started a newspaper, *The African Vanguard*, which was dedicated to nationalism in Sierra Leone.

He founded a political party called the People's Party and agitated for one Sierra Leone and for unity between the citizens of the colony and the citizens of the protectorate. For this, he earned the hostility of some radical Krios, who felt that the status quo should be preserved.

Later, he joined with Dr Milton Margai, the leader of the Sierra Leone Organisation Society (a strictly protectorate political organization), and they agreed to form a single political party in the country, which would embrace both the people of the colony and the people on the protectorate. The Sierra Leone Organisation Society and the Peoples Party therefore merged and thus was born the Sierra Leone People's Party (SLPP) with Dr M.A.S. Margai as its president and Lamina Sankoh as the vice president.

Sankoh was so motivated by his desire to unite Sierra Leone's people and for the country to be granted independence that, after the merger of the two political parties, he transferred the ownership of *The African Vanguard* to the SLPP.

On account of his desperate efforts to unite the people of the colony and those of the protectorate, he was scorned and ostracised by some Krios, who wanted to maintain the status quo. But he maintained his conviction.

Unfortunately, the members of the protectorate in the SLPP did not treat Sankoh well, and they more or less abandoned him. For all his sincere and desperate effort to unite the people and his agitation for independence, after Sierra Leone had become independent, Sankoh was not appointed to any ministerial post or to any official position in the government. He became a frustrated and disillusioned man, and he died more or less a pauper. It was the Hon. Sanusi Mustapha who provided funds for his funeral.

Dr H.C. Bankole Bright

A strong political leader who fought for the grant of independence and for the preservation of standards, Dr Bankole Bright was a pioneer of the rights and status of the Creoles (Krios) of Sierra Leone. He might have been overenthusiastic in his desire to preserve the heritage of the Creoles (Krios), and so he lambasted the indigenous people of Sierra Leone, rather than lambasting the British colonialists.

He was president of the National Council of Sierra Leone, a political party that was strongly opposed to the SLPP. Dr Bright struggled to keep the status quo of the Krios and wanted Freetown to remain a purely British colony. He even advocated that the colony be granted independence and be made a separate country from the protectorate.

But all his efforts were rejected by the British, who wanted the whole of Sierra Leone to be one country under one ruler.

Even though Bright strongly opposed the British colonial government, it was known by a few citizens that one of the colonial governors was secretly in touch with him, always seeking his advice. The governor would secretly invite Dr. Bright to his official Fort Thornton residence for dinner. Bright died without being appointed to any official government position.

Mrs Constance Agatha Cummings-John

Constance Cummings-John was a nationalist and an educationist. She was also the first woman mayor of Freetown.

Constance was born to a prominent Creole family in Sierra Leone in 1918. She attended the Annie Walsh Memorial Girls Secondary School and later the Freetown Secondary School for Girls. After completion of her secondary education in Freetown, she was sent to Britain to attend Whitelands College in Putney, England, where she was trained as a teacher.

While in Britain, she participated in the activities of various radical organisations fighting for the independence of West African colonies from Britain. Among such radical organisations in which she was a member were the West African Students Union (WASU) and the League of Coloured People.

In 1930, she went to the Unites States of America to study at Cornell University. There, she suffered racial insults as well as misunderstanding from even the blacks in America. All these sad experience affected her political thinking. She returned to London, and, in 1937, married Ethanan Cummings-John, a young lawyer. They both returned to Freetown that same year.

In Freetown, Cummings-John was appointed principal of the AME Girl's Industrial Institute, which was then struggling for its existence as a secondary technical school. With youthful zeal, as well as other sterling qualities, Cummings-John quickly reorganised the school, and it developed under her regime.

In 1938, she joined the West African Youth League, which had been founded by Wallace-Johnson. Cummings-John participated in educational and civic affairs aimed at developing Freetown. In 1951, she organised the Women's Movement, a popular movement joined by thousands of women of all classes in Freetown.

She established and was the first principal at the Roosevelt Secondary School for Girls in Freetown in the early 1950s.

She participated in many political affairs. Later, she became a member of the SLPP. She participated actively in the affairs of the

Freetown City Council and was eventually elected councillor. A few years later, she was elected mayor, becoming the first woman to fill that position in Freetown. During her term as mayor, she carried out various improvements to the city, including sanitation, education, and more.

Cummings-John was also one of those who agitated for Sierra Leone' independence, and she was a member of the delegation to London in 1960 on the constitutional conference before Britain granted Sierra Leone independence.

Sir Ernest Samuel Beoku-Betts

Ernest Samuel Beoku-Betts was a jurist and civic leader in Freetown. He was one of those who won recognition by the British colonial government in the forties.

Beoku-Betts was born in 1895 in Freetown to Creole parents. He was educated at Leopold Educational Institute, after which he attended Fourah Bay College, where he earned a bachelor of arts. He later proceeded to London. He studied law at London University and was called to the bar in 1917.

He returned to Freetown and set up his own private legal practice. He participated very actively in civic affairs and became a councillor and, eventually, mayor of the City Council of Freetown. Whilst he was mayor, he carried out major reorganisation and development of the city council.

He was the first African to be nominated by the British governor as member of the Legislative Council during colonial era.

In 1937, he quit politics and his civic duties for the bar and was appointed by the colonial government as police magistrate, where he acquitted himself well. In 1945, the colonial government appointed him as the first Sierra Leonean puisne judge. The country was still a British colony, and the British judges in Sierra Leone frowned on an African being appointed a judge equal in status to them. That was why the colonial government compromised and named his post "puisne judge" (inferior in rank to the other British judges in Sierra

Leone). In 1946, the colonial government appointed him the first Sierra Leonean West Africa Court of Appeal Judge. He was awarded knighthood, and thus the title of sir, by Queen Elizabeth II in 1957. He died the same year.

EMMANUEL COLE – HERO OF THE "GUNNERS REVOLT"

Emmanuel Cole was born in 1908 of ordinary Krio parents. He was educated in Freetown, and when the Second World War started in 1939, he volunteered to join the army in Sierra Leone. This was at a time when only semi-literate and illiterate men from the protectorate would join the army. The pay being given to Sierra Leonean soldiers was a pittance. They were not permitted to wear boots and were never promoted above the rank of sergeant major. No Sierra Leonean soldier could then be promoted to senior ranks. All the senior ranks in the army were held by British officers. Even most of the sergeant majors, sergeants, and corporals (non-commissioned officers) were British.

Nevertheless, Cole and a few other young Creole men joined the army and were posted to the Royal artillery heavy battery section at Murray Town Barracks.

On account of the meagre wages these Sierra Leone soldiers received and the refusal by their British officers to allow them to wear boots, Cole convinced the other soldiers to join with him in send a written complaint to their British commanding officer.

On receipt of the letter of protest, the British commanding officer was infuriated. He ordered that Cole and the others be arrested and court-martialled. These soldiers were found guilty and given terms of imprisonment ranging from fifteen years to several days. Cole, as the leader, received the severest punishment, sentenced to fifteen years imprisonment for his efforts.

Cole and the others were later pardoned and released from prison. This incident resulted in the British commanding general in Sierra Leone giving approval for the wearing of boots by Sierra Leonean soldiers. In addition, the soldiers received substantial increases in their wages and other amenities. It wasn't until many years later that Sierra Leonean soldiers were promoted to senior ranks in the Sierra Leone Army.

DR MACORMACK CHARLES FARRELL EASMON

This doctor was born of Creole parents in Accra, the Gold Coast (now Ghana), where his father became a doctor in 1890. The young Macormack received his education at the CMS Grammar School in Freetown. He was later sent to Epson College in Britain, where he graduated and was awarded a scholarship to study medicine at the Medical School of St Mary's Hospital in London. He qualified for medicine and surgery in 1912 and, the following year, passed the examination of the London School of Tropical Medicine.

He returned to Sierra Leone in 1913 and applied to be appointed medical doctor in the civil service of Sierra Leone. His application was denied by the British colonial government because of his colour. Despite his excellent qualifications, he was later appointed as medical officer in the lower category of medical officers (African medical officers). There were then two categories of medical officers in Sierra Leone – one for British medical officers, who earned far greater emoluments than their counterparts, the African medical doctors.

The young Dr Easmon campaigned for years against this racial discrimination in the medical service and in the civil service in general, thus earning the antipathy of the British colonial doctors in Sierra Leone, who labelled him "The Yellow Peril". Dr Easmon was of light skin.

During the First World War (1914 to 1917), Dr Easmon enlisted in the army and served as a medical officer with Sierra Leonean soldiers in Cameroon, then a German colony. After the war, Dr Easmon returned to Britain, where he studied and qualified as an obstetrician and gynaecologist.

He returned to Sierra Leone and was posted in several posts in the then protectorate, mainly because the British colonial doctors were opposed to working with a coloured medical doctor, in spite of his superior qualifications. It was later that he was posted to hospitals in Freetown.

Dr Easmon did not give up his quiet fight for equality with British doctors in Sierra Leone. It was many years later and as result of strong pressures by other Sierra Leonean civil servants that the colonial government relented and began to appoint Sierra Leoneans to senior posts in the civil service, including the medical profession, in the fifties. And even then, the colonial government created two categories of senior civil servants – "expatriate senior civil servants" and "African senior civil servants". The former earned higher salaries and other emoluments than did the latter.

DR EUSTACE HENRY TAYLOR-CUMMINGS

Dr Taylor-Cummings was born of prominent Creole parents in Freetown in 1890. He attended the Methodist Boys' High School and then Fourah Bay College. He then travelled to Britain, where he studied at Liverpool University and became the first African to qualify at that university as a doctor.

He was employed as a medical officer in Birmingham for a short period and later returned home to Sierra Leone. He was employed as a doctor in the medical service. But some of the British doctors resigned from their positions as doctors in the Sierra Leone medical service because they did not want to serve with a black doctor, whom they considered inferior. Dr Taylor-Cummings was, therefore, placed in the sanitary department where, despite the obvious snub of him, he advocated for improvement in the sanitation in Freetown and other improvements. He was, in due course, advanced to the rank of senior medical officer before his retirement in1947.

Dr Taylor-Cummings was very active in civic affairs and was elected as councillor of the Freetown City Council. He was later elected mayor in 1948. As mayor, he was instrumental in the establishment of municipal schools in Freetown. He also exerted pressure on the colonial government to build more primary schools in Freetown.

He was a member of the Commission on Higher Education in West Africa, set up by the British colonial government in 1943. That commission recommended the establishment of universities in Ibadan and in the Gold Coast (now Ghana). When the British colonial government wanted to reduce the status of Fourah Bay College, changing it to a technical institute, Dr Taylor-Cummings and others were stoutly opposed. The colonial government eventually relented in 1944, and Fourah Bay College was permitted to maintain its status. Thereby, Fourah Bay College remained the premier college in Sierra Leone.

From 1950 to 1953, Taylor-Cummings served as president of the Fourah Bay College Council, the college's governing body. In 1960, he was awarded the degree of doctor of civil laws by Durham University in England.

Dr Eustace Taylor-Cummings was also a very active churchman. He died in1967.

chapter 27

Unity, Freedom, Justice?

Governor Clarkson's Prayer for Sierra Leone

Of the four British colonies in West Africa, Sierra Leone is unique in that the first governor of the colony, Governor Clarkson, offered a prayer for the Creoles before departing from the colony as result of illness. Formerly, many Creole homes displayed this prayer, known as "Governor Clarkson's Prayer for Sierra Leone", printed on paper and hanging on one of the walls in the parlour (living room). That prayer is cherished by some Creoles, who would refer to it as the source of their protection in the country. A copy of that prayer (Governor Clarkson's Prayer) is in the appendix.

The Decline of the Creoles

Having examined how the Creoles attained such lofty heights, let us now see how they descended from such high pinnacles. This happened for a number of reasons.

The emergence of more highly educated citizens of provincial origins was good for the general development of the country. No Creoles had criticised the ambition of citizens in the provinces to be educated. As has already been pointed out, the Creoles even assisted in the education of provincial citizens.

Freetown and the surrounding villages in the colony were formerly populated mainly by Creoles, with enclaves of groups of citizens from the provinces. But gradually, a substantial number of provincial citizens came to reside in these former Creole settlements. The influx was accelerated during the atrocious civil war from 1991 to 2002, when provincial citizens fled the horrendous atrocities of the RUF rebels, leaving behind their towns and villages to seek shelter in Freetown and its environs. Thus, the demographic makeup of the colony became unbalanced against the Creoles.

In addition, lopsided laws in the country prevent Creoles from purchasing and owing lands in the provinces, whereas citizens of the provinces are free to purchase and own lands in the Western Area (the colony). Antiquated and anachronistic laws stating that the land in the provinces belong to the people are used as a pretext to prevent Creoles from purchasing and owning land in the provinces.

In view of the introduction of universal adult suffrage, which gave provincial citizens political leverage in the country, some political leaders, through distorted perception, unnecessarily harboured hidden animosity against the Creoles. Therefore, they enacted laws designed to give the citizens from the provinces more advantages than the Creoles.

When Sir Milton Margai, Sierra Leone's first prime minister, died suddenly in 1964, he was succeeded by Albert Margai. During the short time in which Sir Albert Margai was in power, he was reported to have mentioned in one of his speeches at a political meeting in Moyamba that the provincials conceded the fact that some of the Creoles had superior education. But he added that, from that time, the Creoles would have to "march time" and wait for their provincial brethren to become equally educated. Then all the citizens as one would together march forward in the development of the whole country. Of course, there was nothing sinister in the provincial citizens accelerating their pace of education. But to make it a policy of government to prevent the educational development of any other group was reprehensible. Report of this speech was in Special Branch.

Furthermore, Dr Siaka Stevens, the first president of Sierra Leone, was assisted by the Creoles in gaining political power. The Creoles felt their position in the country was seriously threatened by Sir Albert Margai's policy. Therefore, during the 1967 general election, which Sir Albert held only because of the great pressure put on him to do so, Creoles turned out in unprecedented numbers to vote for the All Peoples Congress (APC) under the leadership of Siaka Stevens.

The APC won the election but only by a very slight margin. When news spread across Freetown that Governor General Sir Lightfoot Boston, a Creole, was going to invite Siaka Stevens to the State House to be sworn in as the new prime minister, citizens flocked to the State House and the Cotton Tree. Seeing Stevens being driven to the State House, the congregated crowds, many of whom were Creoles, erupted in jubilation, blithely chanting Negro spirituals like "Oh, Oh Freedom" and other religious songs. They were completely oblivious to the fact that they were singing the dirges for the *funeral* of the Creoles.

When Dr Stevens had consolidated his political power, he started gradually but cunningly to whittle down the influence of the Creoles. He later on did not conceal his success. He wrote in his ghostwritten autobiography, *What Life Has Taught Me*, that one of his satisfactions was to have succeeded in reducing the influence the Creoles had hitherto wielded in the country.

Creoles were in no way belligerent. Thus, when at times Creoles who were legitimate owners of vacant lands – lands that had been in their families for generations – attempted to enter their lands only to find that several people had encroached on the properties, they were filled with utmost surprise. They would sometimes be confronted by hostile and rowdy mobs brandishing machetes, clubs, rocks, and other dangerous implements and making menacing gestures. The lawful owners would be forced to retreat from their properties and would resort to taking the matter to court, in hope they would receive impartial treatment and justice in the courts. It was reported that, when some of these cases were taken to courts, the encroachers would produce completely fictitious documents in support of their illegal ownership of the lands. The matter would drag on in court indefinitely for years and without any decision. Justice delayed is justice denied.

Later, ministers of successive governments were known to have become complicit in the illegal encroachment onto people's properties and the illegal acquisition of properties in the colony by citizens from the provinces. It was alleged that one particular minister of lands told the actual landowners (Creoles) who would produce their title deeds, establishing legitimate ownership, that they had acquired the properties illegally and that the lands were state lands.

The behaviour of indigenous politicians toward the Creoles, who have been quietly pushed aside, is nothing short of xenophobia. Creoles are now treated as "foreigners" and as not belonging to Sierra Leone. But as has already been explained, it was the unfortunate consequences of history that placed Creoles in such an invidious position. The Creoles are descendants of various tribes in West Africa. Some Creoles are even the descendants of tribes in Sierra Leone.

The marginalisation of the Creoles is totally against the motto of Sierra Leone – "Unity, Freedom, Justice." Where are unity, freedom, and justice in the country when certain groups of people are being marginalised and justice is brazenly denied to them? Sierra Leone no longer offers a level playing field, in which everyone is allowed to play his or her own part. Rather, the field has been tilted strongly against the Creoles. So I repeat the question; where are unity, freedom, and justice?

The pretence being made by successive governments to bring about unity is nothing more than complete farce. The present political leaders seem to forget the positive contributions the ancestors of the Creoles made in the development of Sierra Leone.

Now, Creoles have been almost completely phased out of important positions in Sierra Leone and made to become nonentities. This is obvious in government ministries and departments, in the educational sector as well as in the award of scholarships. As a result of this blatant unfair treatment, a substantial number of Creoles who could afford to do so have migrated to Britain, America, or to other countries. In a desperate effort to survive, the remainder of the Creoles in Sierra Leone are gradually undergoing a metamorphosis as a group with the other indigenous tribes. In the not too distant future, there may no longer be a group of people in Sierra Leone called Creoles. But the Creole influence and language may outlive the demise of the Creoles as a group. And perhaps the Creole language, in a varied form, will be the *de facto lingua franca* in Sierra Leone and in other countries of the subregion, as it is already to a great extent.

Fortunately, this transition in Sierra Leone did not occur as a result of a violent and bloody revolution, as happened in Rwanda, but by peaceful evolution. However, the peaceful evolution should involve all tribes in the country in keeping with Sierra Leone's motto, "Unity, Freedom, Justice." History will later be the impartial judge of the present political leaders in the country, who are responsible for this unfair treatment of the Creoles of Sierra Leone and who have, in the past, contributed significantly to the development of the country.

I will close this chapter by quoting parts of the hymn: "O God, our help in ages past":

O God, our help in ages past,
Our hope for years to come,
Our shelter from the stormy blast,
Be thou our guard while troubles last
And our eternal home.

chapter 28

THE KRIO DESCENDANTS UNION (KDU)

Note:
Since there are Creoles in the Caribbean and in countries in the Indian Ocean, I will now use the term "Krios" instead of Creoles as Krios refers specifically to the Creoles of Sierra Leone).

An organization known as the Krio Descendants Union (KDU) has been established in Freetown, Sierra Leone. There are also branches of the KDU abroad mainly in some towns in Britain and in the USA.

The main aims of the Krio Descendants Union (KDU) are to preserve the identity, heritage and culture of the Krios of Sierra Leone.

This is quite a laudable organization and the members are to be highly commended.

However, it is observed that in almost all of the branches of the KDU as well as the parent body in Freetown, Sierra Leone, it is women who play dominant roles in all the affairs of this organization. The women should be congratulated for their moral courage in trying desperately to preserve the identity, culture and heritage of the Krios of Sierra Leone.

On the other hand it is disheartening that the young male Krios have taken a backstage and have hitherto been playing a passive role in the branches of the KDU. They seem to have left the women to be in the forefront in the struggle to preserve the identity, heritage and culture of the Krio ethnic group in Sierra Leone.

The parent body of KDU in Freetown and almost all of the branches of the KDU are either headed by women or women play very dominant roles in the various activities of the KDU. The young Krio men are in the background where they only play passive roles in activities organized by the women. When the women struggle to organise dances, dinner parties and other activities, then the men will show up in large numbers. The young men do not seem to be ashamed to have left the women to be in the forefront in the struggle for the preservation of the Krio ethnic group.

The Krios are presently being phased out of all public services in Sierra Leone. This is abundantly clear in all the ministries/departments of government, the diplomatic service, in the Freetown City Council as well as in most other public organisations in the country and in the award of scholarships to students.

It is a shame for the present-day young Krio men to have left the women to struggle for the preservation of the Creole (Krio) ethnic group. Throughout history it is the males who are in the forefront of any struggle for the defence of a country or defence of something very dear to the group. Women are always in the background. But for the Krios of Sierra Leone presently, the men have left the women to be in the forefront. In short, the women have assumed the role of the leadership. This is an indication of moral cowardice as well as moral dysfunction on the part of the young Krio males. It may seem as if the present day Krio young men have neglected their sacred duty to the group.

When I spoke to one of the Krio young men presently in America sometime ago and broached the subject of why the men have not been in the forefront in the efforts to preserve the heritage of the Krios of Sierra Leone but rather have left it to the women, his puerile response was that the government back home will feel that the Krio men of Sierra Leone who are diaspora were fighting against the government.

I despaired then and have lost complete confidence in the emerging Krio men. His response indicates the attitude of Krio young men in confronting problems. They would prefer to be abroad in foreign lands in comfort whilst ignoring their own relatives and friends back home to be denied fair treatment. Is it an offence to make effort to preserve one's identity and cultural heritage?

I am not advocating any physical and violent struggle with any government in Sierra Leone. Far from it and may it never come to that. The Krios of Sierra Leone were never known to be a combative and pugnacious ethnic group. The Krios in Sierra Leone have hitherto lived in peaceful coexistence with all the other ethnic groups in the country. But it should not be seen as an attempt to undermine or subvert any legitimate and progressive government in Sierra Leone by pointing out that there are certain negative tendencies which militate against one particular group of the inhabitants of the country. And this is completely against the country's motto which is: "Unity, freedom, justice."

But the motto is not being adhered to when one group of the inhabitants of the country is quietly being marginalized and being pushed out of all public services as well as in the award of scholarships to students.

I am not advocating the preservation of the dominating position in which the Krio ethnic group once held in the country. Far from it. It is no longer possible nor is it desirable for one group to dominate other groups in the country. Nevertheless there should be a balance. The policy of the late Dr. Milton Margai the country's first prime minister was a balanced policy towards all tribes in the country and this should be emulated by the politicians who are now in power.

I wish to comment on another aspect of the KDU. The staging of dances and dinner parties as well as other activities in countries outside the country of our birth may not be a positive response to the present trend back home wherein the Krios have been marginalized and removed from all public organisations. Not that there is anything wrong in the staging of dances, dinner parties and other activities. In fact these activities are desirable for attracting young Krio men abroad to become members of the KDU. But a situation like this which confronts the Krio ethnic group in Sierra Leone, a more positive response is required

On another matter concerning the KDU. In an organization like this, there should be abundant manifestation of cohesion amongst its various branches in the countries abroad rather than for each branch competing with each other. Remember the adages: "Unity is strength" and "United we stand; divided we fall." These should be the adages of all the branches of KDU abroad as well as with the parent body in Sierra Leone.

In pursuance of these maxims, the emblem of each branch of KDU irrespective of the country or town in which that KDU branch is located should be the same as that of the parent body. This will indicate unity of purpose. At present the emblem of each branch is quite different from the emblem of the others including the emblem of the parent KDU in Freetown. But I am so far not certain that the emblem of the parent body in Sierra Leone is known.

The KDU should take its cue from various international organisations like the Red Cross. Wherever any branch of the Red Cross organisation is located, it will be identified by the red cross emblem. So also are other international organisations.

Perhaps members of the different branches of KDU abroad may observe the above comments.

Unless the emerging young Krio men resolve resolutely to take up the struggle to preserve the Krios of Sierra Leone, the once powerful ethnic group which had formerly contributed greatly in the development of the country will gradually fade into oblivion. History will then be the judge in years to come; and the judgment will not reflect admirably on the male present-day Krios who have neglected their role in fighting for the preservation of the achievements and culture of their ancestors.

The young Krio men at present are delinquent in upholding the traditions of past Krio leaders like Wallace Johnson, Lamina Sankoh, Mrs. Cummings-John and others and even Dr. Bankole-Bright who might have been considered an eccentric but who in some ways was struggling for the preservation of the Krios of Sierra Leone.

PART 5

THE WAY FORWARD

chapter 29

I have been reflecting on parts of my personal life, as well as on the governance of Sierra Leone. These reflections bring me poignant memories of the past that contrast with the present.

I was born during British colonial rule of Sierra Leone. In my youthful days, I had always entertained dreams of what life would be like if my country could be free from the shackles of British colonialism. I was then both idealistic and naive. My dreams were like a peep into Utopia.

I was in my adulthood when Sierra Leone became independent on the 27 April 1961. I was not physically present in Sierra Leone at that time. I was in Glasgow, Scotland, on training in police duties. Even though I was so far away from Sierra Leone, I was jubilant that the country had gained its independence and cut off the shackles of British imperialism without any violent struggle.

Initially, it seemed as if my dreams of Utopia would became reality. Immediately following the granting of independence, the country was on the right path – politically stable and economically prosperous. But after a few years had elapsed, the idealism I had entertained gradually faded and turned into nightmares. It soon became evident that the country was rapidly slipping down a slope to instability and chaos. Serious struggles and acrimony erupted between the two political parties. These resulted in the army frequently stepping in and adding to the chaos already rocking the country.

It became evident that apart from Dr. Milton Margai, the first Prime Minister, most of the other political leaders who emerged were inept and corrupt. Their rhetoric about seeking to enhance the welfare of Sierra Leonean citizenry became a cover for their corrupt activities. The political leaders lost all sense of the sacred obligation they owed to the citizens.

The activities of our political leaders in Sierra Leone surpassed those portrayed in George Orwell's satirical novel *Animal Farm*.

To deceive citizens while misappropriating the wealth of the country, ruling political parties in the country would make cryptic slogans such as "Constructive Nationalism", "Self Help", "Green Revolution", and several others. In spite of all these slogans, citizens would not see any positive signs of development in the country.

I'll give a few examples of corruption and inept administration. Successive political parties ruling the country have promised to develop agriculture so that the country's staple food, rice, will be available to her citizens at a very cheap price. Millions of leones (*the country's currency*) have been spent annually ostensibly on the development of agriculture. Nevertheless, these successive governments continue to spend thousands of dollars annually on the importation of large quantities of rice from countries in Asia. Where has all the money allegedly being spent on the development of agriculture gone? Some of the answers can be found in the auditor-general's annual reports on the finances of the country.

Successive governments have also spent thousands of dollars on the importation of both fertilisers and agricultural tractors. Yet the country still suffers an acute shortage of rice.

In what may be termed the "good-old days" before the country gained independence, there was never a shortage of rice. Rather, rice was abundant. There were only temporary shortages of rice during the Second World War (1939–1945). These shortages were due to the presence of large numbers of soldiers from other West African countries, whose staple food was also rice. Otherwise, in normal times, there never used to be any shortages of rice.

Permanent shortages of rice became a manifestation long after the country had gained its independence.

PAYMENT OF SALARIES TO GOVERNMENT WORKERS

During pre-independence days, all civil servants were paid promptly on the twenty-eighth of each month. In December, salaries would be paid earlier before Christmas. In February, which has twenty-eight or twenty-nine days, salaries would be paid on about the twenty-fifth of the month. There was absolutely no delay in the prompt payment of salaries of civil servants.

Now when Sierra Leone has become independent, late payment of salaries to civil servants is a common manifestation. In some cases, workers including school teachers are not paid for many months. On the other hand, ministers and some officials of government live in luxury. They are never paid late.

DISHONEST PRACTICES IN THE EMPLOYMENT OF WORKERS

Except in war-related work during the Second World War, it was completely unheard of for ghost workers to be on the payroll in any government department. Now that the country has been independent for many years, it is quite common for many ghost workers to be on the payroll of departments. In the education field, apart from ghost teachers in some schools, there were also ghost schools with entire staffs of ghost workers on the payroll. The salaries of these ghost workers were diverted into the private pockets of corrupt senior officials.

SUPPLY OF ELECTRICITY

During British colonial rule of the country, there were never any blackouts. Blackouts, now normal, began to occur after the country had gained independence.

Sierra Leone's government has given spurious reasons why the entire country is facing an electricity shortage. But the real reason for this sad state of affairs seems to be a lack of integrity among both the senior and junior staff, as well as ineptitude of the administrators.

Abundant example is provided in the Bumbuna hydroelectric project. That project was started over thirty years ago. Yet it still has not been completed. Successive governments have given various reasons why that project has still not been completed. Is that progress?

INTEGRITY AMONG SENIOR OFFICIALS

During pre-independence days, all senior officials in departments (there were then no ministries) were British, and every one of them exhibited a high degree of integrity. There was then no indication or the slightest suspicion that any senior officials were engaged in irregular financial activities. Consequently, junior officials emulated senior officials in regard to probity.

Presently, gross financial irregularities are unearthed in almost all government departments and ministries annually. These are revealed in the annual reports of the country's auditor general. Yet there is hardly any evidence of penalties having been inflicted on any government officials for the financial irregularities.

Rectitude among senior officials in public offices, to whom juniors should be able to look for guidance in regard to the standard of probity, has also disappeared. Sierra Leone is now graded as one of the most corrupt countries in the world. It is a shame to the country whose capital, Freetown, formerly earned the accolade of Athens of West Africa. A country that prided itself in the spreading of light to other countries in the subregion has now been enmeshed in the tight embrace of widespread corruption, gross indiscipline and other negative attitudes.

The disclosures in the annual reports of the auditor-general of the country show a perplexing and alarming number of cases involving the misappropriation of public funds and property in Sierra Leone. The large amounts involved in some of the cases, and also the seniority of the officials involved are shocking. Some of these financial irregularities are tantamount to criminal action.

According to the provisions of section 119(4) of the country's constitution, the auditor general must submit the annual report on the finances of the country to Parliament. Despite the serious financial irregularities which are disclosed in the annual reports of the auditor-general, all parliamentarians do now is "debate" the reports and, in some cases, summon the officials responsible for such irregularities for explanation. Generally, that's all any of these issues come to. Hardly any action will be taken by parliamentarians to rectify the irregularities. Nor are there any recommendations for penalising the officials involved in very serious financial irregularities.

In the auditor general's annual report for the financial year ending 2012, the losses in the finances of the country due to the activities of corrupt officials were conservatively estimated at Le.8,146,575,696.00. This is the equivalent of approximately $18.2 million. Hardly any action was taken by parliamentarians to stop this massive drainage of the country's finances.

What legacy do we intend to bequeath to our children and grandchildren? Do we intend them to grow up in an environment in which no one has any scruples about stealing or engaging in other forms of dishonesty – an environment where such activities are regarded not as wrong but as normal conduct?

RESPONSIBILITIES OF PARLIAMENTARIANS

Parliament is the institution to enhance the welfare of the citizens and protect their rights. Unfortunately, parliamentarians who were elected by the citizens into that holy institution as servants to protect their interests have become despots. Rather than serving the people who elected them, parliamentarians in Sierra Leone have become masters. Citizens dare not criticise any parliamentarian. Any citizen who would be so foolish as to make any adverse comments in the press against a parliamentarian would find him or herself summoned before parliamentarians to explain his or her indiscretion (his or her daring to criticise the "almighty" parliamentarian).

Not too long ago, a Freetown newspaper printed an article about a certain parliamentarian who had been arrested for an alleged traffic violation. That parliamentarian, according to the article, had the indecency of reporting to Parliament his arrest, which he termed "obstruction" by the police while he, the parliamentarian, was on his way to attend a meeting of Parliament.

The inspector general of police was, according to the report, summoned to appear before Parliament, where he was excoriated because one of his diligent policemen had had the temerity of arresting a parliamentarian who had allegedly violated the law. The arrest was termed an "obstruction of a parliamentarian while he was proceeding to attend a meeting of Parliament."

Laws of the country are enacted by parliamentarians. Such laws are supreme, and not even the president of the country can violate any law with impunity.

Parliamentarians should also protect the freedom of the press. Unfortunately, in spite of the provisions in Sierra Leone's constitution, a newspaper journalist who might write adverse comments against any parliamentarian may find him or herself being summoned to appear before Parliament like a pupil being made to appear before his or her teacher for having contravened a disciplinary code of conduct.

On the other hand, some journalists in Sierra Leone are most irresponsible. They are not fit to become journalists. They are depraved and have used their positions to vilify and blackmail decent citizens. Some journalists have abased journalism in various ways, and they deserve penalties under the laws of the country. However, parliament should not be turned to a court of law.

The widespread corruption and other forms of immoral behaviour and indiscipline in the county do not augur well for Sierra Leone.

The problems confronting the nation are formidable. In order to extricate the country from the quagmire in which it now finds itself, citizens, especially political leaders and senior officials, should adapt a fundamental change in their attitude. The country also requires someone with an abundance of moral courage who is endowed with Herculean strength to clean this Augean stable. By so doing, citizens will seek to honour the land that we love, our Sierra Leone, as is echoed in the country's national anthem.(See the Appendix)

However, let us not despair. Let us look towards the future with optimism. It is hoped that the country will be like a Phoenix, the mythical bird that, having succeeded in immolating and destroying itself, miraculously rose again from its ashes, refreshed and strengthened. So also let us hope that Sierra Leone, having succeeded in destroying itself by way of vices like corruption, indiscipline, and other forms of immorality, will in due course rise up from its ashes, rejuvenated and ready to take its rightful place in the subregion and once again spread enlightenment throughout the other countries in the region.

Glossary

A/C. Assistant commissioner of police

APC. All People's Congress (a political party in Sierra Leone)

ASP. Assistant superintendent of police

Asst. Com (ACP). assistant commissioner of police

BEM. British Empire Medal (national award during colonial days)

Borbor. Pet name in Creole (Krio) for a small boy

Brig. Brigadier (A military rank)

Cap. or Chap. Chapter of a book

Capt. Captain

CFAO. A French commercial company in Sierra Leone, which is now closed down

C/I. Chief inspector of police

CID. Criminal Investigation Department

CMS. Church Missionary Society (an organisation of the Anglican religion)

Col. Colonel (in the military)

CP or C of P. Commissioner of police

CPO. Chief police officer (the police officer in charge of a police division)

Cpl. Corporal

DC. District commissioner (administrative officer in charge of a district in the provinces –the nomenclature used during British colonial days)

DCM. Distinguished Conduct Medal (A British medal for outstanding conduct and courage)

DCP. Deputy commissioner of police (the second rank in the hierarchy of the police force)

DELCO. Sierra Leone Development Company (a British iron ore mining company in Sierra Leone, which folded in around 1974

DFC. Distinguished Flying Cross (A British medal for gallantry in the Royal Air Force)

DO. District officer (administrative officer in charge of a district in the provinces – the nomenclature used after Sierra Leone became independent)

DOT. Department of Transportation

Dr. Doctor

DSO. Distinguished Service Order (a British medal for distinguished service in the military)

DSP. Deputy superintendent of police (the second to last rank in the hierarchy of the senior officers – not to be mistaken with DCP)

ECOMOG. The military wing of the Economic Community of West African States headed by Nigeria

Elementary school. Primary school

EXCO. Executive Council (the cabinet) during the British colonial administration of Sierra Leone

FTO. Force transport officer (in the police force)

GBO. G.B. Ollivant (a large commercial company in Freetown, which is now defunct

HE. His Excellency

Hon. Honourable

IDM   Illicit Diamond Mining or Illicit Diamond Miner
IG. Inspector general (of police)
Insp. Inspector of police
ISU. Internal Security Unit

JP. Justice of the Peace
JPO. Junior police officer (sub-inspector, inspector, and chief inspector, for example)

Karmajors. Local hunters who, during the Sierra Leone Civil War (1991–2002) took up arms and participated actively in defeating the RUF
Korni Karta. A cunning person who is able to outwit another

Kortor A Temne expression of someone whom you have high respect for or someone of high status

Lappa. A length of decorative cloth that is wrapped around the body of a woman and used to tie a baby tightly on the woman's back
Land Rover. A small and rugged cross-country truck
LEGCO. Legislative Council (The "Parliament" during British colonial days)
Leone. The national currency of Sierra Leone (abbreviated Le)

MBE. Member of the British Empire
Mjr. Major in the military
MP. Member of Parliament
MR. Member of the Order of the Rokel (Sierra Leone nation award)
Mr. Mister
Ms. Miss or misses
MV. Motor vessel (referring to a ship that is powered by internal combustion engine and by steam) or mail vessel (a vessel that carries mails)

MVO. Member of the Victorian Order (a British award). This award was being made whilst Sierra Leone had not yet become a republic.

NC. North Carolina (State in the United States of America)
NC DOT. North Carolina Department of Transportation
NCO. Non-commissioned officer in the military or the police force

O/C. Office in charge of a police district or of a branch in the Sierra Leone Police Force (that nomenclature it is understood has now been changed)
Ojeh. A Creole secret society
Omolankay: A wide two-wheeled push cart used to transport large quantities of variety of   goods. It is generally pushed by one or two men.
OR. Officer of the Order of the Rokel (Sierra Leone National Award)

Pa. Creole salutation to a male elderly person or person in authority by a younger or junior person
parastatal. A quasi-government commercial organisation with its own members of a board of management
PC. Police constable or paramount chief
pekin. Small child (boy or girl)
PIO. Principal immigration officer
plassas. A soup of vegetable leaves boiled in palm oil, together with lumps of meat and fish and condiments
poda-poda. A minibus used to convey passengers and their luggage
Poro Society. A secret tribal society mainly in the south and east of Sierra Leone
POW. Prisoner of war or Prince of Wales School
POW School. Prince of Wales School (A boys' secondary school in Sierra Leone)
poyoh. An alcoholic drink extracted from palm trees
primary school. Elementary school

PsyD. Doctor of Psychology (An American medical qualification in psychology)

PWD. Public Works Department (The department of the government of Sierra Leone responsible for all public works in the country, including roads, government buildings, and the like. Since the country received her independence to the country, the nomenclature has been changed to Ministry of Works.)

PZ. Paterson, Zochonis & Co (a Greek commercial company formerly in Freetown but no longer in Sierra Leone)

QE II. Queen Elizabeth the Second (of Britain)

QE II Quay. Queen Elizabeth the Second Quay (the main quay in Freetown, Sierra Leone, so named during British colonial days when the quay was opened in 1954)

QPM. Queen's Police Medal (A British Medal for meritorious or long service in the police force)

RAF. Royal Air Force (The British Air Force)

Rev. Reverend (A Christian priest)

RN. Royal Navy (The British naval force)

RUF. Revolutionary United Front (the rebel group that waged eleven years of ruthless civil war in Sierra Leone)

SALONE. Compressed form for "Sierra Leone"

SALPOST. The national post office in Sierra Leone

SB. Abbreviation for Special Branch (the police intelligence service)

SCOA. A French commercial company in Sierra Leone, which is no longer in existence in Sierra Leone

SDO. Senior district officer

secondary school. High school

Sgt. Sergeant

Sgt Mjr. Sergeant major

S/I. Sub-inspector of police

SLBC. Sierra Leone Broadcasting Corporation

SLBS. Sierra Leone Broadcasting Service (the former government broadcasting organisation in Sierra Leone responsible for radio and TV broadcasting), now known as SLBC (Sierra Leone Broadcasting Corporation)

SLDC. Sierra Leone Development Company (same as DELCO, a British iron ore mining company in Sierra Leone). This company stopped operating in Sierra Leone around about 1974.

SLPM. Sierra Leone Police Medal (either for long or for meritorious service)

SLPMB. Sierra Leone Produce Marketing Board (a quasi-governmental company for the collection and sale of Sierra Leone produce to overseas markets)

SLPP. ...   Sierra Leone People's Party (a political party)

SLST. Sierra Leone Selection Trust (British Diamond Mining Company in Kono)

S/O. Station officer of a police station (larger than a post) or staff officer

SPO. Senior police officer (the general term used to describe a senior police officer of the rank of assistant superintendent of police (ASP) upwards to inspector general of the police force)

SS. Steam ship (a vessel that is powered by steam engine and not by internal combustion engine)

SSD. Special Security Division (in other words, special armed police force for control of serious civil unrest). This nomenclature has now been changed.

Supt. Superintendent of police

tong. The Creole (Krio) for town

UAC. United Africa Company (a subsidiary of the giant conglomerate Unilever company)

U-boat. A German submarine (in German, *Unterseeboot*)

UDP. United Democratic Party (a political party in Sierra Leone)

UK. United Kingdom (another name for Britain)

USA. United States of America

wahala. A Creole expression that can mean either a problem or trouble or a disaster or serious embarrassment

WESTAFF. West African Frontier Force (a battalion of soldiers in Sierra Leone during British Colonial days)

Appendix
Governor Clarkson's Prayer
for Sierra Leone

O Lord, I beseech thee favourably to hear the prayer of him who wishes to be thy servant, and pardon him for presuming to address thee from this sacred place. O God, I know my own infinity and unworthiness, and I know thine abundant mercies to those who wish to be guided by thy will. Support me. O Lord, with thy heavenly grace, and to enable me to conduct myself through this earthly life that my actions may be consistent with the words I have uttered this day. Thou knowest that I am now about to depart from this place, and to leave the people whom it has pleased thee to entrust to my care. Guide them, O merciful God, in the paths of truth and let not a few wicked men among us draw down thy vengeance upon this Colony.

In graft into their hearts a proper sense of duty, and enable them through thy grace to conduct themselves as Christians, that they may not come to thy house without that pleasing emotion which every grateful man must feel when paying adoration to the Author of life. But I have a great reason to fear, O Lord, that many who frequent thy church do not approach thy presence as becomes them, and that they may partly be compared to the Scribes. Pharisees, and hypocrites. Pardon, O God, their infirmities, and as thou knowest their weakness from the manner in which they have formerly been treated, and the little opportunity they have had of knowing thy will and getting acquainted with the merits of thy Son, our saviour Jesus Christ, look down upon them with an eye of mercy and suffer them not to incur thy displeasure, after they have had an opportunity of being instructed in the ways of thy commandments.

Bless, O Lord, the inhabitants of this vast continent, and incline their hearts towards us that they may more readily listen to our advice and doctrines, and that we may conduct ourselves towards them as to convince them of the happiness we enjoy under thy almighty protection.

Banish from this Colony, O Lord all heathenish superstition and let the inhabitants know that thou art the only true Lord in which we live and move and have our being. If these people who protest thy religion will not be assured of thy superior power, convince them. O God, of Thine anger for their profession without their practice, for thou knowest I brought them here in hopes of making them and their families happy, both in this world and to all eternity.

But I fear they may not be governed by my advice, and that they themselves and their children forever by their perverse and general behaviour. I entreat thee not to let their evil example ruin the great cause in which we have embarked, but I would rather see that place in ashes and every wicked person destroyed, than that the chance we have now an opportunity of bringing to the light and knowledge of thy holy religion should, from the wickedness of a few individuals will continue in their accustomed darkness and barbarism. They know that I have universally talked of their apparent virtue the goodness, and have praised thy name for having permitted me to be the servant employed in so great and glorious a cause. If I have been deceived, I am sorry for it, and may thy will be done; but I implore thee to accept the sincerity of my intentions and my best endeavours to improve the talent committed to my case. Only pardon the intuity of my nature, and I will trust to thy mercy.

Should any person have a wicked thought in his heart or do anything knowledge to disturb the peace and comfort of our Colony, let him be rooted out O God, from off the face of the earth; but have mercy upon him hereafter.

Were I to utter all that my heart now indicates, no time would be sufficient for any praise and thanksgiving for all the mercies. Thou has vouchsafed to show me, but as thou art acquainted with every secret of my heart, accept my thoughts for thanks. I have no words left to express my gratitude and resignation to thy will. I entreat thee, O God, if nothing I can say will convince these people of thy power and goodness, make use of me in anyway thou pleasest, to make an atonement for their guilt. This is an awful and I fear too presumptuous, a request; yet if it should be thy will that I should lay down my life for the cause I have embarked in, assist me, O Lord with thy support, that I may resign it in such a manner as to convince these unbelieving people that thou art God indeed. May the heart of this Colony, O Lord, imbibe the spirit of meekness, gentleness, and truth; and may they henceforth live in unity and godly love, following as far as the weakness of their mortal natures will admit, that most excellent and faultless pattern which thou hast given us in thy Son our Savior Jesus Christ, to whom with thee and the Holy Spirit be all honour and glory, now and forever. Amen.

Sierra Leone National Anthem

High we exalt thee, realm of the free;
    Great is the love we have for thee;
    Firmly united ever we stand,
    Singing thy praise, O native land.
    We raise up our hearts and our voices on high,
    The hills and the valleys re-echo our cry;
    Blessing and peace be ever thine own,
    Land that we love, our Sierra Leone.

One with a faith that wisdom inspires,
    One with a zeal that never tires;
    Ever we seek to honour thy name
    Ours is the labour, thine the fame.
    We pray that no harm on thy children may fall,

That blessing and peace may descend on us all;
So may we serve thee ever alone,
Land that we love our Sierra Leone.

Knowledge and truth our forefathers spread,
Mighty the nations whom they led;
Mighty they made thee, so too may we
Show forth the good that is ever in thee.
We pledge our devotion, our strength and our might,
Thy cause to defend and to stand for thy right;
All that we have be ever thine own,
Land that we love our Sierra Leone.

About the Author

Ezekiel Alfred Coker was born in Freetown, Sierra Leone, West Africa on 11 October 1926. He received his secondary education at St Edward's Secondary School in Freetown from 1942 to 1945. After passed the Cambridge Senior School Certificate Examination in 1945, he served as a schoolteacher for a short period. He later joined the customs department as a customs officer. After serving in that department for nine years, he applied for enlistment in the Sierra Leone Police Force as a sub-inspector in May 1956.

Coker rose through the police force ranks to senior assistant commissioner of police, third in the hierarchy of the Sierra Leone Police Force. From October 1978 to January 1980, he acted as commissioner of police.

He served in every important section of the police force, including his longest stint in the Special Branch, of which he eventually became the head. During his time there, Coker witnessed momentous events, including the political manoeuvrings and wrestling that would eventually result in the overthrowing of successive governmental regimes and, ultimately, political instability in the country.

He was among the senior officers of the army and police force who were arrested and detained in 1968 following an army coup. On his release from detention, he was reinstated in the police force. During his continuing service, he served as chief police officer in Kono, the diamond-mining district; as principal immigration officer; and in the Special Branch.

Whilst in the Special Branch, Coker witnessed the major political tussles and manoeuvrings that wracked Sierra Leone, including the student revolution in 1977, which nearly resulted in the overthrow of President Siaka Stevens and the APC government.

Late in 1977, he was transferred to police headquarters as senior assistant commissioner in charge of police operations. In October 1978, he was appointed acting commissioner of police, Member of Parliament, and cabinet minister by His Excellency the president, Dr Siaka Stevens, in accordance with the provisions of the then Sierra Leone constitution.

Coker retired from the police force in 1981 but was re-employed a few years later on a contract to train middle cadre officers (JPOs) in the CID and Special Branch respectively. In 1997, following the army-led coup that overthrew President Tejan Kabbah and amid the extreme violence that seized Sierra Leone, he escaped to the United States of America with his wife and a few other members of his remaining family.

Coker loves classical music during his leisure, particularly works by Wolfgang Amadeus Mozart and Franz Josef Haydn.

State House, Freetown, Sierra Lenone

Printed in the United States
By Bookmasters